The Covent Garden
COOKERY BOOK

By the same author
The Breakfast Book

The Covent Garden
COOKERY BOOK

Diana Troy

IN ASSOCIATION WITH
NEAL'S YARD WHOLEFOOD WAREHOUSE
Illustrations by Nicki Holt

SIDGWICK & JACKSON
LONDON

First published in Great Britain in 1987 by
Sidgwick & Jackson Limited
1 Tavistock Chambers, Bloomsbury Way
London WC1A 2SG

Copyright © Diana Troy and Michael Loftus 1987

Photographer James Murphy
Home Economist Berit Vinegrad
Stylist Antonia Gaunt
Art Director Jane Willis
Designer Linda Hardaker

ISBN 0 283 99447 9

Phototypeset by Falcon Graphic Art Limited
Wallington, Surrey
Printed in Great Britain by
Butler & Tanner Limited, Frome

Contents

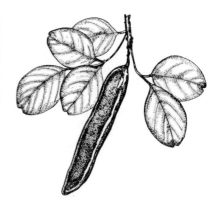

Introduction

The idea of enlivening a grain and vegetable diet with herbs is not new; it has been a feature of peasant cookery for centuries. Historically, meat has been consumed in large quantities only by the rich, and the same is true today; a staple grain or pulse crop, cooked with fruit, vegetables, herbs and spices still forms the basic diet of most of the world's population.

When the choice of foodstuffs is limited it becomes especially important for the cook to season them as interestingly as possible. Thus, simple traditional cookery, for example the rice dishes of the Far East or the lentil dishes of India, often display a more creative use of ingredients than the overcomplicated cuisine of expensive hotels and restaurants. Furthermore, on close inspection they are found to contain a judicious and perfectly balanced combination of ingredients.

In recent years, a network of specialist 'wholefood' shops has greatly increased our access to the staple crops of the whole world. Brown rice, all kinds of dried beans and lentils, buckwheat and millet, as well as a great variety of dried fruit, nuts and soya products are now easily obtainable. The immigrant communities have also 'set up shop', importing many interesting fruits, vegetables and seasonings that were almost unheard of 20 years ago - ginger root, tamarind, chillies, limes, coconut milk, to name a few. So the basic ingredients of not one but many vegetarian diets are available to us, usually at a very reasonable cost. As more and more people doubt the benefits of a diet based on over-refined, additive-laden food and animal products, traditional vegetarian food is becoming increasingly popular. Few would dispute that an imaginative vegetarian diet offers more vitamins, minerals and fibre, as well as *less* saturated animal fat and sugar, than the conventional diet based on meat and fish.

With an ever-increasing range of foreign foodstuffs available to us, many people have begun to take a closer interest in non-European cookery. Writers like Madhur Jaffrey and Claudia Roden have whetted our appetite for the delights of Oriental cookery, just as Elizabeth David inspired interest in French and Italian cookery some years ago. In this book, I have drawn ideas from many different cuisines, particularly those of Europe and Asia. It seems to me that the best way of learning how to prepare unfamiliar ingredients is to study the recipes of the countries in which they originated and have been cooked for centuries. Therefore, I looked to Chinese, Japanese and other Asian cookery traditions for ideas about cooking rice and soya bean products, to India for lentil recipes and to the Middle East for interesting ways of cooking beans. There was no need to look further than Britain for most baking recipes. We have a great repertoire of these because wheat, oats, barley and rye have always been our staple crops.

Perhaps the current influx of new ideas will lead to a renaissance of British cookery, which is long overdue. British cuisine, unlike that of other European countries, seems to have been suffering a steady decline during the last 150 years, particularly with respect to taste and flavourings. From the Middle Ages until the eighteenth century, English food was interesting and well seasoned: the food of the rich was generously spiced and included many daring combinations of sweet and savoury ingredients, while even the poor man's diet used plenty of herbs. The spice trade and all the colonial connections made for a vigorous exchange of ideas and commodities. By the mid-nineteenth century, however, when Mrs Beeton wrote her famous *Book of Household Management*, English cookery had lost much of its flair. This was due mainly to increasing industrialization: people moved from the countryside into towns and cities thus severing the vital link with the land, the link which is the pre-condition for all good cookery. Perhaps the pervading Puritanism of the Victorian age also caused the middle classes to adopt the sober and starchy diet from which we still suffer today. The modern fast food industry has compounded the problem by imposing on the consumer an increasingly tastless and unhealthy diet. This is surely the moment to take advantage of the wealth of ideas and ingredients that are available, and rescue the national diet from the monotony into which it has sunk!

One of the ideas which I hope will become clear to people using this book is that in vegetarian cookery the interests of nutrition and flavour are not mutually exclusive. On the contrary, they often coincide, or, with a little imagination, can be made to do so. Whole grains, for example, not only have a higher food content but also a more appetizing flavour than their refined counterparts. A food with a high vitamin and mineral content often has more natural taste than a less nutritious one; sea salt, for example, with its more varied mineral content, has a more interesting flavour than rock salt. In the same way, substituting unsaturated vegetable fats for saturated animal fats has proven nutritional benefits and need not in any way impair flavour. There are new good-quality hard vegetable margarines on the market which may be used to advantage instead of butter. In my opinion, their lighter, less cloying taste sets off the flavour of the other ingredients with which they are used, even in a traditionally butter-based sauce like Hollandaise.

One of the arts of vegetarian cookery is to combine vegetable ingredients in such a way as to form high quality proteins. In fact, traditional vegetarian recipes often mix ingredients which produce a high protein content as a matter of course. The combination of rice and soy sauce, prevalent in the Far East, is a good example; the addition of a pulse-based sauce to the rice means that the whole range of essential amino acids is present and the body can therefore absorb a useful amount of protein from the meal. The same effect can be achieved by adding a cheese- or nut-based sauce to rice. A vegetarian meal containing varied and well-combined ingredients will have a protein content equal to any containing meat or fish.*

I began this book with the idea that a kitchen stocked with about 30 different seasonings and a range of grains, nuts and pulses would be able to produce an almost infinite number of vegetarian dishes. However, in the process of writing, the list of seasonings has more than doubled – and it is still by no means comprehensive! But to begin with, I think a basic stock of 30 or 40 dried or preserved flavourings augmented by fresh herbs and spices when they are in season is probably enough. This may sound extravagant but I think that a vegetarian cook, who is spending so much less on basic ingredients than one who cooks with meat and fish, can afford the luxury of such a selection.

Fast food freaks and busy cooks may object that using a large number of ingredients will take too long. Although it is true that preparing a good vegetarian dish can be time-consuming, it is also true that such a dish can be a meal in itself and needs no more than a simple accompaniment such as wholemeal bread or a green salad. This kind of dish is sometimes even better the next day, when all the flavours have had a chance to blend together, so it is a good idea, particularly in the case of a complicated recipe, to cook more than is necessary for a single meal. The preparation will take only a little longer and there will be food for another day. (People rarely object to eating the same thing twice if it is really delicious.) Furthermore vegetarian cookery is altogether more flexible than meat or fish cookery in terms of the number of people it can serve. Meals can conveniently be made to 'stretch' and an unexpected guest is rarely a problem.

If vegetarian cookery makes sense in terms of domsestic economy, there is no doubt that it also makes sense in terms of global resources. As it takes between 10 and 30 times more land to feed a meat-eater than a vegetarian, the ecological value of people adopting a vegetarian diet is obvious. Britain, at any rate, seems to have moved from its traditional roast beef-eating image since, with the exception of Greece, it now boasts the lowest consumption of meat in western Europe.

By including as wide a variety of ingredients as possible, and by attempting to give recipes which are not only nourishing but tasty, I hope this book will contribute a few new ideas to an increasingly popular style of cookery. Flavourings, often no more than an afterthought in many cookery books, are the focal point of these recipes and the basis for the subdivision of chapters. In turn, these sections are organized into chapters according to their generic taste: hot, sour, salty, nutty, sweet, spicy, etc. I hope this will lead cooks to experiment further, interchanging flavours of a similar type.

A comprehensive index at the back of the book clearly lists all the various types of recipes – soups, casseroles or rice dishes, for example – as well as individual ingredients. A general recipe chapter describes some of the basic

---

*For more details on this subject see *Protein Balanced Vegetarian Cookery* by David Scott (Rider, 1985). He suggests that the following combinations of ingredients produce high value proteins:
1. Dairy products plus grains, pulses, nuts or seeds
2. Grains (including flour) plus pulses
3. Pulses plus dairy products or nuts and seeds.

---

techniques of vegetarian cookery not otherwise covered in the recipes. There are also a list of soya-based ingredients that may be substituted for dairy produce and some suggestions for useful kitchen equipment. The recipes are generally designed to feed four people, sometimes with second helpings.

Note on salt
I have used Maldon salt in preparing the recipes for this book. The flavour of this salt is much more subtle and less harsh than ordinary table salt and it may be used quite generously. If using rock or a strong-tasting sea salt, use considerably less than I have suggested in the recipes.

Hot tastes

CHILLIES·GIANT WHITE RADISH·GINGER HORSERADISH·MUSTARD·PAPRIKA PEPPER

Paprika

Mustard

Chilli

Ginger

Chillies

Chillies belong to the capsicum family. Originally a South American plant, they were introduced into Asia, via Europe, in the sixteenth century, after which they became an indispensable part of Indian cookery.

Fresh chillies are sold ripe (red) or unripe (green) – the former have a slightly sweeter flavour. Dried chillies should be used very sparingly, especially the tiny 'bird's eye' chillies which can be fearsomely hot. I prefer to use fresh chillies, if possible, because their heat is tempered with a pleasant fruity taste. It is hard to say exactly how many chillies should be used in a recipe because they vary so much in size and pungency. However the seeds and upper part, nearest the stem, are always the hottest. Generally speaking, the smaller the chilli, the stronger its flavour will be. When cooking with fresh chillies, ascertain how hot they are by nibbling the tip of each one, and use them accordingly. Remove the seeds to avoid excessive pungency. The insides of chillies can irritate the skin, so be careful not to rub your face while or just after preparing them.

Chilli powder, cayenne pepper (a dried chilli powder originating in South America), chilli or tabasco sauce can all be used to add chilli flavouring to a dish. Chilli and cayenne powders should be bought in small quantities only, as they go stale quickly.

Although in some countries chillies are used in excess to mask a monotonous diet, when used with discretion they can add a zest to cooking which no other flavouring can quite achieve. Chillies can be cooked, with onions, at the outset of preparing a savoury dish: in this way their warmth pervades all the ingredients. They can be used in all kinds of rice and pulse dishes, as well as in relishes and chutneys, and are especially useful in wholefood cookery where they lift the rather neutral flavours of grains and pulses. Chillies aid the digestion and are rich in vitamins A and C.

AVOCADO AND CHILLI DIP

This is a variation of Mexican guacamole. It is a good recipe to make when ripe avocados are being sold off cheaply.

2 large avocados
1 large clove garlic, crushed
juice of 1 lemon
1–2 tablespoons hot chilli sauce
3 hardboiled eggs
1–2 red chillies
lettuce

Carefully cut the avocados in half. Remove the stones and scoop out the flesh, leaving the skins intact. Mash up the avocado flesh in a bowl and add the crushed garlic, lemon juice and chilli sauce. Spoon the mixture back into the shells and serve topped with a little chopped hardboiled egg and chopped red chilli. Place the avocados on a bed of lettuce surrounded by extra slices of hardboiled egg.

PEPPERS STUFFED WITH RICE AND CHILLIES

You can use either red or green peppers in this recipe. The tomato puree I have used is available packeted, and is not the more concentrated variety found in tins or tubes.

a few inner celery stalks with some leaves
4 red chillies
3 tablespoons vegetable oil
6 large cloves garlic, crushed
250 g/8 oz tomato puree (½ packet) *or* 250 g/8 oz tomatoes, chopped
300 g/10 oz cooked brown long grain *or* short grain rice
175 g/6 oz Gouda *or* Edam *or* Gruyère cheese, grated
salt
black pepper
6 medium red *or* green peppers

Preheat the oven to 180°C (350°F, gas mark 4). Chop the celery and chillies finely and fry them in the oil for a few minutes. Add the crushed garlic and the tomato puree or chopped tomatoes and simmer for a further 10 minutes. Combine this mixture with the cooked rice and grated cheese, and season to taste with salt and pepper. Cut the tops off the peppers, scoop out the seeds and ribs and fill the peppers with the stuffing. Put the lids back on and place them on a greased baking tray, or support them in a high-sided baking tin if they are top-heavy. Bake for about 40 minutes.

PASTIES FILLED WITH SWEETCORN, CHILLIES AND BEANS

This recipe gives quantities for 8 good-sized pasties.

crust
350 g/12 oz wholewheat flour
1 level teaspoon salt (optional)
175 g/6 oz vegetable margarine
6 tablespoons cold water

filling
2 large sweetcorn cobs
250 g/8 oz French beans
2 large red chillies
2 large onions
5 cloves garlic
3 tablespoons vegetable oil
125 g/4 oz Dutch *or* English cheese, grated
1 heaped teaspoon salt
4 tablespoons tomato puree (from a packet) *or* 2 tablespoons tomato ketchup

Make the pastry in the usual way (see p. 218) and set it aside in the refrigerator. Preheat the oven to 190° C (375° F, gas mark 5).

Boil the corn cobs and the French beans separately, in salted water. Deseed the chillies. Chop the chillies, onions and garlic finely and sauté them for 10–15 minutes in the oil.

Drain the sweetcorn and the beans when they are sufficiently cooked. Remove the sweetcorn from the cob with a sharp knife and cut the beans into short lengths. Combine these ingredients with the cooked garlic, onions and chillies and mix in the grated cheese, salt and tomato puree or ketchup.

Divide the pastry into 8 pieces and roll each one into a circle about 20 cm (8 in) across. Divide the filling equally between them and fold each circle over into a semicircle. Trim the edges and seal, using your thumbs or a fork to press the edges together. Put the pasties on to greased baking trays and bake for 40 minutes, or until the pastry is well browned.

PAKORAS

These vegetable fritters are commonly sold on street stalls in India. They are made of vegetables, such as onions, potatoes, cauliflower or green chillies, dipped in chick pea batter and then deep fried. The batter here is seasoned with chilli powder or cayenne pepper. You can add other ground spices if you wish, but it is not essential.

batter
250 g/8 oz chick pea flour
1 level teaspoon bicarbonate of soda
2 teaspoons salt
1 teaspoon chilli powder *or* hot cayenne pepper
500 ml/18 fl oz water

vegetables
3 medium onions, sliced thinly
1 small cauliflower divided into florets *or* 250 g/8 oz broccoli
1 large sweet potato, sliced thinly
a few whole green chillies

vegetable oil for frying

To make the batter, mix all the dry ingredients together, then gradually beat in the cold water. Leave to stand for 10 minutes. Pour the oil into a cast iron pan to a depth of about 7.5 cm (3 in), and heat to about 150° C (300° F). Dip a selection of vegetables into the batter and fry them for 5–8 minutes or until they are well browned. Remove from the pan and press between sheets of absorbent paper to get rid of excess grease. Repeat until all the vegetables have been cooked. Serve hot.

QUICK MANGO CHUTNEY

The sweet, vinegary mango chutney sold in England is one of those Anglo-Indian hybrids, like curry powder, which were originally made for export to Britain but rarely used in India itself. Mango chutney, as I have come across it in India, is usually made from unripe mangoes: it is extremely hot and not sweet at all. The recipe below, which can be quickly mixed up in a blender, is a compromise: it is fruity and refreshing, but can be made as hot as you like by adjusting the quantity of chillies. It can be kept in the refrigerator for a week or more, but is best made for immediate consumption (which will probably be rapid!). The idea for this recipe came from Meera Taneja's useful book on North Indian cookery, *The Indian Epicure**.

2 ripe mangoes
2 small onions
1–2 large fresh red chillies (*or* more to taste if required)
1 small bunch coriander leaves
½ teaspoon salt

Peel the mangoes and scrape the flesh away from the stones. Peel the onions and chop them roughly, along with the chillies and coriander leaves. Add the salt, put the mixture into a liquidizer and blend.

* *The Indian Epicure*, Meera Taneja, Mills and Boon, 1979.

CHILLI 'FLOWERS' FOR GARNISHING

Bright red chillies transformed into long-petalled flowers make a dramatic decoration for salads, especially those of Far Eastern origin like Gado Gado (see p.85). They are easily made by splitting the chillies in half with a sharp knife, starting about 2.5 cm (1 in) down from the stalk end, and then making more vertical slits until eight 'petals' have been cut. Put the chillies in a bowl of iced water and leave them in the refrigerator for 1 hour, by which time the petals will have curled back to make flower shapes.

Giant white radish

This large species of radish grows all over Asia and Africa, and its flavour is something between a small red radish and a young turnip. In the Far East, white radish is often grated and used to flavour sauces. It is especially valued for its digestive qualities and is often served with tofu. In Japan it is sometimes dried, when it acquires a sweeter flavour which is excellent in vegetable soups. Indians generally eat mooli, as they call them, chopped up as an appetizer, rather as we eat red radishes in Europe. Fresh white radish can be bought from Chinese grocers all year round, but for the Japanese dried or pickled radish or daikon you may have to go to a specialist wholefood shop.

VEGETABLE SOUP
WITH DAIKON AND NOODLES

Daikon imparts an interesting flavour to this soup. The stock can be used as a basis for many other soups too.

1.5 litres/2½ pints boiling water
15 g/½ oz daikon, shredded
2½ tablespoons soy sauce
1 level teaspoon chilli sauce
1 large onion, chopped
2 tablespoons vegetable oil *or* 90 g/3 oz vegetable margarine
250 g/8 oz carrot, grated
125 g/4 oz wholewheat *or* buckwheat noodles

garnish
30 g/1 oz parsley, chopped

Make the stock by mixing in a bowl the water, daikon, soy sauce and chilli sauce. Fry the onion in the oil or margarine, and after a few minutes, add the carrot. Pour in the stock and bring to the boil. Allow to simmer, covered, until the carrots are soft. Add the noodles and simmer the soup rapidly for another 5 minutes.
Serve hot, garnished with chopped fresh parsley.

PARATHAS
STUFFED WITH MOOLI AND ONION

In India parathas, an unleavened bread, like chapatis, are made from *ata*, a finely ground, low gluten wholewheat flour. If this is not available, use a mixture of wholewheat and plain white flours, both finely ground. The usual ghee may be replaced by melted vegetable margarine. Stuffed parathas are a popular breakfast or snack in North India; sometimes the stuffing is a spicy potato mixture or a mixture of other vegetables, as in this recipe.

parathas
250 g/8 oz wholewheat flour
125 g/4 oz plain white flour
1 heaped teaspoon salt
60 g/2 oz vegetable margarine, melted *or* ghee
approx 150 ml/¼ pint water

filling
350 g/12 oz white radish *or* mooli, grated
1 tablespoon mustard seeds
vegetable oil for frying
1 large onion, grated
1 green chilli, finely chopped (optional)
2 heaped teaspoons salt

to serve
pickle *or* chutney (optional)

First prepare the parathas. Mix the two flours with the salt. Melt the vegetable margarine or ghee and rub it into the flour mixture, as if making pastry. Add enough water to make a pliable dough and knead well. Leave the mixture aside, in a bowl covered with polythene, while you make the filling.

Press the grated white radish or mooli between kitchen paper to remove any excess moisture. Fry the mustard seeds in a little of the oil and combine all the other ingredients.

Knead the paratha mixture for a few minutes more and then divide it into 6 balls. Indian cooks usually roll out all the dough for a single paratha, put the filling in the middle and, after sealing the filling in the middle of the dough, roll out the dough and filling on a well-floured board. Alternatively, you can roll out 2 thin parathas from a single ball and enclose a layer of filling between them.

Heat a large, cast iron frying pan over a low heat: when it is thoroughly heated, brush with about 1 tablespoon of the oil and cook the first paratha for 2–3 minutes on each side. While the first side is cooking, brush the top with oil. Repeat until all the parathas are cooked.

Serve immediately, perhaps with some pickle or chutney.

Ginger

Ginger is the rhizome of a tropical plant, widely cultivated in southern Asia, Africa and the West Indies. In European cookery, ginger is best known in its dried and powdered form and has mainly been used in sweet confections. The whole root, however, is of great value in savoury recipes and is delicious in all kinds of rice, vegetable and pulse dishes. Indian and Far Eastern cookery make excellent use of root ginger and we should follow their example because ginger goes very well with our northern root vegetables like parsnips, turnips, carrots and potatoes. The Chinese combination of ginger, garlic and soy sauce is a favourite of mine. As ginger is a very warming spice – used in large quantities it produces copious sweating! – it is a particularly good flavouring for winter dishes. Candied stem ginger is a Chinese delicacy made from young, tender ginger roots and sugar. It can be used in desserts and goes particularly well with melons and pears.

When buying root ginger, make sure that it is neither too hard nor too fibrous. It should be peeled very thinly because, as with many roots, most of the flavour is concentrated just underneath the skin. Root ginger may be kept in the bottom of the refrigerator for some weeks. Dried, ground ginger, for use in cakes, biscuits and desserts, should be bought in small amounts because, like most ready ground spices, it goes stale quickly.

CHICK PEA AND GINGER SOUP

175 g/6 oz chick peas
3 tablespoons vegetable oil
2 large onions, chopped
2–3 green chillies, chopped
4 cloves garlic, chopped
900 ml/1½ pints light vegetable stock
salt
45 g/1½ oz fresh root ginger, grated
juice of 2 lemons

garnish
coriander leaves, finely chopped

Soak the chick peas for at least 6 hours, then wash and drain them. Alternatively, parcook them in a pressure cooker. Heat the oil in a large soup pan and add the onions, chillies and garlic. Fry on a low heat for 10 minutes before adding the chick peas and stock. Cover the pan and leave to simmer for 1 hour. After this add the salt, grated ginger and the lemon juice. Cover again, and leave to simmer until the chick peas are quite soft – about 30 minutes. Add more salt to taste, and serve garnished with finely chopped coriander leaves.

VEGETABLE CRUMBLE
FLAVOURED WITH GINGER

175 g/6 oz mushrooms, chopped *or* 15 g/½ oz dried mushrooms
600 ml/1 pint water (for soaking dried mushrooms)
250 g/8 oz onions, thinly sliced
4 tablespoons vegetable oil
250 g/8 oz parsnips, thinly sliced
250 g/8 oz carrots, thinly sliced
5 cloves garlic, finely chopped
30 g/1 oz fresh root ginger, grated
600 ml/1 pint water (only if using fresh mushrooms)
1 small bunch parsley, chopped
3 tablespoons soy sauce

crumble
200 g/7 oz soft oatflakes
60 g/2 oz wheatgerm
125 g/4 oz vegetable margarine *plus* extra for topping
125 g/4 oz cheese (e.g. Cheddar *or* Cheshire), grated
2 tablespoons soy sauce
60 g/2 oz sesame seeds

If using dried mushrooms, soak them in the 600 ml (1 pint) of water. Preheat the oven to 180° C (350° F, gas mark 4). Simmer the onions in the oil, then after 5 minutes add the parsnips, carrots, garlic and ginger. Stir fry for a few minutes, then cover the pan and leave to simmer for 15–20 minutes while you prepare the crumble.

Mix the oatflakes and wheatgerm together and then rub in the margarine and cheese. Season with soy sauce.

Now add the 600 ml (1 pint) of soaking water or, if using fresh mushrooms, 600 ml (1 pint) fresh water, the mushrooms, the chopped parsley and the 3 tablespoons of soy sauce to the vegetables simmering in the pan. Grease a large casserole dish and transfer the vegetable mixture into it. Press the crumble evenly over the top, then add the sesame seeds and a few dots of vegetable margarine. Bake for 45 minutes; cover with a lid for the first 30 minutes of cooking and then allow to brown.

GINGER AND DRIED FRUIT FOOL

350 g/12 oz mixed dried fruit (prunes, apricots, apples, pears etc.)
300 ml/½ pint water
juice of 1 lemon
15 g/½ oz fresh root ginger, pounded *or* 30 g/1 oz preserved stem ginger
350 g/12 oz Greek yoghurt

Soak the dried fruit in the water for a few hours. Pour the water and fruit into a saucepan and simmer until the liquid is reduced by half. Remove the stones from the prunes and put all the dried fruit and juice in a liquidizer. Add the lemon juice, ginger and yoghurt and blend to a smooth puree. Chill the mixture in the refrigerator before serving.

RHUBARB AND GINGER
SEMOLINA PUDDING

Rhubarb seems to have a special affinity with ginger – the warm taste of the ginger offsets the acidity of the rhubarb.

700 g/1½ lb rhubarb
15 g/½ oz fresh root ginger
150 ml/¼ pint water
juice of 1 large *or* 2 small lemons
125 g/4 oz brown sugar
45 g/1½ oz semolina
60 g/2 oz almonds, ground

Wash the rhubarb and peel off the skin unless the stems are very young. Cut into short pieces. Cut off a piece of root ginger and peel it very thinly. Grate or pare with a sharp knife, discarding the centre if it is too fibrous. Put the rhubarb, ginger, water, lemon juice and sugar into a pan (avoid using one made of copper or cast iron because the rhubarb will react with it) and simmer until the rhubarb is quite soft. Liquidize or sieve the mixture and return it to the pan. Slowly bring to the boil, while gradually adding the semolina and the ground almonds. Stir constantly to prevent lumps forming, and when the mixture has thickened take it off the heat, still stirring. Pour into one large bowl or individual bowls, and refrigerate before serving.

Hot tastes: Ginger

PARKIN

This old English cake recipe is very easy to make and produces delicious results. Parkin was traditionally eaten in the North of England at Michaelmas.

350 g/12 oz medium ground oatmeal
175 g/6 oz wholewheat flour
2 level teaspoons ginger, ground
2 level teaspoons cinnamon, ground
1 teaspoon salt
2 level teaspoons bicarbonate of soda
125 g/4 oz brown sugar
175 g/6 oz vegetable margarine
150 g/5 oz black treacle
150 ml/¼ pint milk

Preheat the oven to 180° C (350° F, gas mark 4). Mix all the dry ingredients together. Then melt the margarine in a saucepan and add the black treacle and the milk. Combine the dry and liquid ingredients and mix well. Grease a square baking tin or a 1 kg (2¼ lb) loaf tin and fill it with the cake mixture. Bake for 1 hour. Allow to cool slightly before taking out of the tin, and then cool the cake thoroughly on a wire rack. Put it in an airtight tin and store for 2 weeks before eating.

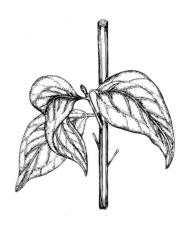

Horseradish

The horseradish plant is easily cultivated all over northern Europe and has traditionally been used in German and Scandinavian as well as in English cookery. Horseradish is best when freshly grated but, as it is rarely found in shops, it is difficult to use it like this unless you have some growing in the garden. If you buy dried horseradish, make sure that it is vacuum sealed because the aromatic oils which give horseradish its flavour are very fugitive. Horseradish preserve, made by mixing the root with vinegar, is readily available and has quite an acceptable flavour.

Horseradish can be used to make some interesting salad dressings, and is especially useful where a strong flavour is needed, for instance to accompany bean salads. It combines well with cheese and can be used to enliven a dull-tasting one. Horseradish mustard (wasabi) is a popular condiment in Japan.

LENTIL SALAD
WITH HORSERADISH DRESSING

Lentils are an excellent food with a very high iron and protein content, but they need a strong seasoning to give them flavour. Horseradish provides the necessary bite in this recipe.

500 g/1 lb brown lentils
1.25 litres/2 pints water
250 g/8 oz mung beansprouts
½ cucumber, diced
1 small bunch parsley, chopped

dressing
2 dessertspoons horseradish preserve
2 tablespoons sunflower oil
juice of 1 large lemon
2 cloves garlic, crushed
2 level teaspoons salt

Soak the lentils for 1–2 hours, then drain and cook in 1.25 litres (2 pints) of water until soft but still whole. Drain, and mix with the raw beansprouts, cucumber and parsley. Combine the salad dressing ingredients and pour them over the lentil mixture. Stir well and leave for some hours so that the flavours penetrate the lentils.

BEETROOT SALAD WITH HORSERADISH AND CURD CHEESE DRESSING

salad
½ clove garlic
350 g/12 oz cooked beetroot
2 tart eating apples

dressing
125 g/4 oz curd cheese
1 heaped tablespoon prepared horseradish *or* 1 level tablespoon dried, grated
horseradish
juice of 1 lemon
4 tablespoons cider vinegar
cold water to mix
1 level teaspoon sweet paprika
salt

garnish
30 g/1 oz parsley *or* alfalfa sprouts, chopped

Rub a salad bowl with the garlic. Cut the beetroot and the apples into cubes and put them in the bowl. In a separate bowl, mix the curd cheese with the horseradish and lemon juice. Beat in the vinegar and add a little cold water to make a good liquid consistency. Season with paprika and salt to taste, and combine with the apples and beetroot in the salad bowl (the beetroot will turn the dressing a beautiful shade of pink!). Garnish with the chopped parsley or alfalfa sprouts.

Mustard

The mustard plant is a native of Europe, and a member of the large family of crucifers, which include the cabbage. There are three seed-bearing varieties of mustard: white, black and brown. The last two are by far the most pungent but black mustard is not much grown commercially due to the unwieldiness of the plant. Traditional English and French mustards are made with the brown seeds, and American mustard with the white.

Unlike many spices, mustard loses nothing in flavour by being ground and used later: its pungency develops, by enzyme action, only when the powder is mixed with cold water. So when you mix up mustard, add water and allow it to stand for 10 minutes before use and before adding to salad dressings or sauces. This 'English' mustard is rather strong and should be used sparingly – though in cooked dishes, a good deal of the flavour will evaporate.

French mustard is produced mainly in Dijon, which still manufactures half of the world's supply, and in Bordeaux. Dijon mustard is blended with wine vinegar and herbs and has a pleasant, sweet taste which offsets its heat. It is very suitable for use in vegetarian cookery. Bordeaux mustard is darker in colour and heavily seasoned with tarragon.

In India, mustard seeds are generally fried whole and used to garnish vegetarian dishes. After frying, most of the seeds' pungency is lost, leaving a pleasant nutty taste. Mustard oil, extracted from the pressed seeds, also adds its distinctive flavour to certain Indian dishes, particularly those of Bengal.

Mustard seedlings, which the seventeenth-century diarist John Evelyn recommended as being of 'incomparable effect to quicken and revive the spirits', can add an interesting flavour to salads all the year round. They can be grown easily on blotting paper or flannel, as many children know. But beware – the boxes of seedlings on sale in greengrocers are not mustard or cress, but rape, which has a much blander taste.

PEASE PUDDING

This traditional English dish is made more interesting by adding a seasoning of mustard and honey. Serve it with a tossed green salad. The mixture would also make a good filling for vegetable pasties.

350 g/12 oz dried green split peas
2 small onions, sliced thinly
4 carrots, grated
a few sprigs mint, chopped
1½ tablespoons Dijon mustard *or* 1 heaped teaspoon English made mustard
1 tablespoon honey
1½ teaspoons salt

Wash the peas thoroughly, bring them up to the boil in plenty of water, wash again and leave to soak for 1 hour. Boil, then simmer them for 20–30 minutes or until they are soft. Drain, and mash with a fork. Mix together the onions, carrots and mint with the peas and season with mustard, honey and salt. Spoon the mixture into a greased 900 ml (1½ pint) sized pudding basin, seal the top with foil and a strong elastic band and place in a large saucepan or steamer. Pour boiling water into the pan to reach halfway up the side of the basin. Put a lid on the saucepan and keep the water simmering rapidly for about 50 minutes.

MACARONI CASSEROLE FLAVOURED WITH MUSTARD

300 g/10 oz wholewheat macaroni
250 g/8 oz leeks, thinly sliced
4 cloves garlic, minced
75 g/2½ oz vegetable margarine
2 level tablespoons plain white flour
600 ml/1 pint milk
175 g/6 oz Gouda *or* Edam cheese, grated
2 tablespoons Dijon mustard
salt
black pepper
175 g/6 oz mushrooms, chopped
250 g/8 oz tomatoes, sliced

Cook the pasta in plenty of boiling, salted water for 10 minutes. Preheat the oven to 180° C (350° F, gas mark 4).

Blanch the leeks in boiling water for 5 minutes.

Fry the garlic in the margarine on a low heat for 1–2 minutes. Keep the heat low while you stir in the flour and then gradually add the milk. Stir continuously until the sauce thickens, then add the cheese and the mustard. Season with salt and pepper, then combine the sauce with the leeks, pasta, chopped mushrooms and sliced tomatoes. Spoon the mixture into a large, greased casserole dish and bake for 30–40 minutes.

GREEN VEGETABLES TOSSED WITH MUSTARD SEEDS

This is an interesting way of serving green vegetables such as runner or French beans, cauliflower, broccoli or sprouts.

Boil the vegetables in salted water until they are just tender. For every 500 g (1 lb) of vegetables, fry 2 tablespoons mustard seeds in 2 tablespoons vegetable oil. When the seeds begin to pop, add the cooked vegetables, stir well and squeeze the juice of a small lemon over them. Serve at once with a seasoning of black or white pepper.

GREEN SPLIT PEAS WITH
YOGHURT AND MUSTARD SEED DRESSING

350 g/12 oz green split peas
1 litre/1¾ pints water
2 medium onions, chopped
2 tablespoons vegetable margarine
250 g/8 oz carrots, grated
1 tablespoon salt

dressing
2 tablespoons vegetable oil
3 tablespoons mustard seeds
300 g/10 oz plain yoghurt
2 level teaspoons garam masala

garnish
1 small bunch coriander leaves, finely chopped (optional)

Wash the split peas, then bring them to the boil in a saucepan of water. Drain and wash, then bring them again to the boil with 1 litre (1¾ pints) water. Leave to simmer for 30 minutes in an open pan.

Fry the onions in the margarine on a low heat for 10 minutes, then add them, with the carrots and salt, to the split peas. Leave the mixture to simmer for a further 10–15 minutes, by which time the split peas should be completely soft and most of the liquid evaporated. In a separate pan, heat the oil and fry the mustard seeds until they pop. Mix together in a basin the yoghurt, mustard seeds and garam masala. Pour this over the split peas immediately before serving. Top with coriander leaves, if liked.

CARROT SALAD
FLAVOURED WITH MUSTARD SEEDS

300 g/10 oz carrots, grated
a few spring onions, chopped
125 g/4 oz mung beansprouts
125 g/4 oz unsalted peanut halves
150 g/5 oz raisins
3 tablespoons mustard seeds
3 tablespoons vegetable oil
juice of 1 small lemon
1 teaspoon salt

Combine the carrots, spring onions, beansprouts, peanuts and raisins in a salad bowl. Fry the mustard seeds in the oil until they begin to pop, then add both the seeds and the oil to the salad: mix all the ingredients together with the lemon juice and salt.

Hot tastes: Mustard

REMOULADE SAUCE

This creamy, mustard-flavoured sauce is excellent in summer with new potatoes and salads of cooked or uncooked vegetables. It is usually made with egg yolks only, but adding the whites creates a lighter texture.

2 hardboiled eggs
1 raw egg yolk
2 teaspoons Dijon mustard
150ml/¼ pint vegetable oil
2 tablespoons wine vinegar *or* cider vinegar
chives, chopped
salt
white pepper

Shell the hardboiled eggs and mash them well with a fork. Mix in the raw yolk and the mustard. Add the oil, little by little, as for mayonnaise (but this sauce is easier to make as it is less inclined to separate). When all the oil has been added, mix in the vinegar, chives, salt and pepper to taste.

FLAVOURED MUSTARD

This tasty mustard can be mixed up in a few minutes, but it should be left a few weeks for the flavour to mature.

6 tablespoons mustard seeds
2 tablespoons honey
4 tablespoons cider vinegar
1 heaped teaspoon salt
1 tablespoon lemon juice
2 tablespoons water

Grind 4 tablespoons of the mustard seeds in a coffee grinder, but leave the other 2 tablespoons whole. Mix all the ingredients together very thoroughly. Put the mustard into a jar with a screw top or a ceramic pot with a tight-fitting cork.

Paprika

Paprika is perhaps most widely used in Hungarian cooking, and it is also a popular seasoning in Spain. It is made by drying and grinding different species of red peppers. Depending on the species used, it can range from hot to rather mild and sweet, and it is therefore usually sold as either 'hot' or 'sweet' paprika. The hot variety should be added, like chilli powder, to taste, but the sweet type may be used generously – 1 or even 2 teaspoons in a single dish.

Paprika should be a brilliant red when you buy it. It is best not to buy too much at a time, because both colour and flavour tend to fade. Like pepper, it should be added if possible at the end of the cooking time because its flavour is fugitive. Paprika is useful for sprinkling on soups and salads – not only for its flavour, but also for its attractive colour. It has a high vitamin C content.

PUMPKIN SOUP
FLAVOURED WITH PAPRIKA

900 g/2 lb pumpkin, peeled and deseeded
2 large onions, chopped
4 cloves garlic, chopped
3 tablespoons vegetable margarine
2 teaspoons salt
2 teaspoons sweet *or* hot paprika
3 tablespoons Greek yoghurt

to serve
Parmesan cheese

Cut the pumpkin into chunks. Fry the onions and garlic in the margarine on a low heat for 10 minutes. Add the chopped pumpkin and salt and cook slowly for 30 minutes. Add the paprika, and transfer the soup to a liquidizer. Blend and return to the pan. Simmer for a few minutes, then take off the heat and stir in the yoghurt.

Serve hot with a bowl of grated Parmesan cheese for sprinkling on top.

JERUSALEM ARTICHOKE
AND CELERY SOUFFLE

Really fresh paprika is a delicate seasoning, well suited to the light and airy texture of a soufflé. The combination of Jerusalem artichokes and celery makes a delicious soup and an equally tasty soufflé. Serve it with a tossed green salad.

350 g/12 oz Jerusalem artichokes, peeled
125 g/4 oz celery heart, chopped
juice of ½ lemon
75 g/2½ oz vegetable margarine
45 g/1½ oz plain white flour
200 ml/⅓ pint milk
60 g/2 oz Parmesan cheese, grated
1 heaped teaspoon sweet paprika
2 cloves garlic, crushed
1 heaped teaspoon salt
4 eggs
15 g/½ oz fresh breadcrumbs, finely grated

Preheat the oven to 200° C (400° F, gas mark 6). Steam the Jerusalem artichokes and celery until just soft. Put them in a blender with the lemon juice and make a smooth puree. Slowly heat a thick-bottomed pan and melt the margarine in it. Stir in the flour and then gradually add the milk, stirring all the time. (When making a thick béchamel sauce like this one, it is a good idea to heat the pan very thoroughly and stir in the flour and milk with the pan off the heat.) Add the grated Parmesan cheese and stir until it has thoroughly melted into the sauce. Add the paprika, crushed garlic and salt.

Set the sauce aside while you separate the egg yolks and beat the whites until they are stiff. Grease a 1.5 litre (2½ pint) soufflé dish and cover the bottom and sides with most of the breadcrumbs. In a bowl, combine the béchamel sauce with the Jerusalem artichoke mixture and then stir in the egg yolks. Take a heaped tablespoon of egg white and beat it into the rest of the ingredients, then lightly fold in the rest of the whites. Transfer the mixture immediately to the prepared soufflé dish and top with the remainder of the breadcrumbs. Put the dish in the oven straightaway, standing on a metal tray, and bake for 25 minutes. If you find that the top of the soufflé is browning too quickly, cover it with a piece of foil (but open and close the oven door gently, and do not leave it open for more than a few seconds). Serve quickly.

BUCKWHEAT TOPPED WITH CABBAGE AND SOUR CREAM

This is a very eastern European combination of ingredients. The sour cream may be replaced by a mixture of yoghurt and curd cheese if preferred.

500 g/1 lb buckwheat, roasted
2 tablespoons vegetable oil
1 litre/1¾ pints boiling water
900 g/2 lb cabbage
5 tablespoons water
60 g/2 oz vegetable margarine
5 tablespoons sour cream
2 teaspoons hot *or* sweet paprika
2 cloves garlic, crushed
2 teaspoons salt

Fry the buckwheat in the oil for 1–2 minutes, then add 1 litre (1¾ pints) of boiling water and let it simmer, uncovered, until all the liquid has been absorbed. By this time the buckwheat should be well cooked, but still retain a slight crunchiness.

Chop the cabbage finely (the greener and fresher the cabbage, the better) and put it in a large saucepan with 5 tablespoons of water. Cook, stirring, with the heat turned up high for 4–5 minutes. Add the margarine and let the pan contents simmer rapidly for a further 4–5 minutes. Take the pan off the heat and mix into it the sour cream, paprika, crushed garlic and salt.

Serve the buckwheat topped with the cabbage mixture.

SWEETCORN AND PAPRIKA FRITTERS

2 large sweetcorn cobs
125 g/4 oz wholewheat flour
2 teaspoons salt, *or* more to taste
1 heaped teaspoon hot *or* sweet paprika
1 egg, beaten
150 ml/¼ pint milk
2 cloves garlic, crushed
60 g/2 oz Parmesan cheese, grated
vegetable oil for frying

Boil the sweetcorn cobs in salted water until soft. When cool, scrape the corn from the cobs with a sharp knife. Put the flour, salt and paprika in a basin and add the beaten egg. Mix in the milk and beat well with a fork. Add the sweetcorn, garlic and cheese, stir, and allow the mixture to stand for at least 15 minutes. Heat a little oil in a heavy-bottomed frying pan and fry the mixture, 1 tablespoon at a time, over a low to medium heat. The fritters should be cooked for 2–3 minutes on each side, until golden brown.

Pepper

The pepper vine, a native of South India, is now cultivated all over southern Asia. Both black and white peppercorns are produced by the same plant, but the method of preparing them is different. Black peppercorns are picked unripe and then left to dry in the sun, whereas white peppercorns are picked ripe before being soaked and skinned.

Peppercorns are nearly always ground before use, except in pickling, when they are used whole and not only enhance the flavour but also inhibit the growth of bacteria. The stronger-tasting black pepper is nowadays more frequently used in cookery than white. The latter has a lighter, almost fruity, flavour and for this reason, and for its appearance, it is often preferred in more delicately seasoned and pale coloured foods like white sauces, mayonnaise and egg dishes. Whatever colour pepper you are using, it is very important to grind the peppercorns freshly just before use, as the aromatic oils which give pepper its flavour are lost soon after grinding. This is why pepper is not usually added to a cooked dish until the end.

Pepper is used almost as universally as salt (Europeans and Americans are currently its largest consumers), and plays such an important part in the savoury diet that it would be impossible to list all its uses. I like to use plenty of black pepper with yoghurt, especially in raitas, in soups, with pasta, cooked cheese dishes, mushrooms and Brussels sprouts.

YOGHURT, CUCUMBER AND PEPPER SOUP

2 medium onions, chopped
60 g/2 oz vegetable margarine
1 large cucumber, diced
1 vegetable stock cube
1 litre/1¾ pints boiling water
1 tablespoon mint, chopped
2 teaspoons salt, *or* more to taste
90 g/3 oz small pasta *or* noodles
300 ml/½ pint Greek yoghurt
1 level teaspoon black pepper, freshly ground

Gently fry the onions in the margarine for 5 minutes. Add the diced cucumber and fry for a few minutes more. Make the stock by dissolving the stock cube in boiling water, then add it, with the chopped mint, salt and pasta, to the soup pot. Cover, and leave to simmer until the pasta is soft. Turn the heat down low and stir in the yoghurt and black pepper. This soup is generously seasoned and the final flavour should be distinctly peppery.

Serve either hot or chilled.

CHEESE AND WALNUT BREAD

This savoury bread is almost a meal in itself, and very useful for sandwich lunches.

Follow the basic wholewheat loaves recipe on p. 216 and for each 500 g/1 lb flour, add:
90 g/3 oz walnuts, broken
90 g/3 oz cheese, e.g. Cheddar *or* Gloucester, grated
½ teaspoon black pepper, freshly ground

Add these ingredients while kneading the bread for the first time.

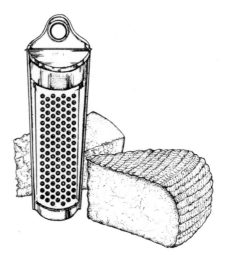

Sour tastes

AMCHOOR
LEMON GRASS
LEMONS AND LIMES
SORREL
TAMARIND

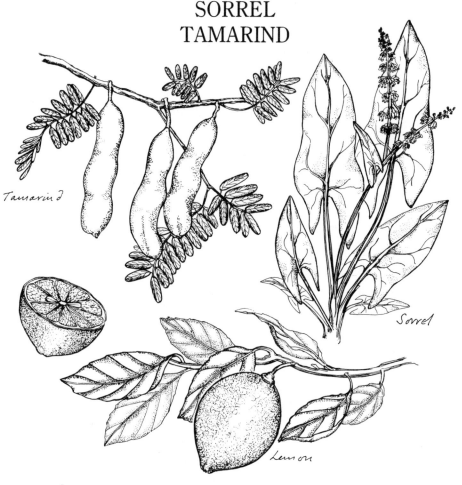

Tamarind

Sorrel

Lemon

Amchoor

This pleasant, fruity-tasting spice made from dried, unripe mangoes is useful when only the hint of a sour taste is required. Amchoor is generally used in combination with Indian spices such as cumin, cardamom, ginger and chilli powder, but in our less spicy European food, I think there is scope for using it on its own. It is sold in powdered form and, since the taste is light, should be used in fairly generous quantities.

DHAL FLAVOURED WITH AMCHOOR

175 g/6 oz red lentils
175 g/6 oz green split peas
300 g/10 oz onions
300 g/10 oz carrots
4 cloves garlic
4 tablespoons vegetable oil
2 heaped teaspoons amchoor
2 heaped teaspoons salt
500 ml/18 fl oz hot water
2 level teaspons garam masala (optional)

to serve
chopped parsley *or* coriander leaves

Wash the lentils and split peas in several changes of water. Chop the onions, carrots and garlic quite finely. Fry the onions and garlic in the vegetable oil for 5 minutes. Add the amchoor and continue to fry, stirring, for another 1–2 minutes. Add the lentils, split peas, carrots, salt and hot water. Bring to the boil, then cover and simmer over a low to medium heat for 45 minutes. Stir occasionally to make sure that the mixture is not sticking to the bottom of the pot (lentils have a habit of burning). Lower the heat if necessary. Add 2 teaspoons of garam masala at the end of the cooking time if you prefer a more spicy mixture. Allow to cool slightly before serving.

Serve with a bowl of chopped parsley or coriander for sprinkling.

SUMMER FRUIT SALAD
FLAVOURED WITH AMCHOOR

Amchoor adds an interesting tang to very ripe summer fruits. Experiment with different soft fruits in season. In India, street food vendors sell fruit salads flavoured not only with spices, but also with salt and pepper – a welcome combination in very hot weather.

3 large, very sweet peaches
2 large, ripe pears
1 ripe mango
juice of 1 lemon *or* lime
2 level teaspoons amchoor

garnish
wild strawberries
a few mint leaves *or* lime zest

Cut the fruit into slices and arrange it on a large plate. Squeeze the lemon or lime juice over the top and then sprinkle on the amchoor. Leave to chill for 1 hour or more. Garnish with mint leaves before serving.

Lemon grass

This is a tropical grass, the bulbous stem of which is used extensively in South-east Asian cookery as a souring agent. Lemon grass is a useful flavouring in rice and vegetable dishes. Although it is similar in flavour to lemons (both contain the same essential oil, citral), there is a subtle difference which makes it well worth using for certain recipes. Use the fresh bulb, rather than the dried version, if possible: it is often obtainable from Chinese grocers. One large bulb, bruised and chopped, is usually enough for a single dish.

AUBERGINE AND LEMON GRASS PUREE WITH BEANSPROUTS

This aubergine dish, cooked with a blend of Far Eastern flavours – lemon grass, ginger and soy sauce – is delicious with brown rice.

700 g/1½ lb aubergines
1 onion, chopped
2 tablespoons vegetable oil
4 cloves garlic
15 g/½ oz fresh root ginger
1 level teaspoon salt
2 small bulbs lemon grass, finely chopped
2 tablespoons soy sauce
300 ml/½ pint water
125 g/4 oz mung beansprouts

to serve
90 g/3 oz sesame seeds

Grill the whole aubergines until they are soft. Skin them, put them in a wire sieve, and press with a wooden spoon to extract the bitter juice. Fry the onion in the oil for 5 minutes. Chop the garlic and peel and grate the ginger, then add them to the onion. Continue to cook for 1–2 more minutes. Add the aubergine, salt, finely chopped lemon grass, soy sauce and water. Leave to fry gently over a medium heat for a further 30 minutes, by which time the ingredients will have cooked down to a fairly liquid puree. Stir in the beansprouts and serve. Roast the sesame seeds under the grill and serve them in a separate bowl for sprinkling on top.

SPICY RICE COOKED WITH LEMON GRASS

The idea for this recipe, in which hot and sour flavourings contrast with the creaminess of coconut milk, comes from South-east Asia. Blocks of creamed coconut, which may be dissolved in hot water, are available from Chinese grocers.

500 g/1 lb brown rice, preferably long grain
3 large cloves garlic
1 small red pepper
2 red chillies
30 g/1 oz fresh root ginger
1 large bulb lemon grass
2 tablespoons vegetable oil
175 g/6 oz creamed coconut dissolved in 750 ml/1¼ pints hot water
1 teaspoon salt
125 g/4 oz mung beansprouts
2 eggs

garnish
1 bunch spring onions

to serve
soy sauce

Soak the rice in cold water for about 15 minutes. Chop the garlic, red pepper and chillies finely. Bruise and chop the ginger and lemon grass. Heat the vegetable oil in a heavy-bottomed pan and add the chopped chillies, garlic, lemon grass, ginger and red pepper. Fry gently, stirring occasionally, for about 5 minutes. Drain the rice and add it to the pan: stir fry for a few minutes more. Next add the coconut milk and a little of the salt and cover the pan. Turn down the heat as low as possible (you may need to use a heat-diffusing pad), and leave to cook until the rice is soft and all the liquid has been absorbed. When the rice is cooked, transfer the contents of the pan to a serving dish and mix in the beansprouts. Keep the dish warm in the oven while you make a simple omelette by beating the eggs and frying them with a little salt. Cut this omelette into strips. Garnish the rice dish with the omelette strips and the spring onions.

Serve with a dish of soy sauce.

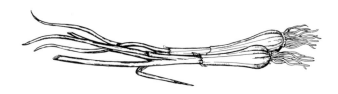

Lemons and limes

The lemon tree, originally from the Far East, is now widely cultivated in all parts of the world which enjoy a Mediterranean climate. Fortunately, in Britain fresh lemons are available throughout the year, imported from a variety of countries. No kitchen should be without them, for their flavour – mainly concentrated in the peel – is essential in cookery and the vitamin C content of the juice makes lemons, according to Mrs Grieve's *Herbal* (published in 1931), 'probably the most valuable of all fruit for preserving health'.

Lemons play such an extensive part in cookery that it would be impossible to list all their uses. In North Indian cookery they are the commonest souring agent in vegetable dishes. In Chinese and Persian cookery they provide the 'sour' ingredient of 'sweet and sour' dishes. In some parts of the Middle East powdered lemon peel is used as a condiment, like pepper. In European cookery we very often offset the sweetness of sugar or honey with the sourness of lemon peel or juice. In pickles, salad dressings, drinks and fruit desserts lemons are invaluable. Vegetables are often cooked in acidulated water (water with a squeeze of lemon juice) so as to preserve their colour – red cabbage or beetroot should be cooked in this way and so should white vegetables like cauliflower or salsify. Some people like to add a squeeze of lemon juice to the water when mixing up pastry dough.

Whereas lemons grow best in temperate regions, limes are more suited to tropical climates. They are becoming more easily available in Britain now and, since they keep very well in the refrigerator, it is worth buying a stock of them whenever possible. Limes have a strong yet subtle flavour which, like that of lemons, is especially concentrated in the peel. They are excellent in relishes and chutneys and in salad dressings, as well as with cream and curd cheeses. In really hot weather, there is nothing more refreshing than freshly squeezed lime juice diluted with iced water and a little sugar syrup.

ASPARAGUS
WITH LEMON HOLLANDAISE

Lemon juice is the traditional flavouring for this delicate sauce which is usually served with rather luxurious foods like asparagus and artichokes. I do not think the sauce suffers from being made with a good vegetable margarine instead of butter and with rather more lemon juice than is usual: the result is less rich than the traditional Hollandaise sauce.

Serve this dish with new potatoes or, as Elizabeth David* suggests, with *oeufs mollets* (eggs boiled so that the whites are set but the yolks are still soft).

500 g/1 lb asparagus

sauce
2 egg yolks
175 g/6 oz vegetable margarine
juice of 1 small lemon
white pepper

To cook the asparagus, tie it in a bundle and stand it, tips uppermost, in a saucepan of rapidly boiling water. If you do not have a high-sided saucepan, extend the height of the saucepan with foil. Cook for about 10 minutes, or longer if the stems are very thick.

For the sauce, heat some water in the bottom of a double saucepan, or in a saucepan into which a heatproof ceramic bowl will fit. The water should be kept just below boiling point while the sauce is being made. Drop the egg yolks into the top of a double boiler. Have the margarine ready, cut into a dozen or so pieces. Whisk the yolks and add the pieces of margarine one at a time, whisking continuously. Allow each piece of margarine to melt thoroughly before adding the next. The sauce should thicken slightly as you proceed (but not too much – if it seems to be thickening too quickly, add a few drops of cold water). When all the margarine has melted, take the sauce off the heat and add the lemon juice and pepper. Serve at once, or keep warm over hot water.

LIME JUICE AND HONEY DRESSING

This is a delicious dressing for green salads.

1 small clove garlic
5 tablespoons sunflower oil
juice of 1 lime
2 teaspoons honey
½ teaspoon hot *or* sweet paprika
salt

Crush the garlic and mix it with the oil. Add the lime juice and honey and mix well. Season with paprika and salt to taste.

* *French Provincial Cookery*, Elizabeth David, Michael Joseph, 1960.

LIMES PRESERVED IN OIL
WITH GINGER AND CHILLIES

Claudia Roden's *Book of Middle Eastern Food** gives a recipe for lemons or limes preserved in oil. I have added ginger and chillies (you could try adding garlic as well) to create a full-flavoured relish for use especially with vegetarian rice dishes. This preserve seems to become tastier the longer it is kept, and it will stay in good condition so long as all the ingredients are completely covered with oil.

Use any oil left in the jar for salad dressings.

600 g/1¼ lb limes *or* lemons
2 tablespoons salt
45 g/1½ oz fresh root ginger
45 g/1½ oz red chillies
450 ml/16 fl oz sunflower oil

Scrub the limes or lemons and put them in the freezing compartment of the refrigerator overnight. Next day, cut them into thin slices, sprinkle with the salt and leave them in a colander for a couple of hours. Peel the ginger very thinly, and wash and chop the red chillies. Put the limes, ginger and chillies into a 1 kg (2¼ lb) Kilner jar and then pour in the oil, making sure that there is a clear 1.5 cm (½ in) of oil covering the topmost ingredients (this is essential to prevent mould forming). Seal the jar and leave the contents to mature for at least 2 weeks.

INDIAN SOUR PICKLE

This is a good pickle to eat with brown rice. In summer it will only take about 10 days to mature, in winter rather longer. All home-made pickles have different shelf-lives and are best kept in the refrigerator.

6 limes *or* lemons, *and* juice of 4 more
60 g/2 oz red chillies, *or* more to taste
60 g/2 oz fresh root ginger
2 tablespoons mustard seeds
2 tablespoons salt
3 tablespoons brown sugar
2 teaspoons kalonji (nigella seeds)

Scrub the limes in hot water. Cut them in half lengthways, then crossways, into thin slices. Remove the seeds from the chillies, unless you want a very hot pickle. Slice the chillies and ginger finely. Mix all the ingredients together in a basin. Stir well. Transfer to a 1 kg (2¼ lb) jar and press the ingredients well down. Stand in a warm place, preferably in sunlight, covered with a lid. Give the bottle a good shake two or three times a day.

* *Book of Middle Eastern Food*, Claudia Roden, Thomas Nelson, 1968.

FROZEN LIME CHEESECAKE

base
125 g/4 oz vegetable margarine
175 g/6 oz digestive biscuits

filling
2 eggs
juice of 2 limes *and* peel of 3, grated
90 g/3 oz brown sugar
250 g/8 oz curd cheese

garnish
thin slices of lime

Make the base: first melt the margarine, then crush the digestive biscuits with the end of a rolling pin and mix them well with the melted margarine. Press this mixture evenly into the bottom of a 20 or 23 cm (8 or 9 in) flan dish.

To make the filling, first separate the eggs. Set a heatproof china bowl over the top of a saucepan of boiling water and break in the yolks. Add the lime juice, peel and sugar and stir the mixture for about 15 minutes, or until it thickens. Take the bowl off the heat and beat in the curd cheese. Beat the egg whites until stiff and fold them into the lime mixture. Pour all these ingredients over the base and put the cheesecake into the freezer to set (this may take several hours). Decorate the top of the cheesecake with thin slices of lime.

DATE AND WALNUT LOAF FLAVOURED WITH LEMON ZEST

In this recipe plenty of lemon zest and a hint of cardamom counteract the sweetness of the dates.

175 g/6 oz dates
peel of 3 lemons, grated *and* juice of 1
2 eggs
200 g/7 oz vegetable margarine
400 g/14 oz wholemeal flour
2 teaspoons baking powder
1 level teaspoon salt
seeds from 4–5 cardamom pods, ground
125 g/4 oz walnuts, broken

Preheat the oven to 150° C (300° F, gas mark 2). Simmer the dates very slowly in a little water and lemon juice. The total amount of liquid should be only about 100 ml (4 fl oz). When the dates are soft and most of the liquid has been absorbed, put the dates, lemon peel and eggs in a liquidizer and blend. Put this mixture into a bowl and cream it with the margarine. Combine the flour, baking powder, salt, ground cardamom seeds and broken walnuts in a separate bowl, then gradually beat them into the date and margarine mixture.

Grease a 500 g/1 lb loaf tin, turn the cake mixture into it and bake for 50 minutes. Allow to cool thoroughly before serving.

LIME MARMALADE

This is arguably the most delicious of all marmalades. Lime peel is very hard, so use a very sharp knife to pare it. This recipe makes about 3.5 kg (8 lb) marmalade.

1.5 kg/3 lb limes
3.5 litres/6 pints water
3 kg/6 lb demerara sugar

Cut the limes in half and squeeze out the juice. Pare the skins as finely as possible. Put the juice and peel in a large basin and pour in the water. Leave to soak for 24 hours. Put the sugar in a low oven to heat. At the same time, heat the jam jars. Pour the lime juice, peel and water into a preserving pan and very slowly bring it to the boil. Add the sugar when the mixture is boiling. Continue to boil rapidly until setting point has been reached (test a spoonful of the boiling liquid on a cold saucer to see whether it gels). Pour the marmalade into the warmed jars and cover with waxed paper discs. Allow to cool thoroughly before sealing the jars.

LEMON BARLEY WATER

This is a good alternative to commercially made soft drinks, which are usually laden with sugar and additives. It is also very economical.

250 g/8 oz pearl barley
2 litres/3½ pints water
6 lemons
125 g/4 oz brown sugar *or* 4 tablespoons honey

Put the barley in a large saucepan, just cover it with water and bring to the boil. Strain and wash under the cold tap. This removes any scum from the grains. Return the barley to the saucepan and add the water. Bring up to the boil again, and then lower the heat so that the liquid is gently simmering. Squeeze the juice from the lemons into a separate bowl and leave aside. Put the skins from 3 of the lemons into the pan with the barley, cover and leave to simmer for 1 hour. Then strain the liquid through a fine-meshed sieve (press the residue with a wooden spoon) and add the lemon juice and sugar or honey. Stir well and chill before drinking.

Sour tastes: Lemons and limes

Sorrel

Sorrel is an extremely useful flavouring. The taste is sour rather than bitter – there are even old recipes for making lemonade using sorrel leaves – and just a few leaves will impart a distinctive flavour to any dish in which they are used. Along with its wild relation, the wood sorrel, it was once popular in English cookery, especially in salads and 'green' sauces. The seventeenth-century diarist John Evelyn wrote that sorrel leaves impart 'so grateful a quickness to salads that they should never be left out'.

It is a great pity, therefore, that sorrel is rarely available in Britain nowadays, but that disadvantage is partly compensated for by the fact that sorrel is very easy to grow. The seeds germinate rapidly and the plants, once established, are hardy and perennial. In France, it is common to find a patch of sorrel growing in country gardens, and French cookery books always contain plenty of recipes for sorrel (*l'oseille*).

Sorrel has a high vitamin C and iron content which should recommend it to us as much as it did to the old herbalists. It can be quickly boiled down to form a puree and is a useful ingredient in soups, sauces, lentil and bean dishes. Sorrel is excellent in combination with bland-tasting vegetables like potatoes and Jerusalem artichokes. Elizabeth David highly recommends sorrel puree and cream as a filling for omelettes*.

When cooking sorrel, avoid using an iron pan as the acid content will react with the iron in an unpleasant way.

SORREL AND POTATO SOUP

700 g/1½ lb potatoes
2 large cloves garlic
150 g/5 oz sorrel leaves
60 g/2 oz vegetable margarine
300 ml/½ pint lightly flavoured stock
salt
200 ml/⅓ pint single cream
1 egg, beaten
black *or* white pepper

Boil the potatoes until they are very soft. Crush the garlic and fry it gently with the sorrel leaves in the margarine for about 5 minutes, until the leaves have softened and can be broken up with a wooden spoon. Take the pan off the heat and sieve in the potatoes. Add the stock and 1 teaspoon of salt. Stir well and bring to the boil. Simmer for 10 minutes, then take the pan off the heat and stir in the cream and the beaten egg. Season well with pepper and more salt to taste. This soup can be served hot or chilled.

* *French Provincial Cookery*, Elizabeth David, Michael Joseph, 1960.

SORREL, CHEESE AND EGG TART

This recipe makes either one large or two smaller tarts, which can be served warm or cold with a green salad.

crust
250 g/8 oz wholewheat flour
125 g/4 oz vegetable margarine
4 tablespoons cold water

filling
200 g/7 oz sorrel leaves
150 g/5 oz Gouda cheese
60 g/2 oz Parmesan cheese
15 g/½ oz vegetable margarine
30 g/1 oz plain flour
250 ml/8 fl oz milk
1 large clove garlic, crushed
white pepper
2 eggs, beaten

Make the pastry in the usual way (see p. 218), and set it aside in the refrigerator while you prepare the filling. Preheat the oven to 180° C (350° F, gas mark 4).

Wash the sorrel and simmer it for a few minutes until it is softened (there is no need to add extra water). Break the sorrel up with a wooden spoon. Grate the cheeses. Melt the vegetable margarine in a pan and stir in the plain flour. Gradually add the milk, stirring all the time. Add the sorrel and the grated cheeses and continue to stir until the sauce is well blended. Take the pan off the heat and add the crushed garlic, a good seasoning of white pepper and lastly, when the mixture has cooled a little, the 2 beaten eggs.

Roll out the pastry and line a greased 25 cm (10 in) flan dish or two smaller (15 cm/6 in) dishes. Pour in the filling and bake for 30 minutes.

GREEN LENTILS COOKED WITH SORREL

250 g/8 oz green lentils
2 large onions
4 cloves garlic
60 g/2 oz vegetable margarine
1–2 teaspoons salt
600 ml/1 pint water
150 g/5 oz sorrel leaves
black *or* cayenne pepper

garnish
4 hardboiled eggs

Soak the lentils for 1–2 hours. Chop the onions and the garlic and fry them gently in the vegetable margarine for 10 minutes. Drain and wash the lentils, then add them, with 1 teaspoon of salt and the measured water to the onions and garlic. Cover the pan and leave to cook at a rapid simmer for 30 minutes.

Wash the sorrel and add it to the onions and lentils after they have been cooking for 30 minutes. Stir well, and cook for a further 15 minutes with the pan uncovered. Season the lentils with more salt to taste plus plenty of black pepper or, if you prefer a hot taste, some cayenne pepper.

Serve in individual bowls and crumble a hardboiled egg on top of each bowl.

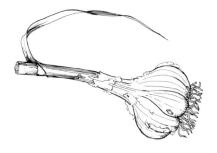

Tamarind

Tamarind trees grow not only in their native India but also in West Africa and the West Indies. Their long, brown seed pods have an interesting flavour since they contain citric, tartaric and malic acids and also some sugar. Whereas other sour seasonings, such as lemons, contain only a single acid, tamarind pods, containing three plus some compensating sweetness, have a more complex flavour which is very useful in cookery. Indian and Indonesian cuisines make good use of tamarind in rice and vegetable dishes, relishes and chutneys; it goes particularly well with tomatoes, peanuts and mint.

Tamarind pods are usually sold in dried, compacted blocks and the 'juice' is prepared by soaking the pods in boiling water and then pressing the resulting pulp through a sieve. To make tamarind 'juice', soak 150 g (5 oz) of dried tamarind pods in 300 ml (½ pint) of boiling water for at least 2 hours. Press the resulting mixture through a wire sieve with a wooden spoon. Add a little more boiling water to the remaining pulp and press through the sieve again. This liquid will keep in the refrigerator for a few weeks.

GREEN PEPPERS AND PEANUTS COOKED WITH TAMARIND

This spicy vegetable mixture is good served with brown rice.

175 g/6 oz peanuts, lightly roasted
500 g/1 lb green peppers
2 medium onions
5 tablespoons vegetable oil *or* ghee
3 teaspoons coriander, ground
2 teaspoons ground cumin
90 g/3 oz desiccated coconut
2 teaspoons amchoor powder
1 teaspoon chilli powder
4 cloves garlic, crushed
1 tablespoon brown sugar
3 tablespoons tamarind juice
salt
300 ml/½ pint boiling water
90 g/3 oz raisins

Break up the peanuts roughly with a pestle or the end of a rolling pin. Chop the green peppers and the onions and fry them in 3 tablespoons of the oil or ghee for 10 minutes. Set them aside. Combine the coriander, cumin, coconut, amchoor, chilli powder and garlic. Fry these ingredients in the rest of the oil or ghee for 2–3 minutes, stirring. Add the peanuts and continue to fry for a few minutes, stirring all the time. Add the peppers and onions, the brown sugar, tamarind, salt and water. Cover and leave to simmer for 15 minutes, adding the raisins after 10 minutes. Serve hot.

SPLIT PEA DHAL
FLAVOURED WITH TAMARIND

Dhal is a lentil or split pea puree – one of the staple dishes of Indian cookery.

3 medium onions
4 cloves garlic
4 tablespoons vegetable oil *or* ghee
350 g/12 oz green *or* yellow split peas
900 ml/1½ pints water
2 level teaspoons salt
3 tablespoons tamarind juice

Chop the onions and garlic and fry them gently in the oil or ghee for 5 minutes. Wash the split peas well in several changes of water. Add them to the onions and pour in the measured water and the salt. Cover the pan and leave to simmer for 40–50 minutes or until the peas are soft. Add the tamarind about 10 minutes before the end of the cooking time. If the mixture seems too liquid at this stage, let the dhal finish cooking uncovered.

OKRA COOKED
WITH TAMARIND AND CHILLIES

This dish can be made with cauliflower or green beans if okra is not available. It is a good accompaniment to rice, and can be served with yoghurt or raita.

500 g/1 lb okra (also called ladies' fingers and bhindi)
a few small green chillies *or* 1–2 large ones
3 tablespoons ghee *or* vegetable oil
4 cloves garlic, chopped
1 teaspoon coriander, ground
1 teaspoon cumin, ground
a 2.5 cm/1 in piece of fresh root ginger, finely chopped *or* grated
1 teaspoon salt
2 tablespoons tamarind juice
500 ml/18 fl oz water
1½ tablespoons brown sugar
1 small bunch coriander leaves, chopped
2 small teaspoons garam masala

Wash the okra, cut off the stalk ends and cut in half lengthways. Deseed the chillies and chop them into small cross-sections. Heat the ghee or oil in a frying pan and add the garlic, coriander, cumin, ginger and salt. Fry these for about 2 minutes over a medium heat. Add the tamarind, chillies and okra and stir fry for a few minutes. Pour in the water and add the sugar and chopped coriander leaves. Lower the heat, cover the pan and leave to cook for 15–20 minutes, or until the okra is soft. Stir in the garam masala and serve hot.

PEANUT AND TAMARIND RELISH

Serve this dish with brown rice and vegetables.

275 g/9 oz peanuts, unroasted
4½ tablespoons tamarind juice
1 small onion
1 bunch coriander leaves *or* parsley leaves *or* a few sprigs mint
1–2 fresh chillies (optional)
6 tablespoons vegetable oil
6 tablespoons water
salt

Grind the peanuts finely and mix them with the tamarind liquid. Grate or finely chop the onion and chop up the green leaves and chillies (without chillies this relish will be quite mild but still interesting). Combine these ingredients and add enough vegetable oil and water to make a sufficiently liquid consistency. Season with salt.

TAMARIND CHUTNEY

In India, chutneys such as this are often made in the morning to be eaten with the evening meal. The tastes take a few hours to intermingle, so make it well in advance of the meal. This chutney will keep well for a few days in the refrigerator if you want to make it in larger quantities.

4 tablespoons tamarind juice
2 teaspoons brown sugar
1 teaspoon salt
a generous pinch cayenne pepper
10 g/about ¼ oz fresh root ginger
a good handful (15 g/½ oz) coriander leaves

Put the tamarind juice in a bowl and add the sugar, salt and cayenne pepper. Peel the ginger root thinly and chop it finely. Chop the coriander leaves equally finely and add both to the tamarind mixture. Leave in a warm place for several hours.

Salty tastes

CAPERS · ITALIAN CHEESES · OLIVES · SALT
SEAWEED · SOY SAUCE AND MISO
UMEBOSHI PLUMS · YEAST EXTRACT

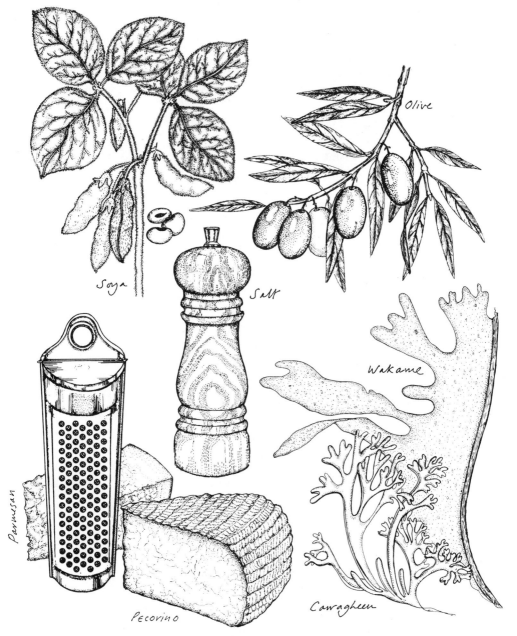

Olive

Soya

Salt

Wakame

Parmesan

Pecorino

Carragheen

Capers

Capers are the pickled, unopened buds of a small climbing plant which grows in Mediterranean regions. If the buds are allowed to open the plant bears a delicate, pink flower, but for edible purposes the buds are picked early in the morning and dropped immediately into salted vinegar.

Capers have an interesting flavour: the pickling medium makes them salty on the outside, but inside they are slightly bitter and aromatic. They should be used sparingly because they are rather strong. Capers go well with cheese, eggs and pizzas and can also be added to salads, particularly those containing tomatoes. They can be stored in vinegar for a long time without deteriorating, so it is worth keeping a jar on the shelf for occasional use. The British substitute for capers is pickled nasturtium buds, which have a similar flavour.

HARDBOILED EGGS IN CAPER SAUCE

This dish can be served as a first course, or as an accompaniment to rice, millet or cracked wheat.

60 g/2 oz vegetable margarine
4 cloves garlic, chopped
30 g/1 oz plain flour
450 ml/16 fl oz milk
black *or* white pepper
1 level teaspoon salt
2 good tablespoons drained capers
6 hardboiled eggs, shelled

garnish
1 small bunch parsley, chopped

Melt the margarine in a pan and add the chopped garlic. Fry very gently for a few minutes. Stir in the flour and then add the milk gradually, stirring all the time. Slowly bring to the boil, then turn down the heat and season well with pepper, salt and capers. Slice the hardboiled eggs and put them in a bowl. Pour the sauce over them and garnish generously with chopped parsley.

TARTARE SAUCE

This is a caper-flavoured mayonnaise delicious with eggs and some salads. Make the mayonnaise as described on p.59 and flavour it with the following:

1 heaped tablespoon chopped capers
3–4 spring onions, finely chopped
a little tarragon, chopped

Use 2 teaspoons of the pickling vinegar from the capers instead of wine vinegar or cider vinegar for making the mayonnaise.

Italian cheeses: Parmesan and Pecorino

These hard, low-fat, Italian cheeses are excellent to use in vegetarian cookery not only for their concentrated flavour but also because, ounce for ounce, they contain up to twice as much protein as meat. They are fairly expensive, but can be used to good effect in small quantities. Sometimes they can be used in combination with a less full-flavoured cheese – in a casserole or a cheese sauce, for example.

There are two main types of Parmesan cheese: Parmigiano Padano and Parmigiano Reggiano (though the Italians make further distinctions – according, for example, to the time of year when the cheese is produced). Parmesan cheeses are matured for at least six months and up to three years; they are considered to be at their best after two years. Although Parmesan is often sold conveniently ready-grated, it is better to buy it on the piece and grate it as required – ready-grated 'Parmesan' is often mixed with cheaper, less flavoursome cheeses.

Parmesan is particularly well known as an accompaniment to pasta and to soups. It is an essential ingredient in gratin dishes and in many cheese sauces, and it goes very well with grains such as millet and bulghur wheat.

Pecorino cheese is made from sheep's milk: two of the best-known varieties are Pecorino Romano and Pecorino Sardo (from Sardinia). These cheeses are generally saltier than Parmesan and are useful in baked dishes where a robust flavour is called for. Pecorino Sardo is traditionally used for making a pesto sauce, arguably the best accompaniment to pasta dishes.

NOODLES AND BEANSPROUTS WITH PARMESAN CHEESE

When you only have about 10 minutes to make a meal, this is a good recipe. It makes a very fast, tasty and well-balanced dish.

300 g/10 oz wholewheat noodles
75 g/2½ oz vegetable margarine
125 g/4 oz mung beansprouts
125 g/4 oz alfalfa sprouts
125 g/4 oz Parmesan cheese, grated

Bring a large saucepan of salted water to the boil. Drop in the noodles and boil for 5 minutes (thin noodles) or 10 minutes (thick noodles). When they are soft, drain them and melt the margarine in the same saucepan. Toss the noodles in the melted margarine and then mix in the mung and alfalfa sprouts and half of the grated cheese. Serve topped with the rest of the cheese.

PASTA BAKED WITH CREAMY AUBERGINE AND PARMESAN SAUCE

500 g/1 lb aubergines
300 g/10 oz wholemeal pasta (spirals, twists *or* rings)
4–5 cloves garlic
60 g/2 oz vegetable margarine
45 g/1½ oz plain white flour
450 ml/16 fl oz milk
150 g/5 oz Gouda cheese, grated
75 g/2½ oz Parmesan cheese, grated
1 small bunch parsley (3–4 tablespoons when chopped)
1 bunch spring onions
salt
black *or* white pepper

Grill the aubergines on all sides until they are soft. Skin them and put them in a wire sieve. Press with a wooden spoon to extract all the bitter juices. Chop them roughly and leave aside.

Put the pasta into a saucepan of boiling, salted water and cook for about 5 minutes. Strain and leave aside. Preheat the oven to 180° C (350° F, gas mark 4).

Make the cheese sauce in the usual way. First chop or crush the garlic, then melt the margarine in a frying pan and add the garlic. After 1–2 minutes add the flour and mix in. Gradually add the milk, stirring all the time. When the sauce has thickened, turn down the heat and stir in the grated Gouda cheese and 60 g (2 oz) of the Parmesan. Add the chopped aubergine and stir over a low heat until the aubergine is well integrated with the sauce. Mix in the chopped parsley and spring onions, and season with salt and pepper.

Put the pasta into a greased casserole dish and pour the sauce over. Top with the remaining 15 g (½ oz) of Parmesan and cover the dish with foil. Bake for 35 minutes. Take off the foil covering for the last 10 minutes of cooking, to allow the top to brown.

Salty tastes: Italian cheeses

FRIED CELERIAC TOPPED WITH PARMESAN CHEESE

Celeriac is an excellent vegetable when grated raw, lightly fried or roasted whole. In this recipe it is fried in small chips.

1 large *or* 2 smaller celeriac bulbs weighing about 500 g/1 lb
3 large cloves garlic
30 g/1 oz parsley
vegetable oil for frying
salt
black pepper
2 tablespoons grated Parmesan cheese

Scrub and peel the celeriac and cut it into thin chips. Chop the garlic and parsley finely. Gently fry the celeriac with the garlic in the oil for 10–15 minutes. Season with salt and pepper and stir in the chopped parsley. Put these ingredients in a serving dish and cover with grated Parmesan.

CAULIFLOWER CHEESE COOKED WITH WALNUTS

2 large onions
3–4 cloves garlic
4 tablespoons vegetable margarine
1 medium cauliflower
125 g/4 oz walnuts, broken
white pepper
125 g/4 oz Parmesan cheese, grated
200 g/7 oz macaroni (optional)

Chop the onions and garlic and gently fry them for 10–15 minutes in the margarine. Break the cauliflower into small florets and add them to the onions and garlic. Cover the pan with a tight lid or plate and steam the cauliflower until it is just soft. Preheat the grill on medium setting. Mix in the broken walnuts and season well with white pepper. Cover with grated Parmesan and put the whole dish under a medium grill for 10 minutes.

If macaroni is included, this recipe becomes a meal in itself. Boil the macaroni separately in salted water, then drain well and mix it in with the other ingredients at the same time as the walnuts. Cover with grated cheese and finish off under the grill as above.

CHARD AND POTATO GRATIN

Chard is related to sugar beet. The plant is eaten mainly for its stalks and thick leaf spines, which are pleasantly juicy and taste rather like celery. The green part of the leaves may be cooked like spinach and served separately as a puree.

500 g/1 lb Swiss chard
250 g/8 oz potatoes, thinly sliced
90 g/3 oz vegetable margarine
4 cloves garlic, crushed
2 level tablespoons plain flour
600 ml/1 pint milk
90 g/3 oz Parmesan cheese, grated
1 teaspoon salt
white pepper
1½ tablespoons fresh wholemeal breadcrumbs

Preheat the oven to 180° C (350° F, gas mark 4). Tear off the green part of the chard leaves and chop the stalks and spines into convenient lengths. Blanch the latter in boiling water for 1–2 minutes. Drop the sliced potatoes into boiling, salted water for 2–3 minutes.

Butter a shallow oven dish (an oval shape is traditional for gratin dishes) and sandwich a layer of chard between two layers of potatoes. Now make the sauce: first melt the margarine and gently fry the crushed garlic for 1–2 minutes. Stir in the flour and add the milk gradually, stirring all the time. Add 60 g (2 oz) of the grated Parmesan and a seasoning of salt and pepper. When the sauce is quite thick, take it off the heat and pour it over the vegetable mixture. Top with the rest of the grated cheese and the breadcrumbs, and bake for 35 minutes.

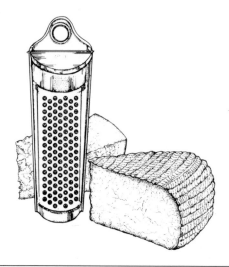

Salty tastes: Italian cheeses

CHEESE STRAWS

350 g/12 oz wholemeal flour
125 g/4 oz Parmesan cheese, grated
1 heaped teaspoon salt
2 teaspoons hot paprika
175 g/6 oz vegetable margarine
2 egg yolks
sesame seeds (optional)

Preheat the oven to 200° C (400° F, gas mark 6). Sift the flour, grated cheese, salt and paprika together. Melt the margarine and add it to the mixture with the egg yolks. Form the mixture into a dough, adding a very little water if it seems too dry. Roll out to a thickness of about 2 cm (¾ in). Lightly press the sesame seeds over the surface of the dough. Cut the dough into strips about 10 cm (4 in) long and 2 cm (¾ in) wide. Lay the straws on a greased baking tray and bake for 10–15 minutes. Cool them on a wire rack and store, if necessary, in an air-tight container.

CHEESE AND HERB SCONES

Cheese scones are excellent when flavoured with Parmesan cheese. Use about one third of Parmesan and two thirds of a mild, higher-fat cheese. This recipe makes about 15 large scones.

350 g/12 oz wholemeal flour
125 g/4 oz plain white flour
1 heaped teaspoon baking powder
250 g/8 oz vegetable margarine
125 g/4 oz mild cheese, e.g. Gouda, grated
60 g/2 oz Parmesan cheese, grated
2 tablespoons fresh herbs, e.g. thyme, savory, marjoram, *or* 1 tablespoon dried
white pepper
100 ml/4 fl oz milk
sesame seeds

Preheat the oven to 190° C (375° F, gas mark 5). Mix the flours and baking powder together. Rub in the margarine and then the grated cheeses. Add the herbs and season with pepper. Mix in the milk to form a stiff dough. Roll out to a thickness of about 2.5 cm (1 in) and cut out the scones with a 7.5 cm (3 in) cutter. Top with sesame seeds. Place the scones on a greased baking tray and bake for 20 minutes. Cool them on a wire rack.

Olives

The gnarled grey branches and the silvery green leaves of the olive tree are one of the most familiar sights of the Mediterranean. Although olives grow in places as far apart as California and China, the tree really belongs to the Mediterranean, where it has been cultivated – even revered – since ancient times. In Greece and Rome the victors of sport and war were wreathed with olive leaves, and olive oil was used to fuel the sacred temple lamps. The olive branch was also a symbol of peace. Olive trees are very long-lived and very slow-growing, and in ancient times one of the worst acts of aggression was to cut down an enemy's olive grove!

When picked, the ripe black olives as well as the unripe green ones are extremely bitter. They have to go through a lengthy washing process and must then be left to steep in brine before they are palatable. Olive oil is extracted by pressing the ripe fruit. The first pressing produces the purest and the strongest-tasting oil, which should be reserved for salad dressings and for making mayonnaise. Subsequent pressings produce a less strongly flavoured oil which may nevertheless be quite suitable for cooking. People living in Mediterranean countries often choose olive oil with the same discrimination and knowledge of regional variations which they might other-wise reserve for choosing wine. In more northerly countries this expertise is hard to acquire; indeed, many people find the taste of cold-pressed olive oil altogether too strong. When buying olive oil, it is a good idea to look out for the cheaper Greek or Spanish oils, which are often in no way inferior to the more expensive Italian product.

Green olives are often sold stuffed with pimentos. If you can get hold of a French implement called a *chasse-noyau* for pitting olives, you could try stuffing them with, for example, pine nuts or slivered almonds. Olives can also be flavoured by bottling them in oil with herbs and spices.

Olive paste is a useful flavouring to keep in the kitchen: its strong, salty taste goes well with eggs and it can also be used in sauces to accompany pasta. Whole olives may be used in summer and winter salads and can be baked in casseroles and savoury (particularly cheese) tarts.

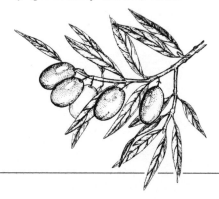

HARDBOILED EGGS
WITH BLACK OLIVE STUFFING

This combination of hardboiled eggs and olive paste is a tasty one, useful for hors d'oeuvres. Use finely chopped olives if you don't have any olive paste.

8 hardboiled eggs
1½ tablespoons olive paste *or* 60g/2oz black olives
2 small tomatoes
a few sprigs of parsley
4 cloves garlic
1½ tablespoons grated Parmesan cheese

to serve
lettuce leaves

Preheat the grill. Shell the hardboiled eggs and cut them in half lengthways. Scoop out the yolks carefully and put them into a bowl. Chop the olives (if using them instead of paste), tomatoes and parsley and crush the garlic. Combine these ingredients with the egg yolks and Parmesan cheese. Put the mixture back into the hollowed-out eggs and place them under a hot grill for 5 minutes, until just brown on top.

Serve on a bed of lettuce.

PASTA SALAD WITH OLIVES

300g/10oz pasta spirals *or* twists *or* shells
½ clove garlic
2 green *or* red peppers
a few young carrots
1 small bunch chives
1 small bunch parsley
175g/6oz Gouda *or* Emmenthal *or* Gruyère cheese
1 cos lettuce
125g/4oz small black olives, pitted
60g/2oz stuffed green olives

to serve
vinaigrette dressing

Cook the pasta in plenty of boiling, salted water until it is just soft. Drain well. Rub a large salad bowl with the garlic and put the pasta in the bowl. Slice the peppers and carrots, chop the chives and parsley, and cut the cheese into small cubes. Shred the lettuce. Combine all these ingredients, plus the olives, with the pasta.

Serve with vinaigrette dressing made with olive oil.

BULGHUR SALAD
WITH OLIVES AND TOMATOES

250 g/8 oz bulghur (cracked) wheat
600 ml/1 pint cold water
250 g/8 oz firm, well-flavoured tomatoes
1 bunch chives *or* spring onions
a few sprigs fresh herbs, e.g. savory *or* mint *or* basil
125 g/4 oz small black olives
6 tablespoons olive oil
1 tablespoon cider vinegar *or* wine vinegar
juice of ½ lemon
1 teaspoon salt
white pepper

Soak the cracked wheat in the cold water for 30 minutes. By this time it should have absorbed all the water and become soft but not soggy. Chop the tomatoes finely, also the chives or spring onions and herbs. Take the stone out of the olives if you have a suitable implement, otherwise cut them away from the stones with a knife. Mix the oil, vinegar, lemon juice and salt together and pour them over the other ingredients. Season with plenty of pepper and chill before serving.

OLIVE OIL VINAIGRETTE

This is a basic recipe which has infinite variations: vinaigrette dressing can be made with all types of oils and vinegars and can be flavoured with the whole range of herbs and spices. Always be generous with the oil and sparing with the vinegar or lemon juice. Sometimes it is a good idea to add a little honey. This recipe allows enough dressing for a single salad for four people, but vinaigrette can be mixed up in quantity and stored in the refrigerator in a screw-top jar.

1 clove garlic
4 tablespoons olive oil
1 level teaspoon cider vinegar
½ teaspoon lemon juice
1 level teaspoon Dijon mustard
a pinch salt
a pinch black *or* white pepper

Crush the garlic and mix it with the olive oil. Stir in the vinegar, lemon juice and mustard and season with salt and pepper.

MAYONNAISE

Like vinaigrette, mayonnaise can be flavoured with many different fresh herbs, mustards and vinegars. Oil is always the main ingredient, however, so it is worth using a good one. Typically, mayonnaise is made with cold pressed olive oil, but substitute another good-quality oil if you prefer.

2 egg yolks
150 ml/¼ pint olive oil
2 teaspoons cider vinegar *or* white wine vinegar *or* tarragon vinegar
salt
white pepper
1 tablespoon fresh herbs, chopped (optional)

Make sure both the eggs and the oil are cool. Beat the yolks with a fork. Begin to add the oil to them drop by drop, stirring constantly with a wooden spoon. It is very important to add only tiny drops of oil at first, otherwise the mixture will separate (don't try to pour the oil straight out of the bottle, because sooner or later one's hand always slips). After about a third of the oil has been poured in, the rest can be added in slightly larger quantities. If the mixture does, unfortunately, separate, start again with a fresh egg yolk and very gradually add the unsuccessful mixture to it. When all the oil has been added, stir in the vinegar and season with salt, pepper and herbs to taste.

OLIVE BREAD

This is a delicious bread and most enticing smells waft from the oven while it is being baked.

Make the bread according to the recipe on p.216, but for one third of the wholemeal flour substitute plain white flour. For every 500 g (1 lb) of flour take 90 g (3 oz) small black olives, stoned and chopped, and 1 crushed clove of garlic. Add these ingredients as you knead the dough for the first time.

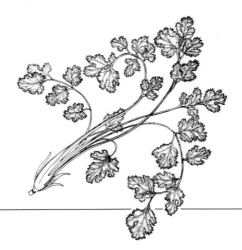

Salt

Salt is in a different category from the other flavourings in this book, since it is an essential part of our body chemistry. The requirement for salt varies from one person to the next, but everyone needs it to some degree. People who want – or need – to reduce the salt content of their diet should stop eating processed foods, which are nearly always over-salted and over-sweetened, rather than give up salt in their own cooking. The amounts of salt suggested in the recipes in this book should not be taken as absolutes: wherever possible, add half the salt at the outset of preparing a dish and the rest, to taste, at the end. More salt can always be added at the table if necessary. When cooking pulses it is generally best to add the salt towards the end of the cooking time.

Sweet and salt tastes seem to be the ones which our palates naturally find most satisfying – a liking for sour and bitter tastes generally has to be acquired. Salt also has the cardinal virtue of bringing out the flavour of other foods with which it is used. Anyone who has eaten either bread or potatoes cooked without salt will realize the importance of the catalytic effect of salt upon other flavours. If fruit is stewed with a pinch of salt, its natural sweetness is enhanced, often making the addition of extra sweetening unnecessary. Eggs, nuts, pasta and lentils all come to life with the addition of salt.

Salt is also, of course, one of the chief agents for preserving food – and before the invention of refrigeration was the principal one: salted meat and fish were the mainstays of the winter diet up until the last century. Salt is essential for all kinds of pickling, whether used by itself or in combination with vinegar or oil.

There are two basic types of salt available: sea salt, which is panned from sea water, and rock salt, which is mined from deposits in the earth which the sea left behind millions of years ago. Sea salt is richer in minerals, especially trace elements, and for this reason is often preferred to rock salt. All the recipes in this book have been tested with Maldon salt, a sea salt which has been panned along the Essex coast for perhaps 2,000 years. It has a soft, pleasant taste, probably due to its high mineral content. The risk of spoiling a dish by accidental over-salting is much reduced by using Maldon salt.

Mixtures of salt and ground spices used to be very popular in the kitchen, and today there are also a great many 'seasoned' salts in the shops, such as garlic salt and celery salt (the latter is especially useful). Gomashio, a Japanese condiment, is made by mixing salt with roasted, ground sesame seeds. The best way to store salt is in a traditional, wide-mouthed salt jar. I keep one near the stove, so that I can easily dip in my hand when cooking.

Because salt is such a vital substance, governments down the ages have often tried to control its supply. From Roman times salt was considered an appropriate item for heavy taxation; Roman soldiers were often paid in salt –

---

their *salarium* has become our 'salary'. French peasants laboured under the salt tax known as the *gabelle* in pre-Revolutionary France, and for thousands of years pack animals toiled over the Himalayas to bring the commodity to the saltless regions of Central Asia. In British India the government held a monopoly over salt making which Gandhi chose to defy in one of his most symbolic acts of passive resistance.

We should consider ourselves fortunate in being able to go out and buy a modestly priced packet of salt in our local supermarket!

SALTED ALMONDS

Elizabeth David describes how she learned to prepare salted almonds from her servant in Egypt*. The almonds were mixed with a very little almond or other oil, spread out on a baking tray and put in a slow oven for about 50 minutes. They were then mixed with salt, cooled and *hidden*, unless for immediate consumption. This method does produce a delicious result.

Another, quicker, method is to dip the almonds in a saturated solution of salt (dissolve some sea salt in hot water until a deposit of salt is left at the bottom of the dish), and then toast them under a hot grill for about 4 minutes on each side. There is no need to blanch or split the almonds for either of these methods.

FRIED, SALTED CASHEWS

Salted cashews are very expensive to buy, but very simple to make at home. Everyone knows how delicious they are.

For every 60 g (2 oz) of cashews or cashew pieces, heat 1 tablespoon of vegetable oil. Add the cashews and fry them gently until they are golden brown. For every 60 g (2 oz), add ½ teaspoon salt. When they are done, lay the nuts on sheets of absorbent kitchen paper to cool and become crisp.

* *Spices, Salt and Aromatics in the English Kitchen*, Elizabeth David, Penguin, 1970

SAVOURY SNACK

This is an economical salted snack which might be useful when there are a lot of hungry children around. In India, the smaller pulses are often roasted and eaten as snacks: they are tasty but rather hard, so in this recipe I have suggested soaking them in boiling water for a few minutes before frying.

90 g/3 oz small yellow split peas (chana dhal) *or* small white lentils (urad dhal)
90 g/3 oz peanuts
90 g/3 oz sunflower seeds
vegetable oil for frying
90 g/3 oz currants
1 heaped tablespoon salt

Put the chana or urad dhal in a bowl of boiling water to soak while you fry the peanuts and the sunflower seeds separately: use about 2 tablespoons of oil for each batch of nuts or seeds. When they are just browned, take them out of the pan and spread them on kitchen paper to absorb the excess oil. Drain the dhal thoroughly and fry it, stirring, until it begins to turn golden brown. Mix all the ingredients, including the currants and salt together in a large bowl.

JAPANESE SALT PICKLE

This pickle could alternatively be made with cauliflower, turnips, carrots or parsnips. The process of steeping vegetables in salt in order to draw out the fluid in which micro-organisms flourish and make the vegetables go bad is basic in pickle making. This is the simplest kind of pickle; in warm weather it should be eaten within 2–3 days.

In Japan, salt pickles are often served with rice.

250 g/8 oz giant white radish (mooli)
2 heaped tablespoons salt, preferably Maldon

Chop the radishes into thin slices. Spread them out on a large plate in layers, sprinkling each layer with salt. Cover with another plate of the same size and place a heavy weight on top of the second plate. Leave for 24 hours, draining off three or four times the water which will accumulate. The pickle will then be ready to eat.

Seaweed

The inclusion of seaweed in our diet helps to maintain the delicate balance of minerals, especially trace minerals, which is necessary for health. Chemical farming may destroy essential minerals in food grown on land, but the sea – so long as it remains unpolluted – is a limitless source.

Hundreds of different species of seaweeds, admittedly not all of them edible, grow around the British coast. Carrageen, laver and dulse are used in traditional Irish and Welsh dishes. Most of the seaweeds at present in the shops, however, are imported from Japan, where seaweeds are both gathered and cultivated along the extensive coastline. Hiziki, wakame, arame, nori and kombu are the main varieties.

The best way to cook with seaweed is to use it as a seasoning. Like salt, seaweed has the ability to enhance other flavours: vegetables, brown rice and beans can all be cooked with a little dried seaweed instead of salt. Kombu is a strong-tasting seaweed, useful – especially in combination with dried mushrooms and soy sauce – for flavouring stock. Any seaweed may, in fact, be used in the preparation of soup stock. Dried nori, which is usually sold in thinner-than-paper sheets, makes a delicious condiment which can be sprinkled over all kinds of brown rice and vegetable dishes: simply hold it over a flame or under a grill for a few seconds and then crumble it between your fingers. Sheets of nori are traditionally used to wrap portions of Japanese sushi rice. Kelp, which is sold in powdered form, can also be used as a condiment.

As well as being used in small quantities as a seasoning, seaweed may be used in more substantial quantities to make a number of tasty vegetable (especially root vegetable), rice and even pasta dishes. Seaweeds are especially good in combination with onions, ginger, soy sauce and dried mushrooms.

VEGETABLE STOCK MADE WITH SEAWEED AND DRIED MUSHROOMS

This recipe makes just over 600 ml (1 pint) of stock.

700 ml/nearly 1¼ pints boiling water
10 g/about ¼ oz dried seaweed
2 dried shiitake mushrooms
2 tablespoons soy sauce

Pour boiling water over the seaweed and mushrooms and leave to soak for a few hours. Then simmer the liquid, covered, for about 30 minutes. Add the soy sauce. The stock may then be strained or, better, put in a liquidizer and blended.

DULSE SOUP

Dulse, one of the most delicately flavoured and textured of the seaweeds, makes an excellent soup.

1 large onion
2–3 cloves garlic
2 tablespoons vegetable oil
1 litre/1¾ pints stock (the stock recipe given on p.202 is ideal)
15 g/½ oz dried dulse
salt *or* soy sauce

to serve
English *or* Dutch cheese, grated

Chop the onion and the garlic finely and fry them gently in the vegetable oil for 10 minutes. Add the stock and the dried dulse and allow to simmer for 20–30 minutes. Season to taste with salt or soy sauce, and serve after sprinkling on the cheese.

RICE BALLS MADE WITH NORI

700 g/1½ lb cooked rice (about 400 g/14 oz uncooked weight)
5 cloves garlic, crushed
3 tablespoons soy sauce, *or* more to taste
125 g/4 oz alfalfa sprouts
90 g/3 oz sesame seeds
10 g/about ¼ oz nori
a little flour
vegetable oil for frying

The secret of making rice balls is to cook the rice until it is quite sticky. Use long or short grain rice, but cook it with more water than usual (about 750 ml/1¼ pints for the above quantity) and leave it to cook until all the water has been absorbed. If, exceptionally, you still have trouble in getting the rice balls to cohere, add a little rice or wheat flour.

Mix the cooked rice with the crushed garlic, soy sauce and alfalfa sprouts. Roast the sesame seeds under the grill and grind them in a coffee grinder. Roast the nori for an instant under the grill, crumble it, then mix both the sesame seeds and the nori with the rice.

Form the mixture into about 15 balls, pressing them together tightly with clean, slightly wet hands. Roll the rice balls lightly in flour. Pour oil to a depth of 10 cm (4 in) in a deep pan or wok, and heat to 180° C (350° F) – about the temperature needed for frying chips. Fry the rice balls, a few at a time, until they are well browned. Drain on absorbent paper.

NOODLES WITH DULSE

45 g/1½ oz dulse
salt
500 g/1 lb wholewheat noodles
1 large bunch spring onions *or* 2 medium onions
125 g/4 oz vegetable margarine
soy sauce to taste

Soak the dulse for 30 minutes in warm water. Drain, but reserve the water for cooking the noodles. Make the water up to about 1.75 litres (3 pints), add a little salt and bring it to the boil. Add the noodles and cook them al dente (small ones will take only about 5 minutes and large ones not more than 10). Chop up the dulse and the spring onions and fry them gently in the margarine.

When the noodles are cooked, strain them thoroughly and add them to the dulse and spring onion mixture. Toss all the ingredients together, add the soy sauce and serve at once.

HIZIKI AND VEGETABLES

45 g/1½ oz hiziki
600 ml/1 pint hot water
2 onions
4 cloves garlic
3 tablespoons vegetable oil
300 g/10 oz carrots
300 g/10 oz potatoes *or* parsnips
a 2.5 cm/1 in piece fresh root ginger
3 tablespoons soy sauce
1 teaspoon salt, *or* to taste
black pepper

to serve
mung beansprouts (optional)

Put the seaweed in a bowl and pour the hot water over it. Leave aside while you prepare the other ingredients. Chop the onions and the garlic and fry them gently in the vegetable oil (use a large cast iron frying pan or any large, open pan). Scrub the carrots and potatoes or parsnips and cut them into thin slices. Peel the ginger thinly, then chop and bruise it. Add the potatoes, carrots and ginger to the pan, raise the heat and stir fry for a few minutes. Now add the seaweed and the water in which it was soaked, the soy sauce and the salt. Leave the pan to simmer gently, without a lid, until the root vegetables are cooked. Season with pepper and serve, perhaps with some mung beansprouts sprinkled on top.

LAVERBREAD AND ONION SAUCE

In South Wales laverbread, a boiled puree of seaweed that can be bought readymade, was traditionally rolled in oatmeal and fried for breakfast. It may also be used in sauces.

350 g/12 oz onions
60 g/2 oz vegetable margarine
250 g/8 oz laverbread
juice *and* peel of 2 oranges, grated
juice of 1 lemon
½ teaspoon salt
black *or* white pepper

Chop the onions finely and fry them gently in the margarine for 10–15 minutes. Stir in the rest of the ingredients and simmer for a further 10 minutes. This sauce is good served with brown rice and vegetables.

KOMBU RELISH

This is a Japanese speciality, sweet and salty, which is served with rice dishes. Mirin is a sweet rice wine obtainable from Chinese grocers.

15 g/½ oz dried kombu *or* other seaweed
150 ml/¼ pint hot water
150 ml/¼ pint mirin (sweet sake)
100 ml/4 fl oz soy sauce

Cut the seaweed into small pieces with kitchen scissors. Soak it in hot water for 1–2 hours. Put the seaweed and the water in which it was soaked into a saucepan with the mirin and soy sauce. Simmer gently until most of the liquid has evaporated.

Soy sauce and miso

In the Far East, the very high food value of soya beans has been appreciated for thousands of years. They contain up to 36 per cent protein and are one of the few vegetable substances to contain all the amino acids necessary to form a complete protein. The main disadvantage is that in their natural state they are difficult to digest, but over many centuries people in countries like China, Japan and Indonesia have developed techniques for fermenting them and producing not only nutritious but also tasty and digestible foods.

Tempe, natto, miso and soy sauce are all fermented soya bean products, containing beneficial enzymes which, like those in yoghurt, aid the digestion. All these soya bean products were designed to accompany a staple diet of rice – not only to make it more interesting but also to add protein content.

Soy sauce, or shoyu, is made from soya beans fermented with roasted wheat and salt and then diluted with water. The strong, salty taste of soy sauce goes exceptionally well with brown rice and can be used to flavour many soups, sauces, casseroles and bean and vegetable dishes. It may even be used as an alternative to salt. Always take care to buy good-quality soy sauce, free from additives and preservatives. Soy sauce which has been fermented in the correct way contains a live enzyme, so wherever possible add it at the end of cooking.

Miso is made by fermenting soya beans with cereal grains and salt. There are several different kinds: mugi miso is made with soya beans and barley, komé miso with soya beans and rice, and hacho miso with soya beans alone. Generally speaking, the darker-coloured miso contains more soya beans and more salt and has a stronger flavour. From a culinary point of view, I think the lighter-coloured (yellow or white) miso, which contains a high proportion of rice and is lightly salted, is preferable.

Because of their high salt content, both miso and soy sauce can be used as pickling mediums for vegetables: the vegetables are simply sliced and covered with the paste or liquid. Miso and soy sauce should be stored at room temperature, and not in the refrigerator.

SOY, TOFU AND TAHINI DIP

Tofu is an excellent high-protein food. It has little taste of its own, however, and provides good scope for ingenious seasoning. Soy sauce is the obvious complement to tofu, as both are soya bean products, but many other tastes may be added as well.

500 g/1 lb soft tofu
6 good tablespoons tahini
2–3 cloves garlic
4 tablespoons soy sauce
juice of 2 lemons
4 tablespoons sesame seeds
1 bunch spring onions
1 small bunch parsley

Mash the tofu with a fork, then mix it well with the tahini. Crush the garlic and combine it with the soy sauce and lemon juice. Toast the sesame seeds. Finely chop the spring onions and parsley. Mix all the ingredients together well, and chill before serving.

MISO SOUP

This is a very sustaining soup often eaten at breakfast as well as at dinner in Japan, and served in special lacquered wooden bowls. The lighter, yellow-coloured miso is generally used; if you are using a darker type of miso, reduce the amount by a half or one third.

a few strips of kombu (see p.63)
4 dried shiitake mushrooms
900 ml/1½ pints boiling water
4 tablespoons yellow miso
1 bunch spring onions
125 g/4 oz white radish (mooli)
250 g/8 oz hard tofu (optional)
vegetable oil for frying

Make the stock by soaking the kombu and mushrooms in the water for 30 minutes, then bringing the liquid to the boil and simmering for 15 minutes. After this you can either remove the kombu and mushrooms or chop them finely and return them to the pot. Turn the heat right down and stir in the miso, continuing to stir until it has completely dissolved. Chop the spring onions, including most of the green parts, and grate the white radish. Add these to the soup. Keep the soup warm over a very low heat while you cut up the tofu and fry it in oil until it is crisp and slightly browned.

When you serve the soup, add a few pieces of tofu to each bowl.

QUICK MISO SOUP

For every 200 ml (⅓ pint) of boiling water, stir in 1 tablespoon yellow miso or 2 teaspoons dark miso. Do not let the liquid boil after the miso has been added. To this simple yet nourishing soup you can add a little crumbled nori (see p.63), some chopped spring onions, a few sprigs of watercress or a little chopped parsley.

SAVOURY MUSHROOM TARTLETS

Mushrooms and soy sauce always go well together. This recipe makes about 18 medium-sized tartlets, which are very good to take on a picnic.

crust
350 g/12 oz wholemeal flour, *or* part plain if you prefer
175 g/6 oz vegetable margarine
1 level teaspoon salt
6 tablespoons cold water

filling
6 cloves garlic
60 g/2 oz vegetable margarine
500 g/1 lb mushrooms
3 tablespoons soy sauce
1 celery heart
1 bunch spring onions
175 g/6 oz Gouda *or* mild Cheddar cheese

Make the pastry in the usual way (see p. 218) and chill it for 15 minutes in the refrigerator. Preheat the oven to 180° C (350° F, gas mark 4). Roll out the pastry and, using a 10 cm (4 in) pastry cutter, make 18 circles. Grease a tartlet tin and fill it with the pastry cases. Bake blind for 10 minutes.

Meanwhile, make the filling. Chop the garlic and fry it gently in the margarine for 2 minutes. Wash the mushrooms and slice them quite thinly. Add them to the pan and fry, stirring all the time, for a further 5 minutes. Take the pan off the heat and mix in the soy sauce. Finely chop the celery and spring onions, grate the cheese and mix all the ingredients together, reserving a little cheese to put on the top of each tartlet. Fill the pastry cases with the mixture, return to the oven and bake for another 20 minutes at the same temperature.

SOY-FLAVOURED PANCAKES STUFFED WITH ALFALFA SPROUTS

1 egg
250 g/8 oz finely ground wholemeal flour *or* 80% flour
400 ml/¾ pint milk *or* soya milk
4 tablespoons soy sauce, *or* more to taste
vegetable oil for frying
125 g/4 oz alfalfa sprouts

Beat the egg and mix it in with the flour. Add the milk or soya milk and soy sauce gradually, beating until a smooth batter is obtained. Leave to stand for at least 30 minutes. Heat a cast iron frying pan for 10 minutes over a low heat. Raise the heat and add 1 dessertspoon of vegetable oil. When the oil is hot, pour in a small cup of batter. Tilt the pan so that the batter forms a thin layer completely covering the bottom of the pan. Cook for 2–3 minutes on each side. Roll the pancake round a good filling of raw alfalfa sprouts and keep warm. Repeat until all the batter is used up.

NUT ROAST OR RISSOLES
FLAVOURED WITH SOY SAUCE

You can serve either of these dishes with a green salad.

250 g/8 oz mixed nuts, e.g. cashews, hazelnuts *and* almonds
150 g/5 oz carrots
125 g/4 oz cheese (most hard English *or* Dutch cheeses are suitable)
1 large onion
3–4 cloves garlic, crushed
30 g/1 oz parsley
125 g/4 oz fresh wholemeal breadcrumbs
2 eggs (*and* extra egg for frying rissoles)
3 tablespoons soy sauce
1 teaspoon chilli sauce
sesame seeds
a little vegetable margarine (for nut roast)
vegetable oil (for frying rissoles)

If you are making the nut roast, preheat the oven to 180° C (350° F, gas mark 4). Crush the nuts into small pieces using a pestle and mortar. Grate the carrots, cheese and onion. Crush the garlic and chop the parsley finely. Combine all these ingredients with the breadcrumbs, then beat the eggs and stir them in with the soy sauce and chilli sauce. Grease a 500 g (1 lb) loaf tin and press the ingredients into it. Top with sesame seeds and a few dots of vegetable margarine and bake for 30 minutes.

If you want to make nut rissoles instead of a roast, simmer the onions and garlic for 10 minutes before combining them with the rest of the ingredients. Shape the rissoles into a convenient size, then dip them in beaten egg followed by flour before deep frying.

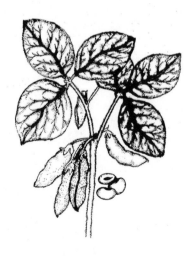

TEMPURA WITH
SPECIAL SOY SAUCE FOR DIPPING

When properly made, tempura is a great delicacy. The vegetables are lightly coated in batter and fried until they are just tender. The thin batter coating should be just crisp. Tempura should be served with individual bowls of sauce for dipping. Unfortunately for the cook, tempura cannot be fried in very large batches and it should be served immediately it is cooked, so it is really necessary for one person to do the cooking while the others eat.

batter
2 egg yolks
1 teaspoon salt
about 350 ml/12 fl oz ice-cold water
200 g/7 oz flour, ½ wholewheat, ½ plain white

dipping sauce
1 dried shiitake mushroom
a little seaweed
400 ml/¾ pint water
3½ tablespoons mirin (sweet sake)
3½ tablespoons soy sauce
a 2.5 cm/1 in piece fresh root ginger
1 large clove garlic

700 g/1½ lb vegetables made up of, e.g:
cauliflower, cut into small florets
broccoli, cut into small sections
small mushrooms
French beans *or* mangetouts
onions, sliced thinly
lotus root, sliced in half

plain flour for dusting
sesame *or* sunflower oil for frying

Make the batter by mixing the egg yolks, salt and iced water together and then beating in the flour. Leave the batter in the refrigerator for 30 minutes.

For the sauce, cut up the shiitake mushroom and the seaweed and put them in a pan with the water. Bring to the boil and then simmer for 30 minutes – the water should reduce by half. When it is ready, strain the stock and mix in the mirin and soy sauce (I have indicated quantities, but you can add more or less according to taste). Peel the ginger, then crush it and the garlic in a garlic press and add them to the sauce. Pour into 4 small bowls.

Wash and cut up the vegetables. It is best to fry vegetables of the same type and of a similar size in the same batch. Dip them into the plain flour before coating them with batter. Take a vessel suitable for deep frying, pour in the oil to a depth of 7.5–10 cm (3–4 in), and heat it to 150° – 180° C (300° – 350° F). Each batch of vegetables should fry for about 4 minutes, so make sure the oil is not so hot that they burn on the outside.

Serve each batch at once with the sauce for dipping.

COURGETTES
FLAVOURED WITH SOY SAUCE

Marrow or pumpkin cubes can also be cooked in this way.

500 g/1 lb courgettes
2 cloves garlic
2 tablespoons vegetable oil
2–3 tablespoons soy sauce

Slice the courgettes and drop them into a saucepan of boiling water for 3–4 minutes. Drain thoroughly. Crush the garlic and fry it gently in the oil for 1–2 minutes before adding the courgettes. Turn the heat up high and stir the courgettes in the oil for another 3–4 minutes. Take the pan off the heat and add the soy sauce. Serve at once.

EXTRA SPECIAL BUBBLE AND SQUEAK

Sunflower seeds roasted with soy sauce have a most enlivening effect on potatoes, and this recipe is a good way of using up leftovers.

100 ml/4 fl oz water
350 g/12 oz cabbage *or* spring greens *or* broccoli, chopped into thin strips
90 g/3 oz vegetable margarine
700 g/1½ lb potatoes, cooked
a little milk
1 tablespoon mustard seeds
125 g/4 oz sunflower seeds
4 tablespoons soy sauce
1 large onion
vegetable oil for frying
salt
black pepper

Boil the water and add the thinly chopped cabbage. Cook rapidly, then, after a few minutes, add 30 g (1 oz) of the margarine and cook until all the liquid has been absorbed or has evaporated. Mash the potatoes with the rest of the vegetable margarine and a little milk.

Fry the mustard seeds in a little oil until they begin to pop, then add them to the potato mixture. Dry roast the sunflower seeds in a heavy cast iron pan: stir them over a medium heat until they begin to turn brown, then take them off the heat and mix in the soy sauce, coating the seeds as thoroughly as possible. Add them to the potato mixture. Finally, chop the onion and cook gently in a little oil for 10 minutes. Combine the potato mixture, greens and onion, season with salt and pepper, and serve hot.

STIR FRIED GREEN VEGETABLES
WITH SOY SAUCE

Vegetables cooked in this way go very well with brown rice. Try using different green leaf vegetables and different kinds of seeds – pumpkin, sesame or mustard seeds, for example.

2 medium onions
5–6 stalks celery
3 tablespoons vegetable oil
125 g/4 oz sunflower seeds
4 tablespoons soy sauce, *or* more to taste
3 cloves garlic
1 small Chinese cabbage *or* ½ a large one

Chop the onions and the celery. Heat the oil in a frying pan or wok and fry them over a medium heat for 10 minutes, stirring occasionally. Meanwhile, roast the sunflower seeds in a dry pan (a cast iron frying pan is ideal for this). When they are lightly browned, take them off the heat and stir in 2–3 tablespoons of soy sauce so that the seeds are coated in the sauce. Chop or crush the garlic and shred the cabbage. Add both to the onions and celery. Stir fry for 3–4 minutes, and then add the sunflower seeds and a little extra soy sauce.

HARICOT BEAN AND DRIED MUSHROOM
SALAD WITH SOY SAUCE

350 g/12 oz haricot beans
a few strips dried seaweed, preferably kombu
30 g/1 oz dried shiitake *or* boletus mushrooms
½ clove garlic
4 tablespoons soy sauce, *or* more to taste
1 large bunch spring onions

Soak the beans in cold water for at least 2 hours. Drain them, put them in a saucepan with the seaweed and plenty of fresh water, and bring to the boil. Turn down the heat and simmer until the beans are quite soft. Meanwhile, soak the dried mushrooms in water for about 30 minutes. (I prefer not to cook the mushrooms for this dish, so that they retain a nice chewy texture.) Rub a dish with the garlic, then drain the beans and seaweed and put them in the dish. Pour in the soy sauce and mix well to distribute it evenly. Chop the spring onions and the drained mushrooms and combine them with the rest of the ingredients. Leave in a cool place for 1–2 hours before serving. Add a little more soy sauce if you think it is required.

Umeboshi plums

These pickled plums are a speciality in Japan, where they are considered very beneficial to health. As they are very heavily salted, they should be used only very sparingly in cooking. They are best when mixed, in small amounts, with grains and pulses – for example, a small piece of umeboshi plum may be placed in the middle of a rice ball before frying.

UMEBOSHI AND CHICK PEA SPREAD

This nourishing spread can be mixed up more or less to taste. Chick peas make a good base for spreads, especially when other very strong-tasting ingredients are added.

250 g/8 oz chick peas
1–2 umeboshi plums
juice of 1 lemon
a few spring onions *or* 1 small onion
about 150 ml/¼ pint water to mix

Soak the chick peas for a few hours or overnight, then cook them until they are very soft. Put all the ingredients in a liquidizer and blend to a smooth paste. Alternatively, put the chick peas, umeboshi plums and onions through a food mill and mix in the lemon juice and water afterwards.

Yeast extract

Brewer's yeast, as opposed to the live yeast used in baking, is one of the few sources of the whole B complex of vitamins. As these vitamins are not easily stored in the body, which nevertheless needs the whole range of B vitamins in order to function well, the inclusion of yeast in the diet is clearly a good thing.

Brewer's yeast in powdered form is not to everyone's taste, but yeast extract, in which the yeast is mixed with salt and vegetable flavourings, is much more palatable. It is also a very useful flavouring in soups, stocks and sauces. About 1 level tablespoon of yeast extract dissolved in 600 ml (1 pint) of boiling water makes a good stock.

There are many brands of yeast extract on the market – Marmite and Vecon are probably the best known. They make a tasty base for soups and sauces.

SAVOURY MILLET COOKED IN STOCK

Cooked in this way, millet retains a slight crunchiness and absorbs the flavours in which it is simmered. A green salad is a good accompaniment to this dish.

2 large onions
3 tablespoons vegetable margarine
1 celery heart
275 g/9 oz millet
900 ml/1½ pints stock, made from 1 heaped tablespoon yeast extract *and* boiling water
black *or* white pepper
salt
175 g/6 oz cheese (e.g. red Cheshire *or* Leicester *or* Gloucester)

to serve
1 bunch radishes

Chop the onions and fry them gently in the margarine for 10 minutes. Chop the celery and add it to the pan. Wash the millet well, and add it with the stock to the onions and celery. Leave the pan to simmer, uncovered, for about 20 minutes more or until the millet is just cooked. Preheat the grill. Season the millet with salt and pepper to taste and grate the cheese over the top. Place the pan under the grill for a few minutes until the cheese has melted.

Serve with sliced radishes.

YEAST EXTRACT SAUCE

This sauce is a useful accompaniment to vegetable, rice and other grain dishes. The Greek Avgolemono sauce, usually flavoured with lemon juice, is made in a similar way. Simmer this sauce very slowly, so that the flour has time to cook.

1 small bunch watercress *or* parsley
2 cloves garlic, crushed
500 ml/18 fl oz stock, made from 1 level dessertspoon of
yeast extract dissolved in boiling water
1 tablespoon plain flour
1 egg

Finely chop the watercress or parsley and put it aside. Stir the crushed garlic into the stock. In a separate bowl, mix the flour with a little cold water to make a smooth paste. Put the stock into a saucepan, heat it to just below boiling and stir in the flour and water paste. Bring to the boil, stirring, then lower the heat and leave the sauce to simmer for a few minutes. Beat up the egg in another bowl and mix with it a few spoonfuls of the sauce, then pour this mixture back into the pan. Add the watercress or parsley and simmer the sauce over a low heat, stirring occasionally, for 10 minutes.

Nutty tastes

ALMONDS · PEANUTS · PINE NUTS
POPPY SEEDS · SESAME AND TAHINI

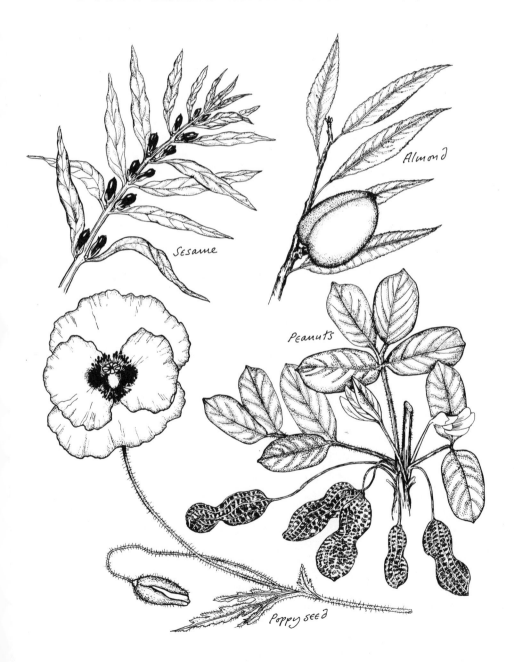

Sesame

Almond

Peanuts

Poppy seed

Almonds

There are two kinds of almonds, sweet and bitter, but it is nearly always the sweet almond which is used in cookery. If bitter almonds are used at all, it is only in very small quantities. Today, almond trees grow mainly around the Mediterranean, in western Asia and in California, though the herbalist Gerard tells us that almond trees were 'in our London gardens and orchards in great plenty' in the sixteenth century.

Almonds are one of the most useful ingredients in wholefood cookery – indeed in any type of cookery – being equally at home in savoury and sweet dishes. In medieval cookery almonds were extensively employed: to thicken sauces (flour was never used for this purpose), to make 'marchpane' (marzipan) and to make 'blanc manger' (blancmange). Indian Moghul cookery also made good use of almonds, especially in extravagant rice dishes, and they are still used a lot in the cuisines of the Middle East. The Spanish excel in confectionery made from almonds, as anyone who has tasted turron will know.

Many recipes call for blanched almonds, and it is easy enough to blanch almonds by soaking them in boiling water for a few minutes and then squeezing them out of their skins. Splitting them cleanly in half is not always so easy, but it is possible with a sharp knife and a little practice.

The flavour of almonds is greatly enhanced by toasting them under the grill (or roasting them in a slow oven: see p.61). Before toasting, the almonds should be split, but not necessarily blanched, and then laid on a piece of foil, insides uppermost. Let them toast until just brown.

Almond oil, which is a light and almost tasteless oil, is often used in the preparation of desserts. Almond essence, which should be genuine and not a synthetic substitute, is a concentrated flavouring useful when making cakes and biscuits.

MACARONI WITH TOASTED ALMONDS AND CRISP CABBAGE

The texture, as well as the taste, of this dish is very pleasing. Its main ingredients are crunchy almonds, crisp cabbage and macaroni, the firmest of all the pastas.

350 g/12 oz wholewheat macaroni
4 cloves garlic
2 tablespoons vegetable margarine *or* butter
1 Chinese cabbage weighing about 500 g/1 lb
1 small bunch coriander leaves
12 stems Chinese chives *or* 1 bunch spring onions
150 g/5 oz almonds, split and toasted
salt
cayenne pepper

Drop the macaroni into boiling, salted water and boil rapidly for 12–15 minutes. Chop the garlic and fry it gently in a large pan with the margarine or butter. Chop the Chinese cabbage, coriander leaves and Chinese chives or spring onions.

When the macaroni is cooked, drain it well and stir it for a few minutes, with the garlic and butter, over a low heat. Add the green ingredients and the toasted almonds, combine well and then remove the pan from the heat. Season to taste with salt and cayenne pepper.

Serve at once – this dish should be warm rather than hot, with the cabbage almost raw.

MILLET WITH ALMOND SAUCE

A serving of leeks, cauliflower or mushrooms would go well with this dish.

350 g/12 oz millet
1 level teaspoon salt
60 g/2 oz vegetable margarine *or* butter
3–4 cloves garlic, chopped
125 g/4 oz almonds, ground
450 ml/16 fl oz milk
black pepper
seeds from 2 cardamom pods, ground
2 tablespoons Parmesan cheese, grated
2 bunches spring onions, chopped

Put the millet in a pan and bring it to the boil with enough water to cover. Drain, and wash under the cold tap to get rid of any dirt and prevent scum forming while the millet is cooking. Return the millet to the pan and add 750 ml (1¼ pints) of water. Bring to the boil and then simmer, uncovered, for 15–20 minutes, by which time the water should all have been absorbed and the grain should be soft but still retaining a slight crispness. Add some of the salt 5 minutes before the end of cooking time. Put the millet in a sieve and wash it again under the cold tap, this time to separate the grains. Put it into a bowl and reheat in a very low oven.

Meanwhile, melt the margarine or butter in a frying pan and add the chopped garlic. Fry gently for a few minutes. Stir in the ground almonds and gradually add the milk. Stir continuously over a medium heat until the sauce comes to the boil. Season with black pepper, salt, ground cardamom and Parmesan cheese and turn the heat right down. Add the chopped spring onions and let the sauce simmer very slowly for about 10 minutes, stirring occasionally. Serve with the millet.

TOASTED ALMOND AND CARROT SALAD

300 g/10 oz carrots
1 tart eating apple
1 small bunch spring onions
90 g/3 oz almonds, split *and* toasted
1 bunch watercress

dressing
5 tablespoons sunflower *or* sesame oil
1 large clove garlic, crushed
2 teaspoons cider vinegar
1 level teaspoon salt
black *or* white pepper

Grate the carrots, dice the apple and chop up the spring onions. When the toasted almonds are cool, combine them with all the other salad ingredients.

To make the dressing, combine the oil with the crushed garlic, stir in the vinegar, then season with salt and pepper. Don't add the dressing to the salad until just before serving – otherwise the almonds will loose their crispness.

ALMOND AND APRICOT CHEESECAKE

crust
200 g/7 oz wholemeal flour
100 g/3½ oz vegetable margarine
4 tablespoons cold water

filling
60 g/2 oz dried apricots
90 g/3 oz almonds, split *and* toasted
250 g/8 oz curd cheese
2 eggs, beaten
90 g/3 oz brown sugar
peel of 2 lemons, grated

Make the pastry crust in the usual way (see p.218) and leave it in the refrigerator while you are preparing the filling. Preheat the oven to 180° C (350° F, gas mark 4).

Chop the apricots finely. Break the almonds into smaller pieces with a pestle or the end of a rolling pin. Mix together the curd cheese, eggs, sugar, lemon peel, apricots and almonds. Roll out the pastry and line a greased 25 cm (10 in) flan dish. Spoon the filling into the piecrust and bake for 30 minutes. Allow to cool a little before serving.

Nutty tastes: Almonds

ALMOND AND CHERRY YEASTED CAKE

Yeasted cakes do take longer to prepare than other cakes, but they are worth making occasionally for their light and unusual texture. As the process is quite lengthy, it is worth making a large cake or two small ones at a time. Sufficient ingredients for this are given below.

300 g/10 oz wholewheat flour
175 g/6 oz plain white flour
½ teaspoon salt
1 teaspoon dried yeast *or* 2 teaspoons fresh
150 ml/¼ pint warm water
100 g/3½ oz brown sugar
150 ml/¼ pint warm milk
150 g/5 oz vegetable margarine
3 eggs
90 g/3 oz almonds, ground
1 teaspoon almond essence
peel of 2 lemons, grated
175 g/6 oz glacé cherries

to decorate
almond halves, toasted
glacé cherries

Mix the flours and the salt together. Dissolve the yeast in the warm water with a little of the sugar. When it is ready, mix it into the flour. Add the warm milk. Knead, then leave this very dry dough to rise in a warm place for 1 hour.

Meanwhile, beat together the margarine and the rest of the sugar. Separate the eggs and beat the yolks in with the margarine and sugar. Stir in the ground almonds, almond essence, lemon peel and glacé cherries.

When the dough has been standing for 1 hour, combine it with the margarine mixture. Beat up the separated egg whites and fold these in last: as with a soufflé, it is best to take a large spoonful of egg white, beat it in well with a fork to moisten the mixture, and then lightly fold in the rest of the whites.

Grease two 20 cm (8 in) cake tins, about 7.5 cm (3 in) in depth, and divide the cake mixture between them. Leave to stand in a warm place until doubled in size. Meanwhile, preheat the oven to 190° C (375° F, gas mark 5). Bake the cakes for 15 minutes at this temperature, then turn down the oven to 180° C (350° F, gas mark 4) and bake for a further 25 minutes. Place them on a wire rack to cool.

As the cakes are cooling, decorate with toasted almonds and glacé cherries.

FRESH FRUIT PASTRIES

Almond pastry makes an excellent base for all kinds of fruit tarts and is easily made by substituting finely ground almonds for one third of the flour in a standard pastry recipe. This recipe makes about 16 little pastries.

250 g/8 oz wholewheat flour
125 g/4 oz almonds, ground
pinch salt
30 g/1 oz brown sugar
175 g/6 oz vegetable margarine
1 egg
500 g/1 lb soft fruit, e.g. strawberries, cherries, chopped peaches, apricots
whipped cream (optional)

Combine the flour, ground almonds, salt and sugar and rub in the margarine. Beat the egg and then add it to the other ingredients to form a soft dough. Put in the refrigerator for 15 minutes to cool. Preheat the oven to 180° C (350° F, gas mark 4).

Roll out the pastry to a little under 1.5 cm (½ in) thick. Cut out about 16 circles 7.5–10 cm (3–4 in) across and put them into a well-greased tartlet tray. Bake for only about 15 minutes.

Allow to cool and fill each tart with fresh fruit as suggested above. Top with whipped cream if liked.

ALMOND BISCUITS

125 g/4 oz almonds, ground
250 g/8 oz wholewheat flour
75 g/2½ oz sugar
1 level teaspoon salt
150 g/5 oz vegetable margarine
1 egg yolk

Preheat the oven to 190° C (375° F, gas mark 5). Combine the almonds, flour, sugar and salt. Melt the margarine, cool it a little and then beat in the egg yolk; mix this with the dry ingredients. When you have formed a stiff dough, roll it out on a well-floured board to a thickness of about 1.5 cm (½ in). Cut the biscuits into convenient shapes and place them on a greased baking tray. Cook for about 15 minutes, but check after 10 minutes to make sure that the biscuits nearest the oven sides are not burning. Leave to cool on a wire rack, then store in an airtight tin.

Peanuts

Peanuts are legumes – members of the pea and bean family – rather than real nuts. They originated in South America but are now a very large and important crop in North America, Africa, India and China. The richest source of vegetable protein after soya beans, they contain almost all the amino acids required to make up a complete protein. Peanut oil, which is extracted in huge quantities from the world crop, is nutritionally useful but lacks flavour; use it when a neutral-tasting oil is required, for instance when frying.

When buying peanuts, choose the pale-skinned variety. Under certain conditions red-skinned peanuts (which are grown in subtropical countries) have been found to be infected with a poisonous fungus called aflatoxin. This has never been discovered in pale-skinned peanuts (which are grown in China and the United States).

Peanuts are used to particularly good effect in South-east Asian cookery, where they form the basis of many delicious sauces. Brown rice, peanut sauce and a few salad vegetables make a simple yet satisfying meal. When making a peanut sauce use freshly ground peanuts, rather than peanut butter, because the latter will not integrate smoothly into the sauce. Ground peanuts are also useful to bind together vegetable bakes, rissoles and pâtés. Peanut butter is a useful spread, particularly sustaining because of its high protein content. Try mixing chopped spring onions, chives, parsley or watercress into peanut butter for sandwiches.

PEANUT SAUCE

Serve this sauce hot with vegetable sticks as a tasty dip or with brown rice and a few salad vegetables to make a simple yet delicious meal.

250 g/8 oz peanuts
2 teaspoons coriander seeds
2 teaspoons mustard seeds
4 cloves garlic, crushed
4 tablespoons vegetable oil
300 ml/½ pint hot water
juice of 2 lemons
2 tablespoons soy sauce
salt
1 teaspoon cayenne pepper, *or* to taste
1 tablespoon brown sugar, *or* to taste

Grind the peanuts, coriander and mustard seeds together in a coffee grinder. Fry the crushed garlic in the oil for 1–2 minutes. Stir in the ground peanuts, coriander and mustard seeds and then gradually add the hot water. Add the lemon juice and soy sauce. Season with salt, cayenne pepper and brown sugar to taste. Simmer the sauce over a low heat for another 5 minutes.

VEGETABLE AND PEANUT PATE

This pâté is easy to make: all the vegetables are steamed until soft, then blended or milled and mixed with the ground nuts and seeds. Using roughly the proportions of vegetables to dry ingredients given below, you can make a great variety of pâtés using different vegetables, herbs, spices, nuts and seeds. This pâté should be chilled in the refrigerator for several hours before serving, so make it well in advance.

125 g/4 oz celery heart
175 g/6 oz carrots
125 g/4 oz leeks
125 g/4 oz onions *or* shallots
a few sprigs fresh herbs
125 g/4 oz mushrooms
3 large cloves garlic
4 tablespoons red wine
60 g/2 oz sunflower seeds, ground
150 g/5 oz peanuts, ground
1½ teaspoons salt
white pepper

Roughly chop the celery, carrots, leeks and onions or shallots and remove any thick stalks from the herbs. Put them with the mushrooms and garlic in a steamer or a colander with a lid, and steam until soft (20–30 minutes). Then transfer to a blender with the red wine (or put the vegetables through a mouli and add the wine afterwards). When the vegetables are reduced to a puree, mix into them the ground sunflower seeds and ground peanuts. Season with salt and pepper and put the mixture into a bowl to chill in the refrigerator.

Nutty tastes: Peanuts

GADO GADO WITH
PEANUT AND COCONUT SAUCE

Gado Gado is an Indonesian salad consisting of a mixture of cooked and uncooked vegetables, with a peanut sauce. Use any selection of seasonal vegetables for the salad. Creamed coconut is available in a solid block from Chinese grocers.

salad
250 g/8 oz potatoes
250 g/8 oz carrots
250 g/8 oz French beans
1 bunch spring onions
1 bunch radishes
½ cucumber
2 hardboiled eggs, shelled
1 small lettuce

garnish
green *and* red chillies, *or* peppers

sauce
2 small onions
4 cloves garlic
2 tablespoons vegetable oil
175 g/6 oz unsalted peanuts
150 g/5 oz creamed coconut dissolved in 400 ml/¾ pint hot water
juice of 1 large lemon
salt
1 small bunch coriander leaves

Cook the potatoes, carrots and beans separately so that they are tender but still firm. Chop and arrange all the salad ingredients as decoratively as possible on a very large plate. Indonesian dishes are often elaborately garnished with an artistic eye for colour, not only with vegetables but also with flowers, so if you are making this dish for a party use plenty of imagination (see recipe on p.16 for making chilli 'flowers').

To make the sauce, chop the onion and crush the garlic and fry them in the oil for 10 minutes. Grind the peanuts in a coffee grinder and dissolve the creamed coconut in the hot water. Stir the ground peanuts in with the onions and garlic, then add the coconut milk and lemon juice. Season with a little salt to taste, and stir the sauce over a low heat for a few minutes. Chop the coriander leaves finely and add them just before serving the sauce.

ADUKI BEAN AND PEANUT RISSOLES

Peanut flour serves as a binding agent as well as a flavouring in these tasty bean cakes. This recipe uses aduki beans, but any well cooked and crushed beans could be substituted. This mixture keeps well in the refrigerator cooked or uncooked, so it is worth making a lot at a time. Serve them with a dressed green salad.

350 g/12 oz aduki beans
2 medium onions, finely chopped
3 cloves garlic, crushed
4 tablespoons vegetable oil *and* 100 ml/4 fl oz extra for frying the rissoles
2 teaspoons salt
1 egg, beaten
juice of 1 lemon
2 teaspoons hot *or* sweet paprika
5 tablespoons parsley, finely chopped
175 g/6 oz peanuts, ground
a little wholemeal flour

Wash the beans and put them in a saucepan with plenty of water. Bring to the boil, then leave to stand for 1 hour. Bring to the boil again and simmer rapidly until the beans are quite soft.

Gently fry the onions and garlic in the oil for 10 minutes. When the beans are cooked, drain them and crush them slightly with a potato masher.

Combine all the ingredients except the flour and frying oil in a large bowl and, with wet hands, shape the mixture into rissoles about 2.5 cm (1 in) thick. Coat the rissoles lightly with wholemeal flour. Heat the rest of the oil in the bottom of a pan (there is no need to deep fry these rissoles) and fry them in batches for about 4 minutes on each side. Keep the heat fairly low so that the ingredients have a chance to cook through.

Nutty tastes: Peanuts

Pine nuts

Various species of pine trees produce edible kernels, but those generally used in cookery are the product of the stone pine, a beautiful tree which figures in many Italian landscape paintings. Although the stone pine is a native of the Mediterranean regions, it also grows extensively in China, which is now the main exporter of pine nuts.

The flavour of pine nuts is quite subtle – faintly resinous and not noticeably sweet. It blends with both sweet and savoury ingredients, and is an especially good complement to pasta. Pine nuts are ground with basil, cheese and garlic to make the delicious pesto sauce. As the texture of pine kernels is softer than that of other nuts, they are good to use in salads. Pine kernels combine well with dried fruit, in either fruit salads or tart fillings. When lightly roasted and sprinkled with salt, they make a tasty snack.

PASTA VERDE WITH PINE NUTS

350 g/12 oz green pasta
4 cloves garlic, crushed
60 g/2 oz vegetable margarine
1 bunch spring onions
60 g/2 oz parsley
a few sprigs mint
90 g/3 oz walnuts, broken
125 g/4 oz pine nuts

to serve
90 g/3 oz Parmesan cheese, grated

Cook the pasta in plenty of boiling, salted water. Gently fry the garlic for a few minutes in the margarine. Chop up the spring onions, parsley and mint and slightly crush the walnuts. Drain the pasta thoroughly and toss it with the fried garlic. Mix in all the other ingredients and stir over a low heat for a few minutes.

Serve with a bowl of Parmesan cheese.

SPINACH PUREE WITH PINE NUTS

Spinach is always best cooked with a little milk or cream, which neutralizes the bitterness caused by the presence of oxalic acid in the leaves.

900 g/2 lb spinach
2 large onions, finely chopped
4 cloves garlic, crushed
90 g/3 oz vegetable margarine
about 5 tablespoons milk
salt
pepper
75 g/2½ oz pine nuts

Wash the spinach and remove the thick stems and spines. Gently fry the onions with the garlic in the margarine for about 5 minutes. Add the spinach and stir the mixture over a medium heat for a further 5 minutes. Add the milk, and leave to simmer until the spinach is pureed and most of the liquid has evaporated. Season with salt and pepper to taste, and stir in the pine nuts just before serving.

PINE NUT AND BULGHUR SALAD WITH YOGHURT DRESSING

300 ml/½ pint boiling water
175 g/6 oz bulghur (cracked) wheat
175 g/6 oz pine nuts
½ cucumber, diced
2 tablespoons mint, chopped
2 tablespoons chives, chopped

dressing
300 g/10 oz Greek yoghurt
2 cloves garlic, crushed
1 tablespoon cider vinegar

Pour the boiling water over the bulghur wheat and leave it to stand for 30 minutes. Then mix into it the pine nuts, cucumber, mint and chives.

Make the dressing by combining the yoghurt, garlic and vinegar. Mix the dressing into the salad, and serve.

Poppy seeds

Edible poppy seeds come from *Papaver somniferum*, the opium poppy, which grows all over Europe and Asia. (Opium is only present in the unripe seed pods, however, not in the ripened seeds.)

The seeds are often used to top bread rolls and loaves, not only for their flavour but also because they help the digestion. These tiny seeds have such a good flavour – and one which blends into both sweet and savoury dishes – that it is well worth using them often. Indian cookery uses them in savoury vegetable dishes, and they are ground up with dried fruit and nuts to make the delicious filo pastries of Greece and the Middle East. Eastern European cookery probably makes the most imaginative use of poppy seeds, putting them in sweet and savoury tarts and in salads, in cakes and with noodles.

Poppy seeds are usually soaked in boiling water before use, though sometimes they are ground in a coffee grinder without soaking. Use a very fine hair sieve to drain the poppy seeds after soaking.

NOODLES WITH POPPY SEEDS AND YOGHURT

The Hungarian and Jewish culinary repertory includes some unusual recipes for sweet noodle dishes, many of them quite elaborate. Here is one which is simple to prepare. Do not be put off by the rather unusual combination of ingredients – the result is delicious.

4 tablespoons poppy seeds
250 g/8 oz cooking apples
1 heaped tablespoon brown sugar
300 g/10 oz wholewheat noodles
3 tablespoons vegetable margarine
4 cloves garlic, crushed
a few spring onions, finely chopped
250 g/8 oz Greek yoghurt
2 heaped tablespoons sweet paprika

Soak the poppy seeds in a small bowl of boiling water while you prepare the other ingredients. Chop the cooking apples and simmer them, with the sugar, in a very little water until they are quite soft. Cook the noodles in plenty of boiling, salted water. When they are cooked, drain them well and put them in a pan with the margarine and garlic. Drain the poppy seeds and mix them in with the noodles. Stir these ingredients together over a low heat, then add the finely chopped spring onions, the cooked apples and finally the yoghurt. Season with paprika.

Serve warm, rather than hot.

POPPY SEED AND
GROUND ALMOND TARTLETS

Sweet pastries with a filling of dried fruit, nuts and spices are a feature of Middle Eastern cookery. The recipe below uses wholewheat pastry, but experiment as well with filo pastry, which is the kind generally used in the Middle East (available from Greek grocers). The following ingredients will make about 12 tartlets.

crust
250 g/8 oz wholewheat flour
125 g/4 oz vegetable margarine
4 tablespoons cold water
a little sugar (optional)

filling
60 g/2 oz poppy seeds, ground
125 g/4 oz almonds, ground
30 g/1 oz walnuts, broken
60 g/2 oz brown sugar *or* honey
peel of 1 orange, grated
1 teaspoon coriander, ground
3 tablespoons orange juice
3 tablespoons orange flower water *or* extra orange juice
90 g/3 oz vegetable margarine

Prepare the pastry in the usual way (see p. 218), adding a little sugar, if using, and put it in the refrigerator for about 15 minutes. Preheat the oven to 180° C (350° F, gas mark 4). Beat together with a fork all the filling ingredients except the margarine, which should be worked in last.

Roll out the pastry, cut it into circles and put them in a greased tartlet tin. Bake blind for 20 minutes, then take them out of the oven and fill with the poppy seed mixture. Return the tartlets to the oven and bake for a further 10 minutes at the same temperature. Serve warm or cold.

Nutty tastes: Poppy seeds

POPPY SEED AND FIG TART

crust
250 g/8 oz wholemeal flour
125 g/4 oz vegetable margarine
4 tablespoons cold water

filling
125 g/4 oz poppy seeds
125 g/4 oz dried figs
60 g/2 oz vegetable margarine
1 egg, beaten
peel of 2 lemons, grated
1 heaped teaspoon coriander seeds, ground

Soak the poppy seeds in boiling water and the figs in cold water, both for 1 hour. Make the pastry (see p.218) and set it aside in the bottom of the refrigerator while you make the filling. Preheat the oven to 180° C (350° F, gas mark 4).

Wash and drain the poppy seeds, using a fine hair sieve. Drain and roughly chop the figs. Put all the filling ingredients into a blender, adding a little water if the blades have trouble turning, and reduce them to a puree.

Roll out the pastry and line a greased 25 cm (10 in) flan dish. Put the filling into the pastry case. Make a lattice with the spare pastry and bake for 35 minutes. Serve warm or cold.

POPPY SEED CAKE

175 g/6 oz poppy seeds
125 g/4 oz vegetable margarine
90 g/3 oz brown sugar
3 eggs
60 g/2 oz plain white flour
1 teaspoon baking powder

Soak the poppy seeds in boiling water for 1 hour. Then empty them into a fine hair sieve and rinse them thoroughly with cold water. Press with a wooden spoon to remove as much water as possible. Preheat the oven to 180° C (350° F, gas mark 4).

Cream the margarine and sugar with the poppy seeds. Separate the eggs and beat in the yolks. Gradually stir in the flour and baking powder. Beat the egg whites stiffly in a separate basin, then fold them into the cake mixture.

Turn the mixture into a greased 20 cm (8 in) diameter cake tin and bake for 35 minutes. After this time test the centre of the cake with a skewer or knife blade, and if it comes out clean take the cake out of the oven. Leave to cool a little before removing from the tin.

Sesame and tahini

Sesame is grown in many parts of Asia and Africa for its seeds and the oil derived from them. Sesame oil is high in linoleic and other essential fatty acids, and the first pressing yields a delicious, nutty-tasting oil. When the seeds are ground and then pressed, a paste called tahini is produced; rich in protein, vitamins and minerals, it is used a great deal in Greek, Turkish and Middle Eastern cookery. Tahini is a very good accompaniment to brown rice (brown rice and sesame together make a complete source of protein). It is tasty in combination with garlic and lemon juice and with soy sauce. Thin it down with water and then mix it with any of a variety of ingredients and make unusual salad dressings. For a snack, spread tahini on wholemeal bread with a little honey.

Roasted sesame seeds add an excellent flavour to rice dishes and salads. They are easily roasted in a cast iron frying pan by stirring them over the heat for a few minutes until they begin to pop. Gomashio, a traditional Japanese seasoning, is made by grinding two parts roasted sesame seeds with one part sea salt. Sesame seeds are also used for topping bread, biscuits, tarts, and baked vegetable and cheese dishes. When ground up and combined with honey, they form the basis of sweetmeats like halva and sesame crunch.

TAHINI DIP

This is a favourite mezze or hors d'oeuvre in the Middle East, where it is usually eaten with pitta bread.

250 g/8 oz tahini
5–6 tablespoons water
juice of 2 large lemons
1 teaspoon roasted cumin, ground
2 cloves garlic, crushed
1 teaspoon salt

garnish
1 small bunch coriander leaves, finely chopped

Beat the tahini with the water and lemon juice to a smooth paste. Mix the cumin and garlic with the paste and season with salt.

Garnish with chopped coriander leaves.

HUMMUS

This is a popular Greek dip of pureed chick peas and tahini with olive oil.

250 g/8 oz chick peas
4 tablespoons tahini
4 tablespoons olive oil
juice of 4 lemons
4 cloves garlic, crushed

garnish
1 teaspoon hot paprika
1 tablespoon olive oil

to serve
parsley, finely chopped

Soak the chick peas overnight or all day, then boil them in fresh water until soft (you may find it convenient to use a pressure cooker).

Put all the ingredients except the parsley and paprika into a blender and liquidize to a smooth paste. If the mixture is too stiff for the liquidizer, add a little boiling water. (It is possible to pound the ingredients together by hand, but it is difficult to achieve a really smooth paste.)

Put the hummus in a serving bowl. Mix the paprika with the 1 tablespoon of olive oil and garnish the surface. Serve with a bowl of finely chopped parsley for sprinkling.

BABA GHANOUSH

This Middle Eastern aubergine and tahini dip is quickly made in a blender. Serve with pitta bread or lengths of fresh vegetables.

500 g/1 lb aubergines
150 ml/¼ pint light tahini
juice of 2 lemons
2 cloves garlic, chopped

garnish
parsley, finely chopped
cucumber, thinly sliced

Grill the aubergines whole: this will take 10–15 minutes, depending on their size. Turn frequently so that they soften right through. Hold the aubergines under the cold tap and remove their skins, then press them through a wire-meshed sieve with a wooden spoon to squeeze out the bitter juices. Transfer the aubergines to a liquidizer and combine with the tahini, lemon juice and chopped garlic. Blend to a soft paste.

Turn out on to a serving dish and garnish well with chopped parsley and slices of cucumber. Chill before serving.

AVOCADOS WITH TAHINI DRESSING

1 clove garlic, crushed
2 tablespoons tahini
2½ tablespoons lemon juice
2½ tablespoons vegetable oil
½ tablespoon wine vinegar *or* cider vinegar
½ teaspoon salt, *or* to taste
2 avocados, halved and stoned

Mix the garlic with the tahini, lemon juice, vegetable oil, vinegar and salt. Beat in several tablespoons of water – enough to make a sufficiently liquid consistency. Serve spooned into the avocados.

NOODLES, BEANSPROUTS AND CABBAGE WITH SESAME SAUCE

sauce
4 cloves garlic, crushed
15 g/½ oz fresh root ginger, grated
3 tablespoons vegetable oil
3 tablespoons sesame seeds, ground
250 ml/8 fl oz hot water
3 tablespoons soy sauce
juice of ½ lemon
black pepper
small bunch Chinese chives *or* spring onions

250 g/8 oz wholewheat noodles
350 g/12 oz Chinese cabbage
175 g/6 oz mung beansprouts

garnish
2 heaped tablespoons sesame seeds, toasted

To make the sauce, fry the garlic and ginger gently in the oil for a few minutes. Stir in the ground sesame seeds and then gradually add the hot water, stirring. Bring to the boil, then lower the heat and add the soy sauce, lemon juice, a good seasoning of black pepper and the Chinese chives or spring onions. Leave the sauce aside in a warm place while you boil the noodles (thick noodles should take about 10 minutes and thin ones about 5). Finely chop the Chinese cabbage.

When the noodles are cooked drain them and mix them with the cabbage and beansprouts in a large serving bowl. Pour the sauce over these ingredients and garnish with toasted sesame seeds.

Nutty tastes: Sesame and tahini

SWEET POTATOES WITH TAHINI
AND SOY SAUCE DRESSING

Allow one sweet potato weighing 150–175 g (5–6 oz) for each person. Scrub the potatoes and boil or bake them until they are quite soft. Split them open, and for every potato mix up a dressing consisting of:

1 tablespoon tahini
1 tablespoon soy sauce
2½ tablespoons water
2–3 spring onions, finely chopped

Serve on a bed of crisp lettuce or with plenty of green vegetables.

BEAN SALAD WITH TAHINI
AND CURD CHEESE DRESSING

300 g/10 oz haricot beans *or* beans of a similar size

dressing
4 tablespoons curd cheese
4 tablespoons tahini
2 cloves garlic, crushed
about 100 ml/4 fl oz water
2 teaspoons salt

garnish
1 bunch coriander leaves *or* watercress

Soak the beans for at least 2 hours – longer if convenient. Throw away the soaking water and bring the beans to the boil in plenty of fresh water. Leave to simmer until they are quite soft.

Beat the curd cheese with the tahini and the crushed garlic. Add the water and salt. Pour the dressing over the beans and leave them to stand for some time to absorb the flavours. Chop the coriander leaves or watercress and garnish the salad just before serving.

CHINESE SALAD WITH SESAME AND GINGER DRESSING

In this salad the vegetables are well coated with a sesame seed and ginger dressing. Add water chestnuts or lotus roots if you can obtain them fresh: lotus roots should be sliced and steamed for about 1 hour, while water chestnuts may be peeled and eaten raw, or boiled for about 15 minutes and then peeled.

1 small Chinese cabbage weighing about 500 g/1 lb
about 12 stems Chinese chives *or* 1 bunch spring onions
175 g/6 oz mung beansprouts
a few water chestnuts *or* slices of lotus root (optional)
60 g/2 oz sesame seeds, toasted

dressing
6 tablespoons sesame oil *or* vegetable oil
2 tablespoons brown rice vinegar
3 cloves garlic, crushed
15 g/½ oz fresh root ginger, crushed
1 level teaspoon salt

Chop the cabbage and the chives or spring onions. Mix all the salad vegetables together in a bowl.

Put the sesame oil in a small bowl, then mix in the vinegar followed by the other dressing ingredients. Add the sesame seeds and the dressing to the salad just before serving.

BEANSPROUT AND SESAME SEED SALAD

For this salad, use beansprouts which have sprouted to about 1.5 cm/½ in.

250 g/8 oz mung beansprouts
1 bunch spring onions
90 g/3 oz sesame seeds, toasted

dressing
2 cloves garlic, crushed
2 teaspoons soy sauce
2 tablespoons sesame oil

Blanch the beansprouts in boiling water for 2 minutes, then drain. Chop the spring onions and combine them with the beansprouts and toasted sesame seeds.

To make the dressing, mix the garlic with the soy sauce and sesame oil. Pour this dressing over the salad, and serve.

Nutty tastes: Sesame and tahini

Hot Tastes: Jerusalem Artichoke and Celery Soufflé with Paprika; Green Vegetables
Tossed with Mustard Seeds; Red Peppers Stuffed with Rice & Chillies;
Chilli 'Flowers' for Garnishing

Sour Tastes: Asparagus with Lemon Hollandaise; Sorrel, Cheese and Egg Tart;
Summer Fruit Salad Flavoured with Amchoor; Lemon Barley Water

Salty and Mushroom Tastes: Fried Rice with Dried Mushrooms and Mangetouts;
Tempura with Special Soy Sauce for Dipping; Miso Soup

Nutty Tastes: Toasted Almond and Carrot Salad; Gado Gado with Peanut and Coconut Sauce; Pasta Verde with Pine Nuts

Onion Flavours: Chollah; Potato and Chive Mayonnaise Salad; Vichyssoise;
Garlic Croutons; Fried Onion Rings

Green Herb Flavours: Winter Salad; Tarragon Vinegar; Tabbouleh;
Mung Bean Pasties Flavoured with Mint

Sweet Tastes: Pancakes with Maple Syrup; Strawberry, Honey and Tofu Tart;
Vanilla Yoghurt Ice Cream

Spicy Tastes: Saffron Buns; Pear and Chestnut Tart Flavoured with Cardamom; Caraway Biscuits; Welsh Griddle Cakes; Cinnamon Carrot Cake

SESAME AND VEGETABLE SAUCE

This makes an unusual sauce for pasta, especially good in winter. It also goes well with brown rice.

250 g/8 oz carrots
175 g/6 oz radishes
60 g/2 oz parsley
4 cloves garlic *or* a few shallots
90 g/3 oz vegetable margarine
150 g/5 oz sesame seeds, ground
400 ml/¾ pint hot water
4 tablespoons soy sauce

Grate the carrots and radishes and chop the parsley. Mince the garlic or chop the shallots and fry them in the margarine for a few minutes. Stir in the sesame seeds gradually. Slowly add the hot water, stirring all the time. Bring to the boil and add the carrots, radishes and parsley. Cover the pan and allow the sauce to simmer for 10 minutes. Season with soy sauce, and serve.

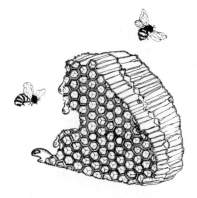

SESAME AND OATMEAL BISCUITS

200 g/7 oz sesame seeds
200 g/7 oz medium oatmeal
1 teaspoon salt
125 g/4 oz vegetable margarine
125 g/4 oz honey

Preheat the oven to 190°C (375° F, gas mark 5). Grind half of the sesame seeds and use the rest whole. Mix the oatmeal, sesame seeds and salt together. Melt the margarine and the honey in a saucepan and then add them to the dry ingredients. Grease a flat, low-sided tin about 25 cm (10 in) square, and press the mixture into it so that it is about 2 cm (just under 1 in) thick. Bake for 30 minutes, or until just brown. Mark the biscuits out into squares just after taking out of the oven, and then leave them to cool before removing them from the tin.

SESAME AND RYE CRISPBREAD

These biscuits can be made in a larger batch if you like, because they keep well for weeks in airtight containers.

175 g/6 oz rye flour
175 g/6 oz wholemeal flour
1 teaspoon salt
175 g/6 oz vegetable margarine
2 heaped tablespoons sesame seeds

Preheat the oven to 190°C (375° F, gas mark 5). Mix the flours and salt together and rub in the margarine. Mix in the sesame seeds and just enough water to make a stiff dough. Roll out, on a well floured board, to a thickness of 0.5 cm (¼ in). Cut into rectangles and prick all over with a fork. Place on greased baking trays and bake for 15 minutes. Cool on a wire rack and then store in an airtight tin.

TAHINI SPREADS

These tasty, nourishing spreads can be mixed up in a few minutes and stored in screw-top jars for some months.

1. For every 3 tablespoons tahini, beat in 2 tablespoons soy sauce.

2. For every 3 tablespoons tahini, mix in 2 scant tablespoons of yellow miso *or* 1 scant tablespoon dark miso.

Onion flavours

GARLIC
LEEKS
ONIONS AND SHALLOTS
SPRING ONIONS, GUCHOY AND
CHIVES

Onion

Garlic

Spring Onion

Garlic

Like the onion, garlic is used as a seasoning in most parts of the world. Cooking mellows its pungency and blends its flavours so subtly with those of the other ingredients that people who swear they never eat garlic rarely guess that there is garlic in the dish which they find so delicious! It is this ability to blend with and enhance other flavours which makes garlic essential to good cookery. It should always be cooked very gently and never burnt. As a rule, the longer it is to be cooked, the more generously it may be used.

In the use of raw garlic, however, discretion is called for (although it is used with complete indiscretion in Mediterranean dishes such as aïoli!). Raw garlic should be crushed in a garlic press, and a single clove is usually enough to flavour a salad dressing – though opinions vary. It is best to start with a single clove and add more to taste, remembering that raw garlic may hang on the breath in a way that cooked garlic never does. A green salad will acquire a delicious hint of garlic by being served in a bowl which has been well rubbed with a cut clove.

Garlic grows best in a warm climate. When bought, it should be neither too old nor too 'green'. The cloves should be firm and well separated, without any signs of decay – never use any which have become brown or spotted. Garlic keeps well when hung up like onions, and it is often economical to buy a whole string at a time.

SKORDALIA

This Greek salad, which also makes a good hors d'oeuvre, is made by pounding garlic with breadcrumbs and almonds and adding oil, drop by drop, as if making mayonnaise. In this recipe here I have added tomatoes, cucumber and olives as well. This salad is sometimes very strongly flavoured with garlic, so increase the quantities if you wish.

125 g/4 oz wholemeal fresh breadcrumbs
125 g/4 oz almonds, ground
2 cloves garlic, *or* more to taste
5 tablespoons olive oil
3 tablespoons cider vinegar
juice of 1 lemon
1 teaspoon salt
250 g/8 oz tomatoes, chopped
½ cucumber, diced
garnish
125 g/4 oz black olives

Mix the breadcrumbs with the ground almonds. Pound this mixture with the garlic and add the oil drop by drop. Add the vinegar, lemon juice and salt and then the chopped tomatoes and cucumber. Garnish with black olives.

QUICK PASTA DISH
FLAVOURED WITH GARLIC

Garlic-flavoured pasta dishes are always a useful standby because they are quick to make and satisfying to eat.

Allow about 90g (3oz) pasta for each person and boil it in plenty of salted water, al dente. Crush 1 large clove of garlic for every 90g (3oz) of pasta and fry it in 30g (1oz) vegetable margarine. Add the pasta and toss it briefly.

Serve hot with plenty of chopped parsley, grated Parmesan and ground black pepper. Chopped watercress, grated carrots and beansprouts are all excellent additions to this dish.

AIOLI

This Provençal sauce is usually made with a great deal of garlic, but in this recipe I have suggested more modest quantities which may be increased to taste. Aïoli is simply a garlic-flavoured mayonnaise which is served with a variety of cooked and uncooked vegetables such as potatoes in their jackets, green beans, green and red peppers, asparagus, courgettes, carrots and cauliflower. Prepare a good selection of vegetables and arrange them on a large plate. Garnish well with watercress, parsley or fresh herbs and serve with a bowl of aïoli.

4 cloves garlic
3 egg yolks
450ml/16floz olive oil
3 tablespoons vinegar *or* lemon juice
salt
pepper

Pound the garlic in a mortar and then mix it with the egg yolks. Add the olive oil, very slowly at first, as when making mayonnaise (see recipe on p.59). When all the oil has been added and the sauce is very thick, season with vinegar or lemon juice and salt and pepper.

GARLIC CROUTONS FOR SOUP

Preheat the grill to hot. Cut a small wholemeal loaf into cubes about 2.5cm (1in) square. Crush 3 large cloves of garlic and fry them in 5 tablespoons of vegetable oil. Toss the bread in the oil and garlic until all the oil is absorbed. Put the croutons under the hot grill to toast, turning them so that they become golden brown on each side.

Leeks

Leeks are a sweeter-tasting relative of the common onion or *Allium cepa*. Very young leeks may be chopped up and eaten raw, but usually they are blanched in boiling water, at least for a few minutes. Leeks are excellent in soups such as Vichyssoise, in a variety of winter casseroles and when served cold with Hollandaise or vinaigrette sauce.

Some cooks find them troublesome to clean because of the mud which tends to collect inside the concentric layers of the stems. If you cut through the leafy stalk end vertically with a sharp knife, however, the mud can easily be washed out under running water.

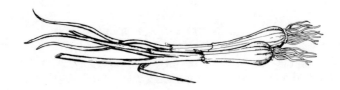

VICHYSSOISE

This is one of the simplest of soups but also one of the best. It is usually served cold in summer.

500 g/1 lb leeks (trimmed weight)
1 medium onion
250 g/8 oz potatoes
60 g/2 oz vegetable margarine
450 ml/16 fl oz water
1 teaspoon salt
150 ml/¼ pint milk *or* 4 tablespoons single cream
white pepper

garnish
chives
paprika

Wash and chop the leeks and onion and slice the potatoes. Melt the margarine in the bottom of the soup pan and fry the onion for 5 minutes. Add the leeks and potatoes and fry them, sttirring, for a few minutes before adding the water and salt. Bring the soup to the boil and then lower the heat. Leave to simmer for 30–40 minutes. Then transfer the soup to a blender and liquidize. Return the soup to the pan and stir in the milk or cream. Season with pepper and chill before serving. Garnish with chives and a sprinkling of paprika.

LEEK, CHESTNUT, AND MUSHROOM CASSEROLE

This casserole is very good served with some wholewheat or spinach pasta.

250 g/8 oz dried chestnuts
500 g/1 lb leeks, chopped
250 g/8 oz mushrooms, chopped
75 g/2½ oz vegetable margarine
3 large cloves garlic, chopped
½ teaspoon black pepper
2 heaped teaspoons salt
45 g/1½ oz plain flour
600 ml/1 pint milk
½ teaspoon nutmeg, grated
45 g/1½ oz hard cheese, grated

Soak the chestnuts for 1–2 hours and then simmer them in a little water until soft. Blanch the leeks in boiling water for 3–4 minutes. Fry the mushrooms for 5 minutes in the margarine with the chopped garlic, some of the pepper and 1 teaspoon of salt. Remove the pan contents with a slotted spoon, retaining the cooking juices in the frying pan. Put the mushroom mixture, leeks and chestnuts into a greased casserole dish, and preheat the oven to 180° C (350° F, gas mark 4).

Now make a white sauce by stirring the flour into the margarine in which the mushrooms were cooked and gradually adding the milk. Bring the sauce to the boil, stirring all the time, and season with the rest of the salt, pepper and nutmeg. Pour this sauce over the ingredients in the casserole dish and scatter the grated cheese over the top. Bake for 50 minutes.

Onions and shallots

Believed to have come originally from Asia, onions have now been culvitated for so many thousands of years that they are no longer found in their wild state. Hundreds of species grow all over the world and there is hardly a national cuisine which does not make use of them – although orthodox Hindus regard onions and garlic with some suspicion. In Britain we not only grow a great many of these 'luscious and tempting vegetables', as the diarist John Evelyn describes them, but according to *The Oxford Book of Food Plants** we are also the world's largest importer. Many varieties of onion are therefore available in the shops, though not usually – unfortunately – the sweet red onions of the Mediterranean which are mild enough to be eaten raw.

Onions form the base flavouring of innumerable soups, casseroles, sauces, grains and legume dishes. Gently frying onions and garlic in oil is often the first step in preparing a savoury dish, and the smell of the onions cooking whets everyone's appetite. Onions should never be cooked too fast or too much, for if they burn they taste bitter rather than sweet. Occasionally a recipe stipulates that onions should be cooked until brown and caramelized (for example, the recipe for onion rings), but generally they should be cooked until just golden.

Only buy onions that are firm and still covered with their brown outer skin. Some of the best onions come from Normandy and can occasionally be bought from itinerant onion sellers, though unfortunately these are a dying breed. It is a good idea to buy good quality onions in the autumn and string them up for use throughout the winter. Do not leave cut, uncooked onions around for any length of time, as they have a facility for attracting micro-organisms and used to be left in sick rooms for this purpose.

Shallots are a kind of onion which forms clusters of bulbs rather than a single bulb. The flavour is strong and distinctive and they are particularly used in French cookery.

* *The Oxford Book of Food Plants*, ed. S.G. Harrison, Oxford University Press, 1969.

ONION SOUP

700 g/1½ lb onions
125 g/4 oz vegetable margarine
750 ml/1¼ pints vegetable stock
2 teaspoons salt
2 cloves garlic, crushed
¼ teaspoon nutmeg, grated
very generous seasoning of black pepper
3 tablespoons Greek yoghurt *or* single cream
1 egg yolk

garnish
chopped chives *or* parsley

to serve
cheese, grated (e.g. Gouda *or* Gruyère)

Chop the onions as finely as possible and fry them gently in the vegetable margarine for 15 minutes. Add the stock and the salt and leave the soup to simmer, in a covered pot, for 30 minutes. After this time, add the crushed garlic, nutmeg and pepper. Beat up the yoghurt or cream with the egg yolk and stir this into the soup after it has been taken off the heat and cooled for a few minutes. Garnish with a few chopped chives or parsley. Serve with hot croutons and grated cheese.

SPANISH POTATO OMELETTE COOKED WITH ONIONS, GARLIC AND CHIVES

500 g/1 lb potatoes
2 medium onions
4–5 cloves garlic
60 g/2 oz vegetable margarine
2 tablespoons parsley, chopped
2 tablespoons chives, chopped
1 tablespoon salt
5 eggs
black *or* white pepper

Boil the potatoes in salted water until they are almost cooked. Chop the onions and garlic and fry them gently in the margarine for 10 minutes. Drain and chop the potatoes and mix them with the chopped parsley and chives. Add these ingredients, plus half of the salt, to the onions and garlic in the pan. Beat up the eggs with the remaining salt and a generous seasoning of pepper, then pour them over the potato mixture. Turn the heat down very low, cover the pan and leave to cook for 15–20 minutes until the eggs are set (take the lid off the pan for the last few minutes of cooking).

Allow the omelette to cool a little before cutting, like a cake, and serving.

BUCKWHEAT, SHALLOT AND MUSHROOM LOAF

This dish may be served simply with a green salad.

250 g/8 oz roasted buckwheat
300 ml/½ pint boiling water
250 g/8 oz shallots, chopped
3–4 cloves garlic, crushed
60 g/2 oz vegetable margarine
250 g/8 oz mushrooms, sliced
125 g/4 oz Cheshire *or* Cheddar *or* Double Gloucester cheese, grated
45 g/1½ oz parsley, chopped
1 egg, beaten
2 teaspoons salt
black pepper
2–3 tablespoons fresh wholemeal breadcrumbs *or* wheatgerm

Preheat the oven to 180° C (350°F, gas mark 4). Rapidly simmer the buckwheat in the boiling water until the water is absorbed and the buckwheat par-cooked. Fry the shallots and garlic in the margarine for 5 minutes. Combine the shallot mixture with the mushrooms, cheese, parsley and beaten egg, and season with salt and pepper. Add enough breadcrumbs or wheatgerm to form a stiff mixture.

Grease a 500 g (1 lb) loaf tin and press the mixture into it. Cover with foil and bake for 35 minutes. Remove the foil 10 minutes before the end of cooking so that the loaf can brown.

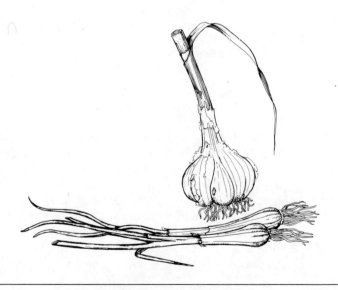

Onion flavours: Onions and shallots

ONION TART MADE WITH YOGHURT AND POPPY SEEDS

Yeasted pastry takes little more effort to make than ordinary pastry. It is light and crisp, and easy to roll out. Classic French onion tarts generally contain cream, but this recipe uses yoghurt, the slight acidity of which offsets the sweetness of the onions.

crust
75 g/2½ oz vegetable margarine
175 g/6 oz wholemeal flour
1 level teaspoon dried yeast
6 tablespoons warm water
½ teaspoon brown sugar

filling
30 g/1 oz poppy seeds
350 g/12 oz onions
60 g/2 oz vegetable margarine
2 eggs
500 ml/18 fl oz Greek yoghurt
1 level teaspoon salt
½ teaspoon black pepper

To make the pastry, rub the margarine into the flour, then dissolve the yeast in the warm water with the brown sugar. Leave to stand for 10 minutes and then add to the flour and margarine. Knead the mixture, then leave it in a warm place to rise for 1–2 hours. (Cover the bowl with polythene as when making bread.) This pastry dough will not rise very much, but the resulting pastry will be springy and light.

To make the filling, first soak the poppy seeds in a little boiling water. Preheat the oven to 180° C (350° F, gas mark 4). Slice the onions into thin rings and fry them in the margarine for 10 minutes. Beat the eggs with the yoghurt and season with salt and pepper.

Roll out the pastry and line a greased 25 cm (10 in) flan dish. Combine the onions with the yoghurt and egg mixture and pour into the pastry case. Drain the poppy seeds and spread them over the top of the filling. Bake for 25 minutes, and allow to cool a little before serving.

FALAFEL

Falafel are a popular street savoury in the Middle East, especially in Israel. Like pakoras and samosas, they are generally made by street vendors who naturally become great experts in their own field, so don't be discouraged if you don't achieve perfect results first time! The uncooked mixture keeps well in the refrigerator, so it is worth making quite a lot at a time and cooking as required. To serve, put 2 falafel in half a piece of pitta bread and fill the remaining space with salad – chopped tomatoes, beansprouts, cucumber and shredded lettuce.

300 g/10 oz chick peas
2 large onions
5–6 cloves garlic
juice of 1 large lemon
1 teaspoon bicarbonate of soda
1 teaspoon salt
2 teaspoons coriander seeds, ground
1 teaspoon roasted cumin, ground
3 heaped tablespoons coriander leaves, finely chopped
1 teaspoon cayenne pepper, *or* to taste
chick pea flour for binding
vegetable oil for frying

Wash the chick peas and soak them overnight or all day. Change the water, bring them to the boil and simmer until soft enough to mash. (You may find it convenient to cook the chick peas in a pressure cooker to save time.) Chop the onions finely and crush the garlic.

Mash the chick peas with a potato masher, and then combine them with all the other ingredients. Allow this mixture to stand for at least 30 minutes. Heat about 7.5 cm (3 in) of oil in the bottom of a pan suitable for deep frying. Take 1 tablespoon of the chick pea mixture at a time, roll it in the palms of your hands with a little chick pea flour and then fry these falafel balls in batches. Each batch will take about 4 minutes.

FRIED ONION RINGS

These onion rings are useful for garnishing rice, bean and other vegetable dishes. Red onions look particularly attractive.

Slice the onions very, very thinly. Using about 1 tablespoon of oil for each medium-size onion, fry them over a medium heat until they are just brown. Stir the onions frequently while they are cooking to ensure that they brown evenly. When they are done, press them between sheets of absorbent kitchen paper to extract the excess oil.

SPICY ONION SAUCE

This is an ideal sauce to serve with nut roasts and rissoles, and vegetable dishes such as stuffed marrows. It also goes well with buckwheat and with brown rice.

2 large onions
4–5 cloves garlic
60 g/2 oz vegetable margarine
1 large cooking apple
1 teaspoon coriander seeds, ground
3 cloves, ground
1 heaped teaspoon hot paprika
1 teaspoon brown sugar
½ teaspoon salt
nutmeg
150 ml/¼ pint water

Chop the onions and garlic and fry them gently in the margarine. Peel and chop the apple and add it to the pan. Add the coriander seeds and cloves along with the paprika, brown sugar, salt and a grating of nutmeg. Pour in the water, bring to the boil and let the sauce simmer, covered, for 15–20 minutes. Serve hot.

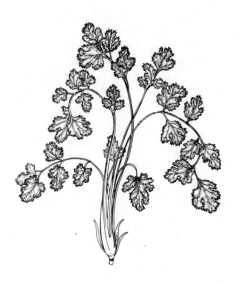

CHOLLAH

This onion-flavoured bread is a Jewish speciality. The dough may be formed into a plaited loaf, or baked in tins in the usual way.

900 g/2 lb wholewheat flour, *or* ⅔ wholewheat *and* ⅓ plain white flour
2 level teaspoons salt
1 level teaspoon dried yeast *or* 2 teaspoons fresh
1 tablespoon black treacle
600 ml/1 pint warm water
125 g/4 oz vegetable margarine
1 small onion, grated
1 egg yolk
a few poppy seeds

Mix the flour with the salt and dissolve the yeast with the treacle in a little of the warmed water. Rub half the margarine into the flour. When the yeast is ready, mix it into the flour mixture and then gradually add the rest of the water. Knead the dough and leave it to rise in a warm place until doubled in size.

Work the onion, egg yolk and remaining vegetable margarine into the dough as you knead it for the second time.

If making a plaited loaf, divide the dough into 3 parts, roll each part into a long sausage shape with the palm of your hand, and plait them together. Leave to rise on a greased oven tray. Otherwise, divide the dough between 2 well-greased 500 g (1 lb) loaf tins. Cover the loaves with poppy seeds and leave to rise again for about 1 hour in a warm place. Preheat the oven to 200° C (400° F, gas mark 6) and bake at this temperature for 10 minutes, then reduce the heat to 180° C (350° F, gas mark 4), and bake for a further 30 minutes. Cool on a wire rack.

Spring onions, guchoy and chives

Spring onions are very useful in dishes where only a light onion taste is needed. They can be chopped and added raw to a cooked dish just before serving, and go well with rice, millet, bulghur and macaroni dishes. Spring onions are also, of course, a useful salad ingredient. Where a recipe of Mediterranean origin calls for raw onion, spring onions may often be substituted.

Guchoy, or Chinese chives, have a very strong onion flavour. Again, they are useful for adding as a garnish to a cooked dish.

The familiar English chives have a much more delicate flavour which is delicious in salads – particularly mayonnaise salads – and with eggs. Chives are used with tarragon, parsley and chervil to make up a bunch of *fines herbes*. They are one of the pleasant tastes of summer and are easy to grow in the garden, or in a pot on a windowsill.

GAZPACHO

This traditional Spanish dish, something between a soup and a salad, has many variants. The characteristic ingredients, however, are always onions, garlic, bread, olive oil and tomatoes. I have used spring onions instead of ordinary onions in this recipe, since the sweet red onions of the Mediterranean are not generally available in Britain. It is best served with slices of wholemeal bread and perhaps some hardboiled eggs on a side dish.

3 heaped tablespoons fresh wholemeal breadcrumbs
3 large cloves garlic
4 tablespoons olive oil
2 teaspoons wine vinegar *or* cider vinegar
1 red pepper, finely chopped
1 bunch spring onions, finely chopped
4 large tomatoes
125 g/4 oz cucumber
1 teaspoon salt *or* to taste
black pepper
1 teaspoon hot paprika
200 ml/⅓ pint iced water

Pound the breadcrumbs and the garlic in a mortar. Add the oil, little by little, to form a thick paste. Mix in the vinegar and finely chopped red pepper and spring onions. Put the tomatoes and cucumber in a blender and liquidize. Mix with the other ingredients and season with salt, pepper and paprika. Stir in the iced water and serve.

SPRING ONION AND CHEESE TART

Oatmeal pastry can be used in this recipe to make a change. Serve the tart hot or cold with a tossed green salad.

crust
125 g/4 oz wholewheat flour
125 g/4 oz fine ground oatmeal
1 teaspoon salt
150 g/5 oz vegetable margarine
4 tablespoons cold water

filling
3 cloves garlic, chopped
45 g/1½ oz vegetable margarine
30 g/1 oz plain white flour
400 ml/¾ pint milk
175 g/6 oz strong Cheddar *or* Gruyère cheese, grated
1 egg, beaten
2 tablespoons mint, chopped
2 bunches spring onions
150 g/5 oz mung beansprouts
½ teaspoon hot paprika
salt
black pepper
1 heaped tablespoon sesame seeds

To make the pastry, mix together the flour, oatmeal and salt. Rub in the margarine and then add the water. Knead the dough and set it aside in the refrigerator while you prepare the filling. Preheat the oven to 180° C (375° F, gas mark 4).

Fry the garlic in the margarine for 2–3 minutes. Stir in the flour and then gradually add the milk, stirring. Bring to the boil and mix in the grated cheese. Take the sauce off the heat and add the beaten egg. Add the mint, spring onions and the beansprouts to the cheese mixture. Season with paprika, salt and black pepper. Roll out the pastry and line a greased 25 cm (10 in) flan dish. Pour the filling into the pastry case, top with sesame seeds and bake for 35 minutes. If you are using a ceramic flan dish, stand it on a metal tray while it is in the oven.

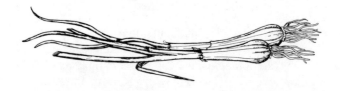

Onion flavours: Spring onions, guchoy and chives

COOKED RICE WITH SPRING ONIONS, LENTILS AND DATES

300 g/10 oz green lentils
300 g/10 oz brown rice
2 tablespoons vegetable oil
400 ml/¾ pint boiling water
150 g/5 oz dates
1 large bunch spring onions
60 g/2 oz vegetable margarine

garnish
parsley, chopped

Soak the lentils for 1–2 hours, then boil them in plenty of salted water until soft but still whole. Drain and set aside.

Fry the rice briefly in the oil, add the boiling water, then turn the heat down to minimum and cover the pan with a few thicknesses of cloth (e.g. a teatowel folded into 4). Cook for about 25 minutes until the rice is soft and all the water absorbed. Chop the dates and spring onions finely. Melt the margarine in a large pan and stir in the rice and spring onions followed by the lentils and dates. Garnish with chopped parsley and serve.

CHIVE, CUCUMBER AND GREEN PEPPER SALAD

dressing
5 tablespoons olive oil *or* other salad oil
2 teaspoons cider vinegar
½ teaspoon salt
1 clove garlic, crushed
black *or* white pepper

1 cucumber
3 green peppers
1 bunch chives
4 hardboiled eggs
1 small bunch radishes

Mix together all the dressing ingredients. Slice the cucumber and green peppers and chop the chives. Arrange these ingredients on a large plate and pour the dressing over them. Chill in the refrigerator for 30 minutes. Slice the eggs, chop the radishes and combine them decoratively with the cucumber, peppers and chives.

POTATO AND CHIVE
MAYONNAISE SALAD

mayonnaise
2 egg yolks
150 ml/¼ pint olive *or* sunflower oil
2 teaspoons cider vinegar *or* white wine vinegar
salt
white pepper

500 g/1 lb new potatoes, scrubbed
500 g/1 lb fresh peas in the pod
1 bunch chives
175 g/6 oz mung beansprouts
60 g/2 oz pumpkin seeds

Make the mayonnaise as described on p. 59. Boil the potatoes until just soft, then drain and cool them. Dice them, unless they are very small. Shell the peas and boil them briefly in salted water. Chop the chives. Combine all the salad ingredients and then lightly mix in the mayonnaise.

Green herb flavours

BASIL · CORIANDER LEAVES · MINT · PARSLEY
AND CHERVIL · SAVORY · TARRAGON · THYME,
MARJORAM AND OREGANO
WATERCRESS

Coriander

Basil

Watercress

Mint

Basil

Basil is a herb which thrives in warm climates and rich soils. A native of India, and sacred to the Hindus, it is grown all round the Mediterranean and in the Middle East for culinary purposes. In cooler climates the plant has to be raised from seed each year, but it is well worth the trouble because the flavour of basil is unique – quite unlike that of any other herb. Fortunately, basil plants are increasingly on sale at greengrocers and garden centres, and if planted in a sunny, sheltered spot, they will produce plenty of well-flavoured leaves throughout the summer.

The basil plant figured in the myths of Greece and Rome as well as those of India; it seems to have had a mixed reputation, sometimes being regarded as very auspicious and sometimes as very unlucky, but always as a plant of considerable power. Even today, a pot of basil can often be seen growing by the doorways of houses in Mediterranean regions, ostensibly to keep away flies but also, perhaps, for older and more superstitious reasons. An orthodox Hindu family will always keep a pot of the sacred *tulsi* or basil growing in or near the house.

When dried, basil loses a lot of its charm as a flavouring. The best way to keep the fresh leaves is to put them in a preserving jar covered with olive oil and use them as required. The leaves will also impart a delicate flavour to the oil, which can be used later for salad dressings; they are excellent with tomato salad and in pasta dishes. Basil leaves should always be shredded, rather than chopped.

TOMATO OMELETTE FLAVOURED WITH BASIL

500 g/1 lb tomatoes
2 medium onions
4 cloves garlic
60 g/2 oz vegetable margarine
6 eggs, beaten
250 g/8 oz Cheddar *or* Cheshire *or* Double Gloucester cheese, grated
2 tablespoons basil, shredded
1 tablespoon parsley, chopped
1 heaped teaspoon sweet paprika

Soak the tomatoes in a bowl of boiling water for a few minutes, then pour cold water over them and remove their skins. Chop them into small pieces. Chop the onions finely and crush the garlic. Melt the margarine in a cast iron frying pan and fry the onions and garlic for 5 minutes. Combine all the other ingredients in a bowl and pour them over the onions and garlic. Put a lid on the pan, turn the heat very low and let the omelette cook for 15–20 minutes, by which time the eggs should be set. If the top of the omelette seems too liquid, take the lid off the pan for the last few minutes of cooking. Allow to cool a little before cutting into slices and serving.

TOMATO, BASIL AND BEANSPROUT SALAD

1 small bunch fresh basil leaves
350 g/12 oz tomatoes
90 g/3 oz beansprouts

dressing
3 tablespoons olive *or* sunflower oil
1 large clove garlic, crushed
1 teaspoon wine vinegar *or* cider vinegar
½ teaspoon salt
white pepper

Spread this salad out on a large plate. Shred the basil leaves. Cut the tomatoes into slices and mix them with the beanspouts and basil.

Make the dressing by mixing the oil and garlic, stirring in the vinegar and then seasoning with salt and pepper. Pour the dressing over the salad, and then leave it in the refrigerator to chill for some time before serving.

PESTO

This traditional Italian sauce, usually eaten with pasta, is made from basil, pine nuts, garlic, cheese and olive oil. A spoonful of pesto can sometimes be used to add flavour to soups and sauces. Pesto can be stored in the refrigerator for a few weeks if not required immediately.

2–3 cloves garlic
125 g/4 oz pine nuts
20–30 g/¾–1 oz basil leaves
90 g/3 oz Pecorino *or* Sardo *or* Parmesan cheese, grated
150 ml/¼ pint olive oil
a little salt (if using Parmesan cheese)

Pound the garlic, pine nuts and basil leaves in a mortar. Add the grated cheese and continue to pound. When you have a thick, well integrated paste, beat in the olive oil a little at a time. Add salt if needed.

SWEETCORN AND BASIL SAUCE

This sauce goes well with pasta or millet.

3–4 sweetcorn cobs weighing about 500 g/1 lb
1 medium onion
2 cloves garlic
30 g/1 oz vegetable margarine
15 g/½ oz basil leaves
1 level teaspoon salt
150 ml/¼ pint milk
black *or* white pepper
60 g/2 oz Parmesan cheese, grated

Cook the sweetcorn cobs in boiling water until soft. Cool them under running water, then, holding the cobs upright, press them down on a wooden board and scrape off the corn with a sharp knife. Chop the onion and garlic and fry them briefly in the margarine. Add the sweetcorn and all the other ingredients except the cheese. Transfer to a liquidizer and blend until the sauce is smooth. Return to the pan, add the grated cheese and heat gently before serving.

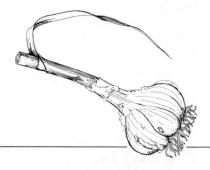

Coriander leaves

The leaves and seeds of coriander bear little resemblance to each other in flavour. Whereas coriander seeds (see p.168) add a warm, spicy taste to any dish in which they are used, the leaves have a sharper, yet still aromatic, flavour. Coriander leaves look rather like flat-leafed parsley, but on closer inspection will be seen to be more rounded and evenly serrated.

Coriander leaves are used most frequently in Middle Eastern cookery, in salads and as a garnish to such popular dishes as hummus, falafel and Baba Ghanoush. They are also used a lot in India and are particularly useful in relishes and chutneys. Like parsley and watercress, coriander leaves can be chopped and added to a cooked dish of grains or pulses just before serving.

WINTER SALAD

This colourful endive, coriander and orange salad is a good combination of sweet, sour and bitter tastes and makes a very pretty starter. It makes good use of the salad stuffs available in winter – coriander leaves are usually available from Chinese and Indian grocers the whole year through. Experiment with other imported fruits and vegetables (e.g. star fruit) which are available in winter.

1 heart celery
125 g/4 oz dates, chopped
1 small bunch coriander leaves
125 g/4 oz walnut halves
1 endive
2 oranges

dressing
4 tablespoons sunflower oil
1 large clove garlic, crushed
juice of 1 small lemon
1 teaspoon salt
1 teaspoon hot paprika
1 teaspoon honey

Chop the celery, dates and coriander leaves and put them in a salad bowl with the walnuts and endive leaves. Add the oranges divided into segments or half segments.

Make the dressing by mixing the oil with the garlic, then adding the lemon juice followed by all the other ingredients. Dress the salad just before serving.

POTATO SAMOSAS

The main ingredient of a vegetable samosa filling is usually potatoes, but you might like to experiment with other vegetables as well. The seasoning is also open to variation – in this recipe I have made coriander, both seed and leaf, the predominant flavour. Using plenty of coriander leaves offsets the heaviness of the potatoes. The pastry should be rolled as thinly as possible before frying – pastry made and cooked in this way is extremely light and flaky. This recipe should make 16 samosas.

crust
175 g/6 oz vegetable margarine
150 g/5 oz wholemeal flour
150 g/5 oz plain white flour
6 tablespoons cold water

filling
500 g/1 lb potatoes
5 tablespoons vegetable oil
1½ tablespoons fresh root ginger, grated
2 tablespoons coriander seeds, ground
2 large onions, finely chopped
4–5 cloves garlic, finely chopped
fresh chillies to taste, chopped
1 tablespoon salt
1 teaspoon dried mint
4–5 tablespoons coriander leaves, chopped
1½ teaspoons garam masala

oil for deep frying

to serve
chutney

To make the pastry, rub the margarine into the flours. Gradually introduce the cold water and knead well for a few minutes. Put the dough in a polythene bag in the refrigerator for at least 1 hour.

Now prepare the filling. Par-boil the potatoes and then cut them into small cubes. Put the oil in a large cast iron pan and fry the ginger and ground coriander for 1–2 minutes. Add the onions, garlic, chillies, and salt and continue to fry, stirring, for 5 minutes. Next, put in the diced potatoes and dried mint. Cook, stirring occasionally, for another 10 minutes. Pour in a little water if the mixture seems too dry. Add the chopped coriander leaves and the garam masala.

Take the pastry out of the refrigerator and knead it again for a few minutes. (Pastry for frying should be very pliable, hence the extra kneading.) Divide the dough into 8 balls, then roll out each ball into a circular piece 23–25 cm (9–10 in) across; cut each circle in half and form into a cone. Fill each cone with the potato mixture, trim the open edges, brush them with a little water and seal. (Making a neat-looking samosa does require some practice.) If you find it easier, you could roll out larger pieces of dough, divide them into rectangles and then make triangular samosas instead. Heat 5–7.5 cm (2–3 ins) of vegetable oil in any container suitable for deep frying – a wok is ideal – and fry the samosas in batches until they are golden brown on both sides (about 3–4 minutes a side). Turn out on to absorbent kitchen paper, and serve with a fruity chutney.

GREEN CORIANDER CHUTNEY

In his excellent book *Herbs, Spices and Flavourings** Tom Stobart remarks: 'There is no better breakfast in the world than chapatis spread with coriander chutney and honey.' This is a popular chutney, particularly in South India, where it is freshly made to accompany rice dishes. If you find it too hot and sour for your taste (this is how it is usually made in South India), reduce the number of chillies and add a little brown sugar dissolved in hot water.

90 g/3 oz coriander leaves
2–3 green chillies
15 g/½ oz fresh root ginger
3 heaped tablespoons fresh *or* dried coconut, grated
juice of 1 small lime *or* lemon
salt

Chop the coriander leaves and chillies finely. Peel and grate the ginger root. Combine these with the other ingredients.

PRUNE AND CORIANDER CHUTNEY

This is a good alternative to mango chutney and can be made when mangoes are not available.

175 g/6 oz prunes
2 fresh red chillies, chopped
1 small bunch coriander leaves, chopped
juice of 1 small lemon
1 heaped teaspoon salt

Soak the prunes overnight or all day in just enough water to cover them. (If you do not have time for this, soak them for as long as possible and then simmer them until soft.) Take out the stones. Put all the ingredients in a blender and liquidize to a smooth puree. Adjust the flavouring to taste: for example, add another chilli if you want a hotter mixture.

**Herbs, Spices and Flavourings*, Tom Stobart, International Wine & Food Publishing Co., 1970.

Mint

There are many species of mint – spearmint, peppermint, apple mint and water mint to name only a few – but the most useful in the kitchen are spearmint and apple mint. Of the two, spearmint is stronger and makes a particularly good flavouring for dishes containing dried pulses as well as for fresh peas and beans. In summer, use spearmint in soups, salads, potato and pasta dishes. Apple mint is excellent in salads and can also be used to flavour cold fruit drinks.

Mint was introduced into Britain by the Romans, and although it is a native Mediterranean plant it is used much more here than in the rest of Europe. Its cooling properties (the essential oil in mint is menthol) are also appreciated in North Africa, India and the Middle East. North African tea is made from fresh mint leaves and unfermented green tea. Mint is also often used in Indian raitas and chutneys.

Apple mint and spearmint are very easily grown – in fact very hard to get rid of once they are established. In winter, dried mint makes a good, strong flavouring for cooked dishes but its flavour does not compare with that of the fresh leaves.

SUMMER SOUP

This mint and cucumber soup is delicious on hot days.

1 large onion
4 cloves garlic
90 g/3 oz vegetable margarine
1 medium cucumber
about 12 large lettuce leaves
1 bunch mint weighing about 15 g/½ oz
2 teaspoons salt
300 ml/½ pint water
500 g/1 lb fresh peas in the pod
white pepper

Chop the onion and garlic and fry them gently in the margarine for 5 minutes. Peel and chop the cucumber and add it to the onion and garlic. Add the lettuce leaves, mint leaves, salt and water. Leave the soup to simmer for about 30 minutes. Then blend the ingredients in a liquidizer and return them to the pan. Shell the peas, add them and simmer for a further 10 minutes to let the peas cook. Season with pepper and a little more mint and salt to taste.

This soup may be served either hot or chilled.

MILLET TOSSED WITH MINT, LEEKS AND COURGETTES

1 tablespoon vegetable oil
300 g/10 oz millet
750 ml/1¼ pints boiling water
2 teaspoons salt
pepper
4 heaped tablespoons grated Parmesan cheese
½ clove garlic
500 g/1 lb courgettes
350 g/12 oz leeks
600 ml/1 pint boiling water
1 small bunch mint

Heat the oil in a pan, then add the millet and stir over a medium heat for 1–2 minutes. Add the 750 ml (1¼ pints) boiling water and leave to simmer fairly rapidly. Skim off any scum which may form on the surface of the liquid as the millet cooks. Season with salt and pepper after 15 minutes of cooking and continue to cook, stirring, for about another 5 minutes, or until the millet has absorbed all the water (it should be soft but still slightly crunchy). Take the pan off the heat and stir in 2 heaped tablespoons of the Parmesan cheese. Rub a serving bowl with the garlic and put the millet into it.

While the millet is cooking, wash the courgettes and chop them into 0.5 cm (¼ in) slices. Wash the leeks and chop them into 1.5 cm (½ in) sections. Have ready about 600 ml (1 pint) of boiling, salted water. Drop in the leeks with a large sprig of mint. Boil rapidly for 4 minutes, then add the courgettes and continue to cook for another 3 minutes. Drain the vegetables well and lightly mix them in with the cooked millet. Finely chop the rest of the mint and add to the dish along with another 2 heaped tablespoons of Parmesan.

Serve warm, rather than hot.

MUNG BEAN PASTIES
FLAVOURED WITH MINT

These pasties are good to take on a picnic or journey. The filling is surprisingly light, yet very sustaining. The quantities given below make 12 pasties.

crust
500 g/1 lb wholemeal flour
1 teaspoon salt
250 g/8 oz vegetable margarine
100 ml/4 fl oz cold water

filling
175 g/6 oz mung beans
350 g/12 oz onions, finely chopped
4 tablespoons vegetable oil
175 g/6 oz carrots, grated
2 tablespoons mint, chopped
2 level teaspoons salt
chilli sauce *or* cayenne pepper to taste
2 tablespoons yoghurt

glaze
1 egg yolk
3 tablespoons milk

Wash the beans and put them in a saucepan with plenty of water. Bring to the boil, then turn off the heat and leave to stand for 1 hour. After this time, bring the water to the boil again and leave the beans to simmer until they are soft – this should take about 30 minutes.

Make the pastry in the usual way (see p.218) and leave it in the refrigerator while you make the filling.

Fry the onions in the oil for about 15 minutes before adding the carrot and mint. Drain the mung beans and add them, and season with salt and chilli sauce or cayenne pepper. Bind the mixture with the yoghurt. By this time the mixture should be moist but not too liquid. Preheat the oven to 190° C (375° F, gas mark 5).

Divide the pastry into 12 equal parts. Roll out each piece of dough quite thinly and cut into a 15 cm (6 in) diameter circle. Put a portion of filling into each circle, fold the pastry over to make a semicircle and trim the edges with a knife. Dampen the edges of each semicircle with a brush and then seal each one using your thumb and forefinger or a fork.

Whisk up the egg yolk and milk to make a glaze. Brush the pasties with the glaze, place them on greased baking trays and bake for 30 minutes or until well browned. Cool them on a wire rack.

Green herb flavours: Mint

POTATO AND MOZZARELLA BAKE FLAVOURED WITH MINT

900 g/2 lb cooked potatoes
30 g/1 oz vegetable margarine
a little milk
3 tablespoons mint, chopped
3 cloves garlic, crushed
2 teaspoons salt, *or* to taste
white pepper
1 large onion
175 g/6 oz Mozzarella cheese
30 g/1 oz Parmesan cheese, grated

Preheat the oven to 180° C (350° F, gas mark 4). Mash the potatoes with the margarine and milk. Season with the mint, garlic, salt and pepper.

Cut the onion into very thin slices and the Mozzarella into slices about 0.5 cm (¼ in) thick. Grease a casserole dish about 10 cm (4 in) deep, and fill it with alternate layers of potato, cheese and onion, starting and finishing with potato. Sprinkle the Parmesan cheese over the top layer. Bake for 30 minutes.

PASTA, MINT AND FRENCH BEAN SALAD

3 good-sized sweetcorn cobs
350 g/12 oz green pasta (spirals, twists *or* shells)
500 g/1 lb French beans
½ clove garlic
a few stems mint, chopped

dressing
125 g/4 oz curd cheese
2 tablespoons lemon juice
2 small cloves garlic, crushed
a few tablespoons water
salt

Boil the sweetcorn on the cob until it is soft: the length of time this takes will depend entirely on the freshness of the cobs. Drain, and allow to cool before scraping the corn off the cob with a sharp knife. Cook the pasta and beans separately, each in salted water, making sure not to over-cook the pasta. Drain both these ingredients well. Rub the ½ garlic clove around a salad bowl, then combine the pasta, beans and sweetcorn in the bowl. Mix in the mint.

To make the dressing, beat the cheese with the lemon juice and crushed garlic. Add the water gradually to obtain a thick pouring consistency. Season with salt to taste. Serve in a separate bowl, to accompany the salad.

MINT, CUCUMBER AND ONION RAITA

Raita, a mixture of yoghurt, herbs, spices and uncooked vegetables, is one of the most popular accompaniments to an Indian meal. It helps the digestion and cools the mouth after eating hot, spicy food.

150 g/5 oz cucumber
1 small onion
1–2 small green chillies (optional)
1 heaped tablespoon mint, finely chopped
5 tablespoons plain yoghurt
½ teaspoon salt
black pepper
pinch cayenne pepper

Dice the cucumber and finely chop the onion and chillies. Combine all the ingredients, except the cayenne pepper, which should be sprinkled on last.

Parsley and chervil

Both these plants belong to the large family of umbellifers, which includes the carrot. Parsley and chervil are related in flavour, though chervil has a much more delicate taste with a hint of aniseed.

Parsley, along with garlic, onions and lemons, is really essential in the kitchen. Its strong flavour makes it a good counterpart to farinaceous or oily food. Its very high Vitamin A and C content makes it a healthy addition to winter dishes, partially making up for the lack of salad vegetables at that time of year. It is also exceptionally rich in iron and contains a variety of other minerals.

In Britain we are most familiar with curly-leafed parsley but flat-leafed parsley – not to be visually confused with coriander leaves – is also available: it has a slightly more bitter flavour. Parsley seeds are notoriously slow to germinate, but once they have done so the plant is not difficult to keep going.

Once established, the plants easily seed themselves so that they may be regarded as perennial. Luckily, parsley is usually on sale in greengrocers throughout the year. Dried parsley is a poor substitute for the fresh plant, since much of the flavour and the vitamin content are lost in drying. Most dishes call for the fresh leaves to be finely chopped but there is also a lot of flavour in the thick stems. Use parsley stems to flavour soups and casseroles, but take them out before serving.

Both parsley and chervil are basic ingredients of the French fines herbes mixture, and chervil is in fact a particular favourite with French cooks. This herb is very easy to grow, even in a box on a windowsill, and unlike parsley it germinates and grows very quickly. Use it chopped in salads, in omelette fillings and as a garnish for soups, but remember that the flavour is light and may be lost with cooking.

WHITE BEAN AND WALNUT PUREE MIXED WITH PARSLEY

Serve this puree as a dip with pitta bread or as a vegetable dish.

500 g/1 lb dried butter beans
2 cloves garlic, crushed
125 g/4 oz walnuts, crushed
200 ml/⅓ pint sour cream *or* olive oil
juice of 2 large lemons
1 tablespoon salt
black *or* white pepper
90 g/3 oz parsley, finely chopped

Soak the beans for at least 1 hour, then rinse them and boil until soft. Drain, and mash well with a potato masher. Combine the garlic and walnuts with the beans. Mix in the sour cream or olive oil (either makes a good puree) and season with lemon juice, salt and pepper. Mix in the finely chopped parsley last of all.

Green herb flavours: Parsley and chervil

AVOCADO AND CHERVIL SOUP

The delicate flavours of avocado and chervil complement each other well. This is a good soup to serve chilled in summer.

1 vegetable stock cube
600 ml/1 pint boiling water
2 large *or* 3 small avocados
about 6 spring onions
1 level teaspoon salt
white pepper
2–3 tablespoons sour cream (optional)

garnish
1 small bunch chervil

Dissolve the stock cube in the boiling water and simmer for 5 minutes. Peel and mash the avocados and chop the spring onions. Add these to the stock and transfer the mixture to a blender. Liquidize and return to the pan. Season with salt and pepper. Warm the soup over a low to medium heat for 10 minutes, but do not let it boil. Stir in the sour cream if liked.

Serve hot or chilled. Finely chop the chervil and sprinkle it over the soup just before serving.

TABBOULEH

This Lebanese salad should contain very generous quantities of parsley. Make the dish some time in advance of serving so that the bulghur wheat has time to assimilate the flavours of the other ingredients.

350 g/12 oz bulghur (cracked) wheat
900 ml/1½ pints water
90 g/3 oz parsley, finely chopped
juice of 2 large lemons
1 bunch spring onions, finely chopped
1 tablespoon mint, finely chopped
3 tablespoons olive oil
salt
black pepper

Soak the bulghur wheat in the water for 45 minutes. Then mix all the ingredients together and leave in the refrigerator to chill for at least 1 hour.

Savory

Savory is an excellent herb to use in cookery. Its flavour, which combines the freshness of mint and the warmth of marjoram or thyme, is strong enough to stand up to lengthy cooking. Savory goes well with eggs, cheese, pulses and grains, and it may be used as a change from mint to flavour boiled beans and peas.

It is possible to use fresh savory the whole year round because there are both summer (annual) and winter (perennial) varieties. This is one of the few Mediterranean herbs to keep its full flavour even when grown in a cooler climate. It also retains a good flavour when dried. Savory is not usually on sale, so it is worth having some plants growing at home.

SCRAMBLED EGGS
COOKED WITH SAVORY AND TOMATOES

1 large onion
1 red pepper
60 g/2 oz vegetable margarine
250 g/8 oz tomatoes
2 dessertspoons savory, chopped
4 eggs
1 heaped tablespoon grated Parmesan
cheese
black *or* white pepper
1 teaspoon salt, *or* to taste

Finely chop the onion and red pepper. Fry them in the margarine for 10 minutes. Chop the tomatoes, add them along with the savory, and simmer until the tomatoes are reduced to a pulp. Beat the eggs with the cheese, pepper and salt. Add them to the tomato mixture and stir over a medium heat for 3–4 minutes until lightly scrambled.

TOMATO AND SAVORY RELISH

This is a fruity relish which is very good with all kinds of egg and bean dishes. It will keep in the refrigerator for 2–3 weeks, so you may find it convenient to double the quantities given in the recipe below.

900 g/2 lb ripe tomatoes
1 large onion
4–5 cloves garlic
1 tablespoon vegetable oil
1 bunch fresh savory (about 4 tablespoons when chopped) *or* 2 tablespoons dried
2 tablespoons brown sugar
2 teaspoons salt
2 heaped teaspoons sweet paprika
150 ml/¼ pint white wine vinegar *or* cider vinegar

Soak the tomatoes in boiling water, rinse them in cold and remove their skins. Chop them up, put them in a lidded casserole and cook them for 40–50 minutes in a low oven, about 110°C (225°F, gas mark ¼). Meanwhile, grate the onion and crush the garlic. Fry them very slowly in the oil for about 20 minutes. Strip the savory leaves off the stalks and chop them up finely. When the tomatoes are well softened, combine all the ingredients except the vinegar in the pan and stir over a low heat for 10 minutes. Take the pan off the heat and stir in the vinegar. Pour the sauce into the warmed jars and allow to cool. Store in the refrigerator.

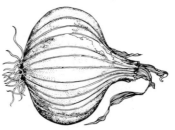

Tarragon

This herb is especially popular in France where its slightly aniseed-like flavour is often used to flavour sauces, egg dishes and salads. It is frequently used to flavour vinegar, mustard and pickled onions as well.

Tarragon should be used fresh whenever possible, because the dried herb loses much of its authentic flavour. Ideally, it needs a dry, sunny climate in which to grow, but English-grown plants can also have a good flavour. There are two species available, French and Russian. When buying plants make sure you get the former, which has a much better flavour.

EGGAH FLAVOURED WITH TARRAGON

Eggah is a Persian omelette which can be baked or cooked slowly in a heavy frying pan on top of the stove. It is quite solid – something like a Spanish omelette – and may contain all kinds of fillings and flavourings. Courgettes, aubergines, wholewheat noodles, pine nuts and fresh herbs are particularly suitable for use in eggah recipes.

300 g/10 oz leeks, chopped
60 g/2 oz vegetable margarine
3–4 cloves garlic
90 g/3 oz walnuts, crushed
a few sprigs tarragon, chopped
6 eggs
2 teaspoons salt
black *or* white pepper

Drop the leeks into some boiling, salted water and cook for about 5 minutes or until just soft. Melt the margarine in a heavy cast iron pan and fry the crushed garlic for 1–2 minutes. Add the cooked and drained leeks. Add the walnuts and tarragon to the pan. Beat up the eggs with the salt and a generous seasoning of pepper. Pour them over the other ingredients in the pan, turn down the heat very low and cover the pan. Allow to cook for 15–20 minutes, until the eggs are solid. Cool before cutting into slices and serving.

If you want to bake this dish, pour the ingredients into a greased oven dish and bake at 180° C (350° F, gas mark 4) for 35 minutes. Keep covered until the last 10 minutes of cooking, then remove the cover to allow the omelette to brown.

TARRAGON VINEGAR

This vinegar is excellent for flavouring salad dressings and mayonnaise.

6 stems tarragon
1 litre/1¾ pints white wine vinegar

Wash the whole stems of tarragon and put them, with the vinegar, in a large jar or bottle. Leave in a warm place (preferably in sunlight) for 3–4 weeks. Test to see whether the flavour of the tarragon has sufficiently permeated the vinegar. Strain, and bottle the vinegar with a fresh sprig of tarragon. Cork the bottle.

Thyme, marjoram and oregano

Thyme is a native Mediterranean plant. Garden thyme, a close relative of the wild Mediterranean thyme, can easily be grown in Britain but needs a warm summer to develop its full flavour. Luckily thyme dries well, retaining most of its characteristic sweetness. In the hills surrounding the Mediterranean thyme actually dries on the plant, deliciously scenting the air, as anyone who has visited those regions in late summer will know.

Thyme is one of the ingredients of a bouquet garni. Its flavour is quite strong enough to withstand long cooking and it is often used in casseroles, particularly those containing tomatoes or wine (thyme blends particularly well with both ingredients). It is also useful in pasta sauces, bean stews and savoury quiches.

Sweet marjoram belongs to the same family as thyme, but is even more 'scented'. It is better used uncooked, in salads or as a garnish, because its flavour is less robust than that of thyme and tends to be lost in cooking.

Oregano, much loved by Italian cooks, is the wild relation of sweet marjoram. Like thyme it can be used to flavour casseroles, sauces and savoury tarts, and it is a traditional Italian flavouring for pizza. Oregano grows quite well in Britain, but for drying purposes the Italian plant is better since the warmer climate produces a fuller, sweeter flavour. Dried oregano is one of the best dried herbs to use in winter: its strong, aromatic flavour will do much to enliven winter food when fresh herbs are hard to come by.

BEAN AND OREGANO SOUP

250 g/8 oz haricot *or* pinto *or* flageolot beans
3 tablespoons olive oil
2 medium onions, chopped
4–5 cloves garlic, chopped
250 g/8 oz carrots, finely chopped
4 stalks celery, finely chopped
1 small bunch oregano *or* 1 tablespoon dried oregano
1 litre/1¾ pints water
1 teaspoon salt
hot paprika *or* cayenne pepper

Soak the beans for a few hours, then drain and wash them. Pour the olive oil into a large soup pot. Fry the onions and garlic in the oil for about 10 minutes over a low heat. Add the carrots and celery and fry for another 5 minutes. If using fresh oregano, strip the leaves from their stalks, chop them and add to the vegetables, reserving some leaves to add just before serving. Add the beans, water and salt to the pot and bring to the boil. Lower the heat and simmer, with a lid, for 1–1½ hours. Add more salt, paprika or cayenne to taste, and the remainder of the herbs.

GLAMORGAN SAUSAGES FLAVOURED WITH THYME

This traditional recipe for vegetarian sausages tastes much more interesting than the ingredients would suggest. It should be well flavoured with aromatic herbs.

1 teaspoon English mustard powder
3 eggs, separated
175 g/6 oz hard English *or* Dutch cheese, grated
175 g/6 oz fresh wholemeal breadcrumbs
1 large onion, grated
2 tablespoons parsley, finely chopped
2 tablespoons thyme, finely chopped *or* 1 tablespoon dried
salt
white pepper
vegetable oil for frying

Mix the mustard with a little water and leave it to stand for 10 minutes. Beat the egg yolks with the made mustard. Combine all the ingredients, except the egg whites, some of the breadcrumbs and the oil for frying. Mix well and form a stiff mixture which can easily be shaped into sausages or rissoles. Add a little water until the required consistency is obtained. Beat the egg whites slightly and dip the sausages first in these, then in the breadcrumbs. Fry in the oil over a medium heat for 4–5 minutes each side.

PIZZA

This recipe makes four medium pizzas.

pizza base
1 teaspoon dried yeast *or* 2 teaspoons fresh
1 teaspoon sugar (if using dried yeast)
180 ml/just under ⅓ pint warm water
250 g/8 oz flour (½ plain white *and* ½ wholemeal)
1 teaspoon salt
1 tablespoon vegetable oil

filling
500 g/1 lb tomatoes
250 g/8 oz small black olives
90 g/3 oz capers, drained
1 level tablespoon dried oregano
black pepper
500 g/1 lb Mozzarella *or* Gouda cheese

If you make bread at home, you can set aside a little of the dough for making pizzas (yeasted dough keeps well for up to 24 hours before being baked). Once the dough is prepared, the pizzas can be made very quickly.

If starting from scratch, dissolve the yeast in a little warm water (add sugar if using dried yeast). Mix the flour with the salt, and stir the yeast mixture into it when it is ready. Add the rest of the warmed water, and lastly the oil. Knead for 1–2 minutes and leave to rise in a warm place for at least 2–3 hours.

After the dough is well risen, knead again for a few minutes. Preheat the oven to 200° C (400° F, gas mark 6). Divide the dough into four pieces and roll out the pizzas on a well floured board. Lightly cover them with oil and transfer to well-oiled oven trays.

Allow the pizzas to stand on a warm surface while you add the filling. First cover them with a layer of thinly sliced tomatoes, olives cut away from their stones, about a dozen capers, a sprinkling of oregano and a good seasoning of pepper. Finally slice or grate about 125 g (4 oz) cheese over the top of the other ingredients. Bake for 10–15 minutes.

'Pizza' means pie in Italian, and a true pizza has a filling enclosed between two layers of dough. To make a pizza pie enclose a double amount of filling between two circles of dough. Pinch the edges together and brush the top layer of dough with oil. Bake for about 15 minutes.

Watercress

Like mustard, watercress belongs to the crucifer family. It grows easily in streams and wet places but should only be eaten when grown in perfectly clean, running water since it can harbour unpleasant parasites. Watercress is intensively cultivated in Britain under controlled conditions, which means that fresh supplies are available for most of the year.

With its fresh, peppery flavour watercress is one of the essentials of good European cookery. It is particularly useful in winter, when other salad vegetables may be hard to obtain or expensive. It is well known in salads, but can also often be chopped and added to a cooked dish just before serving. Its high vitamin and mineral (especially iron) content greatly enriches the nutritional quality of any dish in which it is used. Other herbs combine well with watercress in cooked sauces and in mayonnaise – the sauces vertes of French cookery are made from combinations of watercress, tarragon and parsley or other green herbs. To store watercress for up to a week, keep it standing in a jar of water in the refrigerator, covered with a polythene bag.

WATERCRESS AND POTATO SOUP

This excellent soup is especially good when made in springtime with succulent new potatoes. In France it is known as Potage de Santé because of its health-giving properties. It may be served hot, warm or chilled, and is good with grated chese, especially Parmesan or Pecorino.

4 cloves garlic, chopped
2 medium onions, chopped
90 g/3 oz vegetable margarine
500 g/1 lb potatoes, scrubbed *and* chopped
2 bunches watercress
600 ml/1 pint water *or* lightly seasoned stock
1 level teaspoon salt, *or* to taste (if using water)
1 egg, beaten
3–4 tablespoons single cream (optional)
white pepper

Fry the garlic and onions in the margarine for 5 minutes. Add the potatoes and fry, stirring, for another 5 minutes. Trim the watercress, but use most of the stems, because, like parsley stems, they contain a lot of flavour. Add it to the soup pot with the water and salt or the stock. Cover and simmer for 45 minutes. Liquidize the soup and return to the pot. Stir in the beaten egg and the cream, if liked, and season well with pepper.

TOFU AND WATERCRESS TART

Most open vegetable tarts are made with eggs, cheese or milk, or all three. If you want to avoid using dairy products or simply to have a change, use blended tofu as a base and add different combinations of vegetables.

crust
250 g/8 oz wholemeal flour
125 g/4 oz vegetable margarine
4 tablespoons cold water

filling
500 g/1 lb soft tofu
1 large bunch watercress
4 tablespoons vegetable oil
5 tablespoons soy sauce
125 g/4 oz mushrooms, chopped
1 bunch spring onions, chopped
125 g/4 oz mung beansprouts
3 cloves garlic, crushed
1 level teaspoon cayenne pepper
45 g/1½ oz sesame seeds

Make the pastry dough in the usual way (see p.218) and set it aside in the refrigerator while you prepare the filling. Preheat the oven to 190° C (375° F, gas mark 5).

Put the tofu in a liquidizer with the watercress, 2 tablespoons of the vegetable oil and 3 tablespoons of the soy sauce. Blend to a smooth puree, adding a little water if the blades have difficulty turning. Turn the mushrooms briefly in 2 tablespoons of hot vegetable oil. Season them with the remaining 2 tablespoons of soy sauce. Combine the tofu mixture with the mushrooms, spring onions, beansprouts, crushed garlic and cayenne pepper. Roll out the pastry and line a greased 25 cm (10 in) flan dish. Put the filling into the case, top with sesame seeds and bake for 35 minutes. Serve hot or cold.

WALNUT AND WATERCRESS 'PESTO'

Although the concentrated pesto sauce for pasta is traditionally made with pine nuts, you can vary the original recipe by using different kinds of nuts.

1 small bunch watercress
2 cloves garlic
125 g/4 oz walnuts
2 tablespoons grated Parmesan cheese
6 tablespoons olive oil
2 teaspoons lemon juice
1 level teaspoon salt
black pepper

Roughly chop the watercress and garlic and break up the nuts. Put all the ingredients in a liquidizer and blend until smooth.

WALNUT AND WATERCRESS SAUCE

Sauces thickened with finely ground nuts go particularly well with rice and other grain dishes.

2 cloves garlic, crushed
60 g/2 oz vegetable margarine
150 g/5 oz walnuts
400 ml/¾ pint milk
1 bunch watercress, chopped
1 bunch spring onions, chopped
150 g/5 oz Gouda *or* any good melting cheese, grated
1 level teaspoon salt
white pepper
a few leaves sage, chopped

Fry the garlic in the margarine. Grind 125 g (4 oz) of the walnuts and gradually stir them in. Add the milk little by little, continuing to stir until the sauce thickens. Lower the heat and add the watercress, spring onions, cheese, salt, pepper and sage. Simmer for another 10 minutes, stirring occasionally. Add the remaining 30 g (1 oz) walnuts, broken into small pieces. Serve hot.

SAUCE VERTE

This delicious and refreshing watercress sauce is made on the same principle as mayonnaise; it turns out a brilliant green colour. Serve it with eggs, pasta salads and even delicate grains like millet and bulghur (cracked) wheat.

1 bunch watercress
15 g/½ oz parsley, chopped
15 g/½ oz chives *or* 1 large spring onion, chopped
a few sprigs tarragon
2 egg yolks
200 ml/⅓ pint olive *or* other oil
1 tablespoon white wine vinegar *or* cider vinegar
salt
pepper

Wash and trim the watercress and herbs. Blanch them in boiling water for 1–2 minutes and then press them dry in a cloth; put into a liquidizer with the two egg yolks. When the mixutre is smooth, pour it into a bowl and start adding the oil drop by drop. Beat well until all the oil is added (this sauce may not thicken in the same way as mayonnaise, but it is none the worse for that). When all the oil has been added, season with vinegar, salt and pepper.

Green herb flavours: Watercress

Sweet tastes

CAROB
HONEY, CANE SUGAR PRODUCTS, MAPLE
SYRUP, CONCENTRATED APPLE JUICE AND
MALT EXTRACT · TOMATO PRODUCTS
VANILLA

Tomato

Carob

Honeycomb

Carob

Dried, ground carob pods are often used as a substitute for chocolate in wholefood cookery because they need less sweetening than cocoa powder, and unlike cocoa they do not contain caffeine. Carob pods grow on a Mediterranean evergreen which is also known as a locust tree – it was these 'locusts' which fed St John the Baptist during his sojourn in the wilderness.

Carob powder varies in colour from light to dark brown. It is better to use the lighter powder which is sweeter and needs less, if any, additional sugar. If you like the flavour of carob powder, use it regularly instead of cocoa powder in cakes and desserts.

GROUND RICE AND CAROB PUDDING

125 g/4 oz brown rice
450 ml/16 fl oz milk
90 g/3 oz brown sugar
45 g/1½ oz carob powder
a 1.5 cm/½ in piece of vanilla pod
peel of 1 orange, grated
split almonds, blanched *and* toasted

to serve
whipped cream (optional)

Grind the brown rice as finely as possible in a coffee grinder. Pour the milk into a basin and add the rest of the ingredients. Leave to stand for 1–2 hours so that the ground rice will soften. Then set the bowl above a saucepan of boiling water and stir the mixture frequently until it thickens (20–30 minutes). Remove the vanilla pod. Pour the mixture into a glass bowl, cover and chill. Decorate the top of the pudding with plenty of toasted, split almonds and serve with whipped cream, if liked.

CAROB CUSTARD

Children enjoy this custard served with ice cream. The method is the same as for making a plain vanilla custard.

450 ml/16 fl oz milk
2 tablespoons brown sugar *or* honey
1 dessertspoon carob powder
2 whole eggs *and* 1 extra yolk

Heat some water in the bottom of a double saucepan (or improvise with a bowl fitted into a deep saucepan). In a separate saucepan, bring the milk up to the boil, then stir in the sugar or honey and the carob powder. Put all the eggs into the top of the double boiler and beat them well. Gradually add the carob milk, stirring all the time. Keep the water in the bottom part of the saucepan simmering rapidly whilst you continue to stir the custard in the top. It should thicken in 10–15 minutes. Serve hot or cold.

CAROB AND YOGHURT CAKE

Cakes made with wholemeal flour can be extremely light when yoghurt is included in the ingredients. For a sweeter cake, substitute 90 g (3 oz) brown sugar for the concentrated apple juice in this recipe.

125 g/4 oz vegetable margarine
4 tablespoons concentrated apple juice
2 eggs
150 g/5 oz Greek yoghurt
275 g/9 oz wholemeal flour
2 teaspoons bicarbonate of soda
2 level tablespoons light-coloured carob powder

topping (optional)
see below

Preheat the oven to 180° C (350° F, gas mark 4). Beat the margarine with the apple juice until they form a smooth cream. Whisk the eggs and then beat them in with the vegetable margarine and apple juice. Add the yoghurt gradually. Mix the dry ingredients together, and then combine them with the liquid ingredients, mixing well. Put the cake mixture into a well-greased round 20 cm (8 in) cake tin and bake for 40 minutes.

After cooling the baked cake, you can cover it with a topping composed of equal parts carob powder, vegetable margarine and apple juice. Alternatively, melt a carob bar, mix it with a little hot water and spread it over the top of the cake.

HAZELNUT AND CAROB CAKE

175 g/6 oz vegetable margarine
90 g/3 oz brown sugar *or* 4 tablespoons concentrated apple juice
3 eggs
125 g/4 oz hazelnuts, ground
90 g/3 oz plain white flour
45 g/1½ oz fresh wholemeal breadcrumbs
2 level teaspoons baking powder
2 dessertspoons carob powder

to serve
whipped cream (optional)

Preheat the oven to 180° C (350° F, gas mark 4). Cream the margarine with the sugar or concentrated apple juice. Beat the eggs well and then mix them in. Add the hazelnuts and continue to beat the mixture thoroughly. Combine the flour, breadcrumbs (reserving a few), baking and carob powders and then gradually add them to the liquid ingredients. Grease a round 20 cm (8 in) cake tin and sprinkle the bottom with the reserved breadcrumbs. When the cake mixture is well combined put it into the tin and bake for 30 minutes. Allow to cool thoroughly before turning out of the tin.

This cake can be eaten plain, or with whipped cream. For a special occasion, make two cakes, doubling the above ingredients, and sandwich them together with whipped cream.

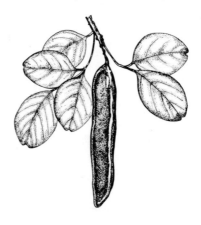

Honey, cane sugar products, maple syrup, concentrated apple juice and malt extract

The first four sweet flavourings of this subsection can be bracketed together because they are, to a large extent, interchangeable in cookery. All contain concentrated sugars, but of different chemical composition, and their individual merits have been the subject of much heated discussion in recent years. The arguments are complex and technical, but it is generally agreed that less refined (i.e. raw brown) sugar is not as harmful as refined white because it offers a less concentrated source of calories, does not have such a disruptive effect on blood-sugar levels and still contains some beneficial minerals. From the point of view of flavour, too, brown sugar does not have such a cloying aftertaste as white. Honey is often thought to be more beneficial to health than either brown or white sugar because of its vitamin, mineral, enzyme and even antibiotic content. Since its sugars have been pre-digested by the bees, they are said to be more easily assimilated into the human body. Concentrated apple juice and maple syrup, which some people might prefer on the grounds of flavour alone, are also easily assimilated because of their simpler chemical structure. For most of the recipes in this book, 1 tablespoon honey, maple syrup or concentrated apple juice can be substituted for 30g (1oz) brown sugar by anyone who prefers to avoid using sugar altogether. My own opinion is that, used in small quantities, brown sugar is not a dietary hazard. And in cookery it is often more convenient to use a dry sweetener than a liquid one. When substituting honey, maple syrup or apple juice in a cake recipe, for example, you will need to add a little more flour to compensate for the extra liquid.

Honey was the only source of concentrated sugar available to man before he discovered how to process sugar cane, and remained so for many centuries. As such, it was highly prized from the earliest times. The flavour of honey depends on the flowers from which the bees have gathered their nectar. Generally speaking, the darker the honey, the higher the pollen content and the stronger the flavour. The aromatic oils which give honey its flavour are easily evaporated in cooking, so use a cheaper, blended honey in cooked dishes and save the more expensive flower honeys for uncooked ones. Honey can be used in all kinds of desserts and in baking; it can also be used for making jams and preserves, though this will be rather expensive because of the quantities required. Fruit fools and purees are best made with honey, as are all kinds of sweet tofu desserts. Finally, honey is useful in salad dressings for counteracting the acidity of the vinegar or lemon juice – the combination of honey and lemon juice is, in fact, one of the most useful in cookery.

Brown sugar comes in varying shades: molasses sugar is very dark and demerara is light, with the muscovado sugars in between. Make sure that the brown sugar you buy is not merely white sugar dyed brown: this can be tested by mixing the sugar with cold water and seeing whether the dye washes off. Nutritionally, the most valuable product of sugar cane is molasses, the dark brown substance, rich in minerals and vitamins, which is left over in the sugar refining process. Unfortunately, most people find the flavour rather unpalatable when taken raw but molasses is excellent in breadmaking, where it helps to cream the yeast as well as adding goodness and a rich colour to the finished loaf.

Maple syrup, another excellent sweetener, is the product of the North American sugar maple. Although very sweet, it is entirely free from any cloying aftertaste. It is very popular in North America, especially to flavour waffles and pancakes. The combination of maple syrup and Greek yoghurt is an ambrosial one, recommended with any breakfast cereal. When buying maple syrup, make sure that it is the pure product and not mixed with sugar syrup.

Concentrated apple juice has recently become popular in 'sugar-free baking'. It is more economical to use than honey or maple syrup and the flavour is not intrusive.

Malt extract, similar in appearance to molasses and also rich in vitamins and minerals, is another nutritious sugar. It is produced when barley is sprouted for malting purposes. Like molasses, malt extract is rather unpalatable in its raw state, but its flavour is transformed when baked in bread. It is therefore a useful addition to wholemeal loaves, particularly those containing dried fruit.

CARROTS COOKED IN HONEY

500 g/1 lb carrots
125 g/4 oz vegetable margarine
3 tablespoons honey
salt
pepper

garnish
parsley *or* chives *or* fennel leaves *or* coriander leaves, chopped

Chop the carrots into fairly thin strips 5–7.5 cm (2–3 in) long. Melt the margarine in a cast iron frying pan and add the honey, then the carrots. Stir well, then leave to simmer over a low heat, with a lid on the pan, until the carrots are soft. Season with salt and plenty of pepper. Serve with a garnish of chopped leaves.

STRAWBERRY, HONEY AND TOFU TART

Tofu, which is available from Chinese grocers and wholefood shops, is made from slightly fermented soya milk. It has an almost neutral taste and can be used in sweet or savoury dishes.

crust
90 g/3 oz vegetable margarine
250 g/8 oz wholewheat flour
1 egg yolk, beaten
2 teaspoons brown sugar

filling
250 g/8 oz strawberries
2–3 tablespoons honey
250 g/8 oz hard tofu
1 heaped tablespoon sesame seeds

garnish
a few extra strawberries

The crust in this recipe is a kind of wholemeal *pâte sucrée* – you can leave out the sugar if you think the pie sweet enough without it. Rub the vegetable margarine into the flour, then mix in the beaten egg and sugar. Form the mixture into a dough and chill in the refrigerator for 30 minutes. Preheat the oven to 180° C (350° F, gas mark 4).

Meanwhile, make the filling by putting half the strawberries, honey and tofu into a liquidizer and blending them to a smooth puree. Mash the rest of the strawberries lightly, and mix with the puree. Roll out the pastry and line a greased 25 cm (10 in) flan dish. Spread the filling evenly inside and top with sesame seeds. Bake for 30 minutes. Cover with foil halfway through the cooking if the pie is browning too quickly. Garnish with sliced strawberries. Serve chilled.

PRUNE, HONEY AND TOFU DESSERT

300 g/10 oz dried prunes
350 g/12 oz soft tofu
2 tablespoons honey
juice *and* peel of 2 lemons, grated

Soak the prunes in just enough water to cover them. If they are left to soak overnight or all day there will be no need to cook them; if you can only soak them for a shorter time simmer them in the soaking water until soft. Stone the prunes, then put all the ingredients in a liquidizer and blend until they form a smooth puree. Pour into a serving bowl and chill.

APRICOT AND ADUKI BEAN TART FLAVOURED WITH HONEY

Aduki beans, also known as dragon beans, are highly prized in the Far East for their nutritive and medicinal qualities. As well as cooking them in the usual fashion as a savoury dish, the Chinese and Japanese make delicious sweetmeats by pounding them with sugar or honey. In this recipe ground aduki beans, tofu and honey are combined with dried apricots to make a delicious tart filling.

filling
250 g/8 oz dried apricot halves
250 g/8 oz aduki beans
3 tablespoons honey
juice of 1 large lemon
175 g/6 oz soft tofu

crust
250 g/8 oz wholemeal flour
125 g/4 oz vegetable margarine
4 tablespoons cold water

to serve
Greek yoghurt *or* cream

Soak the apricots in just enough water to cover them. Wash the beans and put them in a large pan with about three times their volume of water. Bring them up to the boil, then leave them to soak in the hot water for 1 hour. Bring up to the boil again and leave them to simmer until very soft. When the beans are thoroughly cooked, drain them and put them in a blender with the honey, lemon juice and tofu.

Make the pastry in the usual way (see p.218) and set it aside in the refrigerator for at least 15 minutes before rolling it out and lining a greased 25 cm (10 in) flan dish. Preheat the oven to 180° C (350° F, gas mark 4). Fill the tart with the tofu mixture and bake for 30 minutes.

Simmer the apricots in their soaking water until soft. Reduce the liquid to 100 ml (4 fl oz). Let the cooked tart cool slightly, then arrange the cooked apricots on top of the bean mixture. Pour the juices over the top and serve the tart warm or cold with yoghurt or cream.

QUICK FROZEN TOFU AND APPLE DESSERT

This tasty tofu dessert can be served like ice cream, perhaps with some fresh fruit.

250 g/8 oz hard *or* medium tofu
4 tablespoons concentrated apple juice

Put the tofu and concentrated apple juice in a liquidizer and blend to a smooth cream. Pour into a shallow dish and freeze overnight or all day.

PANCAKES WITH MAPLE SYRUP

Ordinary pancakes made with wholewheat flour tend to be a little heavy, but they are very good when leavened with yeast and mixed with buttermilk or yoghurt. This recipe makes about eight thin pancakes. Maple syrup and creamy Greek yoghurt are excellent accompaniments.

15 g/½ oz dried yeast
1 teaspoon sugar
100 ml/4 fl oz warm water
250 g/8 oz finely ground wholewheat *or* 80% flour
1 level teaspoon salt
200 ml/⅓ pint buttermilk *or* yoghurt
2 eggs
vegetable oil for frying

to serve
maple syrup *and* yoghurt

Dissolve the yeast with the sugar in the warm water. In a large bowl mix the flour with the salt and then beat in the yeast and the buttermilk or yoghurt. Leave to stand, covered, for 1–2 hours.

Separate the eggs and beat the yolks into the pancake mixture. Add a little water if the mixture seems too stiff. Slowly heat a heavy cast-iron pan. Beat the egg whites stiffly and then fold them into the mixture. Heat about 1 tablespoon of oil in the pan and then fry the pancake mixture, a small cupful at a time. Tilt the pan so that the mixture covers the bottom as thinly as possible. Cook the pancakes for a couple of minutes on each side over a high heat.

Serve at once with maple syrup and perhaps yoghurt as well.

HONEYED POPCORN

For each person use:

30 g/1 oz popping corn
1½ tablespoons vegetable oil
1½ tablespoons honey
¼ teaspoon salt

Put the popping corn in a large cast iron frying pan and stir constantly over a medium heat. When it begins to pop, cover the pan and turn down the heat a little. Shake the pan to prevent burning until all the corn has popped (discard any which refuses to do so). Take the corn out of the pan and add the appropriate quantity of oil, honey and salt. Return the popcorn to the pan and stir until all the pieces are well coated in honey and oil. Remove from the pan and spread out to cool.

HONEY CAKE

4 heaped tablespoons honey
125 g/4 oz vegetable margarine
3 eggs
peel of 2 lemons, grated
juice of ½ lemon
350 g/12 oz wholemeal flour
1 teaspoon baking powder
1 teaspoon coriander seeds, ground
1 teaspoon cinnamon, ground
a few cloves, ground (optional)
30 g/1 oz split almonds

Preheat the oven to 180° C (350° F, gas mark 4). Warm the honey and then beat it with the margarine. Separate the eggs and beat in the yolks, also the lemon peel and juice. Mix the flour, baking powder and ground spices together and gradually beat them into the honey and margarine mixture. Beat the egg whites until stiff and fold them in. Grease a shallow, rectangular baking tray (30 × 15 cm/12 × 6 in) and pour in the cake mixture (it should be only about 3 cm (1½ in) deep. Top with split almonds and bake for 30 minutes. Cover with a sheet of foil for the first 20 minutes, and then remove it to allow the cake to brown.

This cake is good when sliced and spread with butter or vegetable margarine.

DRIED FRUIT AND NUT CAKE SWEETENED WITH APPLE JUICE

The only sweetening agents in this cake are dried fruit and concentrated apple juice, thus eliminating processed sugars.

175 g/6 oz vegetable margarine
4 tablespoons concentrated apple juice
3 eggs
90 g/3 oz currants
90 g/3 oz sultanas *or* raisins
90 g/3 oz glacé cherries, halved
peel of 1 lemon, grated
300 g/10 oz wholewheat flour
2 level teaspoons baking powder
45 g/1½ oz almonds, ground
1 level teaspoon salt
¼ teaspoon nutmeg, grated
a little milk
30 g/1 oz almonds, blanched

Preheat the oven to 180° C (350° F, gas mark 4). Cream the vegetable margarine with the concentrated apple juice in a large bowl. Whisk the eggs in a separate bowl and then beat them in with the margarine and apple juice. Mix in the dried fruit, cherries and lemon peel. In another bowl combine all the dry ingredients – flour, baking powder, ground almonds, salt and nutmeg – then add the dry ingredients to the liquid ones. Add a few tablespoons of milk to make a dropping consistency.

Transfer the mixture to a greased 23 cm (9 in) cake tin and bake for 1 hour. After this time, insert a knife into the centre of the cake and see whether it comes out clean. If so the cake is done, otherwise bake for a further 10 to 15 minutes. Lightly toast the blanched almonds under the grill and decorate the top of the cake with them when it is cooked. Cool the cake on a wire rack.

HONEY DOUGHNUTS

This recipe makes about 20 medium-sized doughnuts.

350 g/12 oz flour (⅔ wholewheat *and* ⅓ plain white)
1 heaped teaspoon baking powder
a little nutmeg, grated
1 teaspoon cinnamon, ground (optional)
1 egg, beaten
250 ml/8 fl oz milk
3 tablespoons honey
1 tablespoon melted vegetable margarine
vegetable oil for frying

Combine the flour, baking powder and spices. Mix the beaten egg with the milk, honey and melted vegetable margarine. Gradually beat the liquid ingredients into the flour mixture. Leave to stand for 1 hour or more. Slowly heat the oil, which should be at least 7.5 cm (3 in) deep, in any pan suitable for deep frying. Meanwhile, turn out the doughnut mixture, which should be very soft yet just solid enough to hold together, on to a well-floured board. Press it to a thickness of about 2 cm (just less than 1 in) with the palm of your hand. Cut the dough into circles with a glass or biscuit cutter (the dough will swell up in cooking). Thoroughly cover a forefinger with flour and make a hole in the centre of each circle. When the oil is hot (about 180° C/350° F) put the first batch of doughnuts into the pan. Fry for about 2 minutes on each side. Repeat until all the dough has been cooked. Put the finished doughnuts on to absorbent kitchen paper to drain and serve them hot.

FRUIT AND MALT LOAVES

2 teaspoons salt
700 g/1½ lb wholewheat flour
150 g/5 oz vegetable margarine
1 heaped teaspoon dried yeast *or* 1 level tablespoon fresh
2 tablespoons brown sugar
350 ml/12 fl oz warm water
2 tablespoons malt extract
250 g/8 oz raisins *and* currants, mixed

Mix the salt with the flour and rub in the vegetable margarine. Dissolve the yeast with the sugar and a little of the warm water; when it is ready, add it to the flour and mix well. Dissolve the malt extract in the rest of the warm water and gradually add it to the flour, mixing well as you do so. Add the dried fruit. Knead the mixture until you have a smooth dough. Cover the bowl with polythene and leave to rise in a warm place until the dough has doubled in size, probably 2-3 hours. Then knead again and divide the dough between 2 well-greased 500 g (1 lb) loaf tins. Leave to rise, covered, in a warm place until the dough has risen up to the top of the tins. Preheat the oven to 200° C (400° F, gas mark 6). Bake at this temperature for 10 minutes, then reduce the heat to 190° C (375° F, gas mark 5) for a further 35 minutes. Cool the loaves on a wire rack.

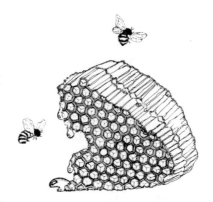

Tomato products: puree, concentrate and ketchup

Tomatoes were introduced into Italy as an exotic luxury from South America in the sixteenth century, but in northern Europe it is only recently that they have become so popular.

A tomato flavour can be introduced into a recipe by adding puree, concentrate or ketchup. Non-concentrated tomato puree (the kind which is bought in packets) by itself does not have a particularly interesting flavour, but it is very good in combination with tomato concentrate, a paste made from sun-dried tomatoes and olive oil. Concentrate is rather expensive, but as its name suggests you only need to use a little at a time: 1 level tablespoon should be enough with 500 g (1 lb) of puree. Good ketchup, free from additives and sugar, is useful for adding a last-minute tomato taste to a cooked dish.

The flavour of tomatoes combines happily with many different seasonings – basil, savory, thyme, mint, olives, capers, garlic, chillies, ginger, lemons and tamarind – and is particularly useful for adding sweetness to a savoury dish. This sweetness can often be used to offset the salty, sour or spicy flavours of other ingredients. Tomatoes also blend well into dishes cooked with wine.

BEANS BAKED
WITH TOMATOES AND GINGER

350 g/12 oz haricot *or* other medium-sized beans
250 g/8 oz onions *or* shallots
2–3 fresh red chillies
30 g/1 oz fresh root ginger
1 small bunch parsley
4 cloves garlic
500 g/1 lb (1 packet) tomato puree
1 tablespoon tomato concentrate
juice of 1 lemon
2 teaspoons salt
1 tablespoon brown sugar
350 ml/12 fl oz water

Soak the beans overnight or all day, or parcook them. Chop the onions or shallots and the red chillies quite finely. Peel the ginger and pound it in a mortar. Chop the parsley finely and crush the garlic. Rinse the beans in clean water. Combine all the ingredients down to the sugar in a large casserole dish. Add the fresh water and cover the casserole with a tight-fitting lid or foil. Bake at 170° C (325° F, gas mark 3) for about 2 hours or until the beans are soft. Test after 1½ hours' cooking and adjust the seasoning.

VEGETABLE COUSCOUS

Couscous, the favourite dish of North Africa, is made from specially prepared wheat and usually cooked in the steam of a tasty sauce. Ready-to-use couscous is now easily obtainable. In North Africa, a double cooking vessel known as a *couscousier* is used for preparing this dish, but a sieve or a colander lined with muslin fitted over a pan will work quite well.

500 g/1 lb couscous
2 large onions
5 cloves garlic
2 green peppers
2–4 red chillies
1 large *or* 2 small carrots
5 tablespoons olive *or* sunflower oil
500 g/1 lb tomatoes, chopped *or* 500 g/1 lb (1 packet) tomato puree
1 tablespoon tomato concentrate
2 teaspoons ground coriander seeds
1 heaped teaspoon sweet paprika
2 teaspoons salt, *or* to taste
1 small bunch parsley *or* coriander leaves, chopped
200 ml/⅓ pint water
90 g/3 oz currants
black pepper

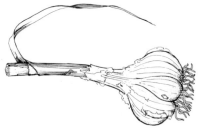

Put the couscous in a basin and add enough water to moisten the grains. Work the liquid into the couscous with your fingers, making sure the grains remain separate. Place in a sieve or colander and set aside while you chop the onions, garlic, green peppers, chillies and carrots, the last into matchstick pieces. Put all these ingredients into a large pan with the olive oil and simmer for 15 minutes. After this time, add the chopped tomatoes or tomato puree together with the tomato concentrate, ground coriander, paprika, salt and chopped parsley or coriander leaves, plus the 200 ml (⅓ pint) water. Simmer for 10 minutes. Now set the sieve or colander over the pan containing the sauce and leave the couscous to steam for 30 minutes. Add the currants to the sauce 10 minutes before the end of the cooking time. When ready, season with pepper. To serve, pile up the couscous on a large plate and pour the sauce over the top of it.

BULGHUR WHEAT
BAKED WITH TOMATOES AND CHEESE

In this recipe I suggest using Pecorino cheese because it has a robust rather salty taste which comes through well in baked dishes.

250 g/8 oz bulghur (cracked) wheat
450 ml/16 fl oz cold water
250 g/8 oz onions
5–6 cloves garlic
60 g/2 oz vegetable margarine *plus* 30 g/1 oz for topping
a few sprigs mint *or* other aromatic herb
60 g/2 oz parsley
175 g/6 oz Pecorino *or* Parmesan *or* Feta cheese
250 g/8 oz (½ packet) tomato puree
1 tablespoon tomato concentrate
salt
pepper

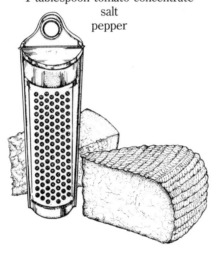

Preheat the oven to 180° C (350° F, gas mark 4). Soak the wheat in the cold water until all the water has been absorbed. Chop the onions and garlic and fry them gently in the margarine for 10 minutes. Chop the mint and the parsley and grate the cheese. Mix all the ingredients together, season with salt and pepper to taste, and turn the mixture into a greased oven dish. Top with a little vegetable margarine and bake for 30 minutes.

TOMATO-FLAVOURED GNOCCHI

Gnocchi is a traditional south Italian dish made from semolina and Parmesan cheese. This recipe has an additional flavouring of tomatoes. Serve the dish with a green salad tossed in a garlic dressing.

600 ml/1 pint milk
1 level teaspoon salt
white pepper
250 g/8 oz semolina
250 g/8 oz (½ packet) tomato puree
2 teaspoons tomato concentrate
90 g/3 oz Parmesan cheese, grated
60 g/2 oz vegetable margarine
2 eggs, beaten

Preheat the oven to 190° C (375° F, gas mark 5). Season the milk with salt and pepper and bring it to the boil. Turn the heat right down and gradually add the semolina, stirring vigorously. Add the tomato puree and concentrate and continue to cook over a low heat for 10 minutes, stirring all the time. By this time the semolina should be thick enough to form a kind of moist dough when it is cooled. Take it off the heat and stir in 60 g (2 oz) of the Parmesan, the margarine and the beaten eggs. Grease a large, shallow tin, and press the semolina mixture into it, forming a layer about 1.5 cm (½ in) thick. Mark out into squares, sprinkle with the remaining 30 g (1 oz) of Parmesan and put it in the oven for 25 minutes.

FRIED TEMPE WITH TOMATO AND TAMARIND SAUCE

Tempe is a kind of soya bean 'cheese' eaten in Indonesia since ancient times, but relatively little known in Britain. It can now be found in specialist wholefood shops and is rich in protein, unsaturated fats and even the rare vitamin B12. I must say I didn't much like its look or smell when I first tried it, but after I discovered Madhur Jaffrey's recipe for fried tempe* it became a favourite food. Tempe invites a fruity, spicy sauce to accompany it, like the one suggested below. If you are in a hurry – and tempe makes a good instant snack – simply dip the fried chips in a sauce made up of two parts tomato ketchup and one part chilli sauce.

sauce
3–4 red chillies
2 tablespoons vegetable oil
4–5 cloves garlic, crushed
350 g/12 oz (¾ packet) tomato puree
2 teaspoons tomato concentrate
2 tablespoons mint, finely chopped
2 tablespoons tamarind juice (see p. 46)
2 teaspoons salt
black pepper

250 g/8 oz tempe
vegetable oil for frying

Cut the chillies in half, deseed them and chop them into small pieces. Fry them gently in the vegetable oil for a few minutes, then add the crushed garlic and fry for 2–3 minutes more. Add the tomato puree and concentrate, then stir in the mint, tamarind juice, salt and pepper. Leave the sauce to simmer, covered, for 15 minutes.

Meanwhile, cut the block of tempe into thin chips 5–7.5 cm (2–3 in) long. Heat the oil to a depth of about 1 cm (½ in) in a cast iron frying pan. When it is quite hot add the tempe chips in batches and fry until dark brown on all sides (2–3 minutes). Absorb the excess oil with kitchen paper and serve the chips hot with a bowl of sauce for dipping.

* *Eastern Vegetarian Cookery*, Madhur Jaffrey, Jonathan Cape, 1983.

QUICK CREAM TOMATO SAUCE

This sauce is perfect served hot with wholewheat pasta cooked al dente.

3–4 cloves garlic
1 tablespoon olive oil
500 g/1 lb (1 packet) tomato puree
1 tablespoon tomato concentrate
fresh basil *or* tarragon *or* savory (if available; if not, use parsley)
125 g/4 oz curd cheese
salt
white pepper

Crush the garlic and fry it gently in the olive oil for 2–3 minutes. Add the tomato puree and concentrate, stir well and leave to simmer while you chop the herbs. Stir in the chopped herbs and the curd cheese, and season with salt and pepper.

ROMESCO SAUCE

The combination of tomatoes and hazelnuts is characteristic of this Spanish sauce, which makes a good accompaniment to pasta. I have added some red wine, which gives it a full, rounded taste.

500 g/1 lb tomatoes *or* 500 g/1 lb (1 packet) tomato puree
3 cloves garlic, crushed
1 red pepper
1 sherry glass red wine
1 good tablespoon tomato concentrate (if using tomato puree)
90 g/3 oz hazelnuts, ground
a few parsley sprigs, chopped

Plunge the tomatoes into boiling water for a couple of minutes, rinse in cold water and then remove the skins. Chop them roughly and put them in a cast iron pan with the crushed garlic. Chop the red pepper finely and add it to the pan. Stir in the red wine (and tomato concentrate if using tomato puree). Leave the sauce to simmer gently for 15–20 minutes. Then stir in the hazelnuts and parsley and simmer for a further 5 minutes before serving.

Sweet tastes: Tomato products

Vanilla

The vanilla pod comes from an orchid which grows wild in the forests of Central America. Its sweet flavour, which develops during the curing process, derives from a substance called vanillin.

Vanilla is best known as a flavouring for dairy foods – ice cream, custards and milk puddings – and vanilla sugar or essence is sometimes used to flavour cakes. Vanilla also goes well with chestnut puree and can be used to flavour tofu desserts. It is generally used by itself – not in combination with other flavourings – because it is easily overpowered by stronger tastes. Sugar readily picks up the flavour of vanilla and a few pieces of pod kept in a jar of sugar will provide a constant supply of vanilla sugar. Alternatively, a small piece of pod can be ground up with the sugar in an electric grinder. When making a milk pudding or a custard, cook a piece of vanilla pod with the rest of the ingredients and take it out just before serving.

A 2.5–5 cm (1–2 in) piece of pod is enough for a single recipe, and it should be split down the middle to release all the flavour. Although vanilla pods are expensive, they can be used over and over again, even after being cooked, so long as they are well washed and dried. Store the pods in an airtight jar. If using vanilla essence, ensure that it is the genuine article and not a synthetic vanillin substitute.

VANILLA YOGHURT ICE CREAM

This is a light, refreshing ice cream that goes well with fresh or dried fruit salad, with maple syrup, or with carob or chocolate sauce.

450 ml/16 fl oz milk
1 vanilla pod
75 g//2½ oz sugar
2 eggs
2 egg whites
150 ml/¼ pint yoghurt

Pour the milk into a saucepan and heat it gently with the vanilla pod. Leave to steep for 1–2 hours. If using brown sugar, grind it in a coffee grinder. Beat the sugar into the eggs and extra whites. Pour some water into the bottom of a double saucepan and bring it to a rapid simmer. Bring the milk to the boil and pour it into the top of the double boiler. Beat in the egg and sugar mixture and stir the custard until it thickens; this will take about 10 minutes. Take it off the heat, whisk in the yoghurt and then pour the mixture into shallow trays or, if you have one, an ice cream maker. Freeze until set, taking it out and beating it two or three times during the freezing process to prevent the formation of ice crystals. Return it to the freezer until 15 minutes before serving.

CHESTNUT AND VANILLA PUREE

Variously known as Mont Blanc or Montebianco, in France and Italy this dessert is made with chestnuts and cream. The version given here is flavoured with vanilla, always good in combination with chestnuts, and instead of cream uses yoghurt, the slight acidity of which pleasantly offsets the richness of the chestnut puree.

250 g/8 oz dried chestnuts
a 5 cm/2 in piece of vanilla pod, split
approx 300 ml/½ pint milk *and* water, mixed
2 egg whites
60 g/2 oz brown sugar
250 g/8 oz yoghurt
garnish (optional)
fresh summer fruit

Soak the chestnuts in cold water for about 30 minutes. Put them in a large pan with the vanilla pod and just enough milk and water to cover them. Simmer slowly until the chestnuts are soft and all the liquid is absorbed. Take out the vanilla pod, which may be washed and reused. Beat the egg whites with the sugar until they are stiff. Put the chestnuts, egg white and sugar mixture and 175 g (6 oz) of the yoghurt into a blender and reduce the mixture to a stiff puree. Mould this puree into a cone shape and leave it in the refrigerator for a few hours to chill thoroughly. Pour the remaining yoghurt over the summit of the 'mountain' just before serving. If it is summer, surround the base of the mountain with fresh cherries or other soft fruit.

BAKED APPLE SNOW
FLAVOURED WITH VANILLA

700 g/1½ lb cooking apples
45 g/1½ oz vegetable margarine
2–3 tablespoons honey
a 2.5 cm/1 in piece of vanilla pod
approx 150 ml/¼ pint water
4 egg whites
45 g/1½ oz brown sugar

to serve
Greek yoghurt *or* cream

Preheat the oven to 230° C (450°F, gas mark 8). Peel and chop the cooking apples and put them in a pan with the margarine, honey, vanilla pod and water. Simmer until the apples are cooked to a puree. Meanwhile, beat the egg whites until they form a peak. Remove the piece of vanilla pod from the apples and put it in a coffee grinder with the sugar. Grind to a powder and beat this in with the egg whites. Transfer the apple puree to a greased heat-resistant dish, cover it with the meringue mixture, and bake for 10 minutes.

Serve hot or cold with Greek yoghurt or cream.

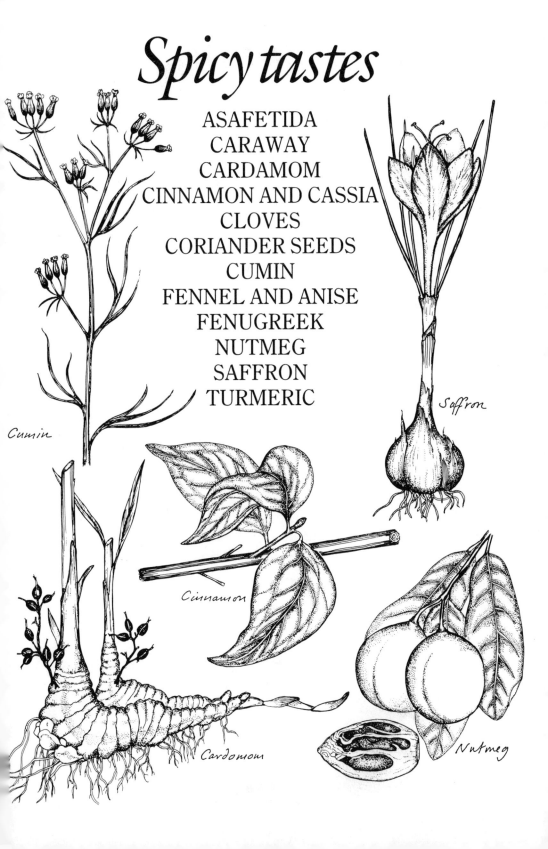

Spicy tastes

ASAFETIDA
CARAWAY
CARDAMOM
CINNAMON AND CASSIA
CLOVES
CORIANDER SEEDS
CUMIN
FENNEL AND ANISE
FENUGREEK
NUTMEG
SAFFRON
TURMERIC

Cumin

Saffron

Cinnamon

Cardomom

Nutmeg

Asafetida

This plant, a native of Afghanistan, is credited with all kinds of medicinal qualities. The part used is the resin which is tapped from the roots. In large quantities this resin is said to have a revolting smell and taste; but when dried and powdered and used in minute quantities it is highly valued – in Indian cookery particularly – for its digestive properties and its ability to bring out other flavours. Indian cooks use asafetida rather as modern Japanese cooks use monosodium glutumate. Use a pinch of asafetida in Indian vegetarian dishes to test its effect as a flavour enhancer.

Caraway

The warm, aromatic taste of caraway seeds is best known as a flavouring for cakes, biscuits and bread. In Germany the Eastern European caraway seeds are also used in savoury dishes, particularly with cabbage and sauerkraut. Caraway seeds, like those of fennel, are helpful to the digestion: 'caraway comfits' – sugar-coated seeds – were sometimes taken for this purpose at the end of a meal.

POTATO BREAD
TOPPED WITH CARAWAY SEEDS

Bread dough made with ⅔ wholemeal flour and ⅓ sieved potatoes produces a light, well-textured loaf which keeps well for up to a week. This recipe makes two 500 g (1 lb) loaves.

700 g/1½ lb wholemeal flour
1 tablespoon salt
350 g/12 oz boiled potatoes, sieved
2 teaspoons dried yeast *or* 1 level tablepoon fresh
1 tablespoon molasses
400 ml/¾ pint warm water
2 tablespoons vegetable oil
1 level tablespoon caraway seeds

Mix the flour with the salt and rub in the sieved potatoes. Dissolve the yeast with the molasses in a little of the warm water. When it is ready, add it to the flour mixture and gradually mix in the rest of the water until you have a firm dough. Knead for 1–3 minutes, working in the oil at the same time, and then leave to rise in a warm place for 2–3 hours until the dough has doubled in size.

Knead the dough for a second time. Grease two 500 g (1 lb) bread tins and divide the dough between them. Top with caraway seeds and then leave to rise until the dough has risen up to the top of the tins, which may take about ½–1 hour. Preheat the oven to 200° C (400° F, gas mark 6). Bake for 10 minutes, then reduce the oven temperature to 190° C (375° F, gas mark 5) and continue baking for a further 35 minutes. Test with a knife blade to make sure the loaves are done. Turn out of the tins and cool thoroughly on a wire rack before storing in a bread tin.

CARAWAY BISCUITS

This recipe makes about 20 biscuits.

150 g/5 oz vegetable margarine
125 g/4 oz fine oatmeal
125 g/4 oz wholewheat flour
75 g/2½ oz brown sugar *or* honey
2 teaspoons caraway seeds
juice *and* peel of 1 lemon, grated

Preheat the oven to 200° C (400° F, gas mark 6). Melt the margarine slowly in a saucepan. Mix together all the dry ingredients and honey, if using. Combine the margarine, lemon juice and peel and the dry ingredients to form a kind of dough. Roll out on a well-floured board and cut out the biscuits with a cutter. Bake on a well-greased tray for 15 minutes, or until just brown underneath. Let the biscuits cool a little before removing them to a wire rack. When they are completely cool, store them in an airtight tin.

Cardamom

The rich, 'perfumed' taste of cardamom is quite unlike that of any other spice. The seeds, which come from a plant native to the forests of South India, are enclosed in a small pod, and when buying cardamom look for the dried seed pod rather than the ready ground spice. When cooking with cardamom, take the seeds out of the pod and grind them in a mortar just before use. Since cardamom seeds are never used in very great quantities in a recipe this is less trouble than it sounds.

The strong flavour of cardamom is partially lost in cooking, so if a dish is to be cooked for some time season it fairly generously. Sometimes cardamom pods are cracked and used whole – always remove them before serving. It is an excellent spice for flavouring white sauces and all kinds of milk puddings: many exotic, yet simple, desserts can be made with a combination of milk, rice or semolina, dried fruit, nuts and cardamom. Indian rice and vegetable dishes make good use of cardamom, and it is a traditional flavouring for coffee in the Middle East.

SWEET RICE COOKED WITH CARDAMOM

300 g/10 oz long grain brown rice
750 ml/1¼ pints milk
seeds of 6 cardamom pods, ground
peel of 2 lemons, grated
grating of nutmeg
90 g/3 oz almonds, ground
90 g/3 oz brown sugar
15 g/½ oz vegetable margarine

garnish
toasted almonds

Preheat the oven to 140° C (275° F, gas mark 1). Wash the rice in several changes of water and soak it for 2–3 hours. Butter an ovenproof dish and put all the ingredients into it, mixed well together. Top with a few pieces of margarine. Cover the dish with a lid or some foil and cook for 1–2 hours, until the milk is just absorbed but the pudding is still quite moist. Decorate with toasted almonds.

This dish can be served warm or completely chilled.

PEAR AND CHESTNUT TART FLAVOURED WITH CARDAMOM

Cardamom makes a good flavouring for pears. In this recipe, the uncooked pears are arranged on a layer of chestnut puree. Only the pastry case is baked.

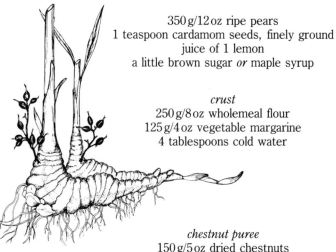

350 g/12 oz ripe pears
1 teaspoon cardamom seeds, finely ground
juice of 1 lemon
a little brown sugar *or* maple syrup

crust
250 g/8 oz wholemeal flour
125 g/4 oz vegetable margarine
4 tablespoons cold water

chestnut puree
150 g/5 oz dried chestnuts
about 300 ml/½ pint milk *and* water mixed, in which to cook the chestnuts
100 ml/4 fl oz milk
a little brown sugar *or* maple syrup

Preheat the oven to 180° C (350° F, gas mark 4). Slice the pears and sprinkle them with the ground cardamom seeds, lemon juice and sugar or maple syrup to taste. Leave them to stand while you prepare the rest of the ingredients.

Make the pastry crust in the usual way (see p. 218) and set it aside in the refrigerator for about 15 minutes. Roll out the pastry and line a greased 25 cm (10 in) flan dish. Prick all over with a fork and bake blind for 30 minutes.

Soak the dried chestnuts in cold water for 30 minutes. Drain them, then put in a pan with just enough of the milk and water mixture to cover them, and let them simmer slowly, uncovered, until all the liquid has been absorbed. Put the chestnuts in a blender with the 100 ml (4 fl oz) of milk and sugar or maple syrup to taste. Blend to a smooth puree.

When the pastry case is cooked, take it out of the oven and allow it to cool before spreading a layer of chestnut puree inside. Arrange the slices of pear on top and pour over them any remaining juice. Allow to cool thoroughly before serving.

SEMOLINA AND CARDAMOM DESSERT

Rice and semolina desserts are worth making in the original Middle Eastern style – with spices and nuts. They bear no resemblance to the degenerate puddings many of us remember from school!

seeds of 5 cardamom pods
60 g/2 oz vegetable margarine
125 g/4 oz semolina
600 ml/1 pint milk
45 g/1½ oz brown sugar
peel of 2 lemons, finely grated
60 g/2 oz almonds *or* pine nuts *or* pistachios, toasted

Take the cardamom seeds out of their shells and grind them in a mortar. Melt the margarine in a pan over a low heat; add the semolina and ground cardamom and fry gently, stirring, for 2–3 minutes. Gradually add the milk, keeping the heat low and continuing to stir. Take the pan off the heat while you add the sugar and lemon peel. Return the pan to the heat and stir until the consistency is that of a very thick sauce. Cool slightly, then pour the mixture into a glass serving dish and chill. Just before serving, crush the nuts slightly and scatter them over the surface of the pudding.

Cinnamon and cassia

Cinnamon and cassia are closely related spices derived from the dried bark of young cinnamon tree shoots. Cinnamon, which is considered the finer flavouring of the two, grows mainly in Sri Lanka. It is harvested during the monsoon and then dried in the sun so that the thin sheets of bark roll up to form quills or sticks. It should be bought in this form and then ground up in a coffee grinder, a little at a time. As with most spices, the quills can be stored for much longer without losing their flavour than can the ready ground powder.

Cinnamon makes an excellent flavouring for cakes and desserts because it has no hint of bitterness. It combines well with nutmeg, cloves and coriander and also goes well with carob powder: an unusual cinnamon toast can be made by mixing cinnamon and light-coloured carob instead of the usual sugar. A warm-tasting spice, it is often used to flavour winter drinks from spiced teas to red wine punch.

Cinnamon also has an interesting potential as a flavouring for savoury food and it goes well with sweet vegetables like onions and parsnips. It is one of the Chinese 'five spices' and is also commonly used in an Indian garam masala mixture.

CINNAMON RICE
MIXED WITH APPLE PUREE

This is a tasty dessert which is quickly made if you have some plain brown rice already cooked. Yoghurt makes a good accompaniment.

700 g/1½ lb cooking apples
90 g/3 oz vegetable margarine
2 tablespoons honey *or* brown sugar
100 ml/4 fl oz water
250 g/8 oz cooked rice
2 teaspoons cinnamon, ground
grating of nutmeg
90 g/3 oz split almonds, toasted

Chop the apples and put them in a pan with 60 g (2 oz) of the margarine, the honey or sugar and the water. Cook until they are well pureed. Fry the rice with the cinnamon and nutmeg for 5 minutes in the remainder of the margarine. Add the apple puree and mix well together. Scatter the almonds over the rice and apple mixture just before serving.

CINNAMON CARROT CAKE

150 g/5 oz vegetable margarine
3 tablespoons honey
150 g/5 oz carrots, grated
2 eggs
175 g/6 oz wholewheat flour
125 g/4 oz plain white flour
1 heaped teaspoon salt
1 heaped teaspoon baking powder
1½ teaspoons cinnamon, ground
peel of 1 lemon, grated
30 g/1 oz split almonds

Preheat the oven to 180°C (350°F, gas mark 4). Cream the margarine with a fork, then beat in the honey followed by the carrots. Beat the eggs in a separate bowl and then combine them with the carrots, margarine and honey. Mix together the flours, salt, baking powder, cinnamon and lemon peel and then gradually beat them into the liquid ingredients. Spoon the mixture into a well-greased 500 g (1 lb) loaf tin and bake for 40 minutes. Then take the cake out of the oven and decorate the top with split almonds stuck in hedgehog fashion. Return the cake to the oven and continue baking at the same temperature for a further 10 minutes. Let the cake cool thoroughly on a wire rack before taking it out of the tin.

APPLE AND CINNAMON CAKE

topping
1 medium cooking apple
juice of 1 lemon
30 g/1 oz brown sugar
1 teaspoon cinnamon, ground

200 g/7 oz vegetable margarine
150 g/5 oz brown sugar
3 eggs, separated
peel of 2 lemons, grated
350 g/12 oz wholemeal flour
2 level teaspoons baking powder
½ teaspoon salt
2 level teaspoons cinnamon, ground

First prepare the topping. Slice the apple. Heat the lemon juice with the sugar and stir in the cinnamon. Put the apple slices in the lemon juice mixture to steep while you make the cake. Preheat the oven to 180° C (350° F, gas mark 4).

Cream the margarine with the sugar and beat in the egg yolks and lemon peel. Mix together in a separate bowl the flour, baking powder, salt and cinnamon. Beat the egg whites until they are stiff. Gradually beat the mixed dry ingredients into the margarine mixture, and then fold in the egg whites. Grease a 500 g (1 lb) loaf tin or a 20 cm (8 in) cake tin and spoon the cake mixture into it. Arrange the apple slices on top of the cake and pour the lemon juice mixture over the top. Bake for 1 hour, covering with foil for the first 30 minutes of baking. Allow the cake to cool thoroughly on a wire rack before removing it from the tin.

WELSH GRIDDLE CAKES

These are almost instant cakes which can be mixed up and cooked in 20 minutes.

250 g/8 oz wholewheat flour
1 teaspoon salt
1 heaped teaspoon cinnamon, ground
30 g/1 oz brown sugar
90 g/3 oz currants
90 g/3 oz vegetable margarine
1 egg, beaten
90 ml/3 fl oz milk
a little vegetable oil

Heat a griddle or a large cast iron frying pan very thoroughly over a low to medium heat. Mix the flour with the salt, cinnamon, sugar and currants. Melt the margarine and add it, with the beaten egg and milk, stirring to form a fairly stiff mixture. Roll out on a well-floured board to a thickness of about 1.5 cm (½ in), and then cut out circles about 7.5 cm (3 in) across. Oil the griddle or frying pan very lightly, turn the heat down to low and cook the cakes, a few at a time, for about 5 minutes on each side.

Cloves

Cloves are the dried buds of a tropical evergreen tree, originally a native of South-east Asia. Their taste is very strong and so they should be used very sparingly – 1–2 cloves are often sufficient for a whole dish.

They are best bought whole, and ground at home in a mortar. In cookery it is best to use them ground, in combination with other spices. A hint of cloves adds zest to both savoury and sweet dishes. They are a standard ingredient of mixed spice and of garam masala.

Coriander seeds

Coriander is an annual plant about 60 cm (2 feet) high, which is naturalized in most parts of the world. The seeds have a delicious, warm, spicy taste which is valuable in both sweet and savoury cookery.

The seeds are generally used ground and in quite generous quantities – perhaps 1–2 teaspoons in a single dish – since their flavour is rather mild. Coriander seed is the best base for an Indian curry powder. In Middle Eastern cookery, coriander seeds are often used with cumin seeds in the proportion of two or three to one. Coriander seeds are very good with dried or baked fruit and they are excellent in all kinds of sweet tarts and crumbles.

Coriander leaves, which taste quite different although they come from the same plant, are described on p. 119.

CORIANDER-SPICED LENTIL SOUP WITH YOGHURT

This lentil soup is flavoured with coriander seeds and leaves. The yoghurt, which is stirred in just before serving, lightens the taste and the texture.

250 g/8 oz green *or* brown lentils
2 medium onions, chopped
3 tablespoons vegetable oil
4–5 cloves garlic, chopped
1 teaspoon roasted cumin seeds, ground
2 teaspoons coriander seeds, ground
2 teaspoons salt
1.25 litres/2 pints water
1 bunch coriander *or* parsley *or* mint
juice of 1 lemon
1 teaspoon garam masala
plain yoghurt

Wash the lentils and leave them to soak for about 2 hours. Soften the onions in the oil. Add the chopped garlic, ground cumin and the ground coriander seeds. Fry, stirring, over a medium heat for 3–4 minutes. Add the lentils, salt and water. Cover the pot and simmer for about 1 hour, or until the lentils are soft.

Mill or liquidize the soup, then return to the pot. Finely chop the coriander, parsley or mint leaves and add them, with the lemon juice, to the soup. Bring to the boil and simmer for 10 minutes more. Add the garam masala and serve hot. Stir in cold yoghurt to taste immediately before serving.

CORIANDER KHICHIRI

This is a traditional dish from western India which is often served as an evening meal, since it is nourishing and easily digestible. There are many variations, but generally the beans are cooked with the onions and spices and the rice is added later. Try making the recipe with other spices such as cumin, mustard seeds or cardamom, or add chillies or chilli powder to taste. Serve with a sour pickle or chutney and some raita.

175 g/6 oz mung beans
250 g/8 oz short grain brown rice
20 g/¾ oz fresh root ginger, chopped
2 level teaspoons coriander, ground
2 teaspoons salt
4 tablespoons vegetable oil *or* ghee
2 large onions, chopped
600 ml/1 pint water
black pepper
1 bunch coriander *or* parsley leaves, chopped

Soak the beans and the rice separately for 2 hours. Fry the ginger, ground coriander seeds and salt in the oil or ghee for 1–2 minutes before adding the onions. Continue to cook for another 5 minutes. Next, add the strained mung beans with the 600 ml (1 pint) water. Simmer these ingredients for 30 minutes in a covered pan, and then add the strained rice. Continue to cook for a further 20 minutes, by which time the rice and beans should be cooked and all the water absorbed. Add a little more water and cook for a little longer if necessary, or, if the mixture seems too liquid, take the lid off the pot and boil off the excess water. Season with pepper.

Just before serving, mix in the chopped coriander or parsley leaves.

Spicy tastes: Coriander seeds

PRUNE AND ALMOND TART FLAVOURED WITH CORIANDER

Many variations of this tart can be made. It is worth experimenting with different combintions of dried fruits and nuts, such as pine nuts, walnuts and cashews, and spices, for instance cinnamon and ginger.

filling
250 g/8 oz dried prunes
juice of 1 lemon
90 g/3 oz almonds, ground
1 level tablespoon coriander seeds, ground

crust
250 g/8 oz wholewheat flour
125 g/4 oz vegetable margarine *plus* 15 g/½ oz
4 tablespoons cold water

Soak the prunes, in just enough water to cover them, for about 3 hours. Make the pastry in the usual way (see p.218) and leave in the bottom of the refrigerator while you make the filling. Preheat the oven to 180° C (350° F, gas mark 4).

Drain the prunes, reserving the water. Remove the stones and blend the fruit into a puree with the lemon juice and half the soaking water. Mix in the ground almonds and ground coriander seeds. Roll out the pastry and line a greased 25 cm (10 in) flan dish. Spread the filling evenly inside the pastry case and cover with a decorative lattice made from leftover scraps of pastry. Dot the surface of the tart with vegetable margarine. Bake for 35 minutes.

FRESH PEACH AND APRICOT CRUMBLE

The ground coriander and apricot kernels add an interesting flavour to this crumble mixture, which might otherwise be rather bland. Ground almonds are another interesting addition to a fruit crumble topping. You can use other soft fruit besides peaches and apricots for the filling.

500 g/1 lb apricots
150 ml/¼ pint water
1–2 teaspoons honey
juice of 1 small lemon
500 g/1 lb peaches

crumble
150 g/5 oz soft oatflakes
60 g/2 oz wheatgerm
125 g/4 oz vegetable margarine *plus* 15 g/½ oz
1 heaped teaspoon coriander seeds
a few apricot kernels
60 g/2 oz brown sugar

Halve the apricots and simmer them for a few minutes in the water with the honey and lemon juice. Slice the peaches and add them, uncooked, to the apricot mixture. Preheat the oven to 180° C (350° F, gas mark 4).

To make the crumble, mix together the oatflakes and wheatgerm. Rub in the margarine until the mixture is coarse and crumb-like. Grind the coriander seeds with the apricot kernels in a mortar. Add them, with the brown sugar, to the crumble mixture. Grease a shallow ovenproof dish and spoon the fruit mixture into it. Press the crumble mixture on top and dot with a few pieces of margarine. Bake for 35 minutes.

CORIANDER MARMALADE

This recipe can also be used with other marmalade fruits apart from oranges. The long soaking period means that the marmalade need only be boiled for a short time, thus preserving most of the flavour of the fruit. The amount of sugar can be reduced if you add artificial pectin to aid the setting process, but if you do so you must keep the marmalade in the refrigerator. This recipe makes about 4.5 kg (10 lb) marmalade.

2.7 kg/6 lb eating oranges *or* a mixture of oranges, lemons *and* grapefruit
1.25 litres/2 pints cold water
15 g/½ oz coriander seeds
2.3 kg/5 lb demerara sugar

Slice the flesh and then the peel of the fruit – thinly for fine cut marmalade and more coarsely for thick cut – having carefully removed the pith. Keep the peel to one side and put the chopped fruit in a large bowl; cover with the water. Lightly crush the coriander seeds, put them in a muslin bag along with the fruit pips and leave this bag in the soaking water. (Do not remove it until the marmalade is ready to be bottled.) Leave the bowl to stand for 24 hours.

After this time, pour all the ingredients into a preserving pan and bring them slowly up to the boil. Then pour them back into the bowl and leave to stand for another 24 hours. Return the fruit to the preserving pan and again bring slowly to the boil. At the same time warm the sugar and the clean jam jars in the oven. When the fruit has reached boiling point, add the sugar and allow the mixture to boil rapidly until setting point is reached (to ascertain setting point, put a spoonful of marmalade on to a cold saucer and see whether it gels as it cools).

Pour the marmalade into the warmed jars and cover each jar with a waxed circle. Allow to cool thoroughly before securing the jars with cellophane covers and elastic bands.

Cumin

There are two kinds of cumin seeds used in cookery – black and white. The latter are actually very pale brown and look rather like caraway seeds. Both kinds have a very strong flavour and should be used with discretion. White cumin seeds are often used in Middle Eastern cookery. Their rather sharp flavour is generally mellowed by dry roasting. Black cumin, commonly used in India, has a more earthy taste. As well as being a standard ingredient in garam masala and curry powder mixtures, it is often the main flavour of the Indian condiment called tarka which is used to enliven lentil dishes.

LENTILS SERVED WITH CUMIN TARKA

Tarka is a crisp, spicy mixture which is added to a lentil dhal on serving. Red, green or brown lentils may be used for this dish. Yoghurt or raita makes a good addition to the meal.

350 g/12 oz lentils
2 large onions, chopped
4 tablespoons vegetable oil *or* ghee
1 tablespoon salt, *or* more to taste
600 ml/1 pint water

tarka
2 long red chillies, chopped
a 5 cm/2 in piece fresh root ginger, grated
3 tablespoons vegetable oil *or* ghee
1 heaped tablespoon cumin seeds

If using green or brown lentils, soak them for 1–2 hours, if possible, to cut down the cooking time. Wash them thoroughly. (There is no need to soak red lentils.) Fry the onions in the oil or ghee for 10 minutes. Add the lentils, salt and water. Bring to the boil, then turn down the heat and simmer the lentils until reduced to a puree. Turn off the heat before the mixture becomes too dry.

To make the tarka, fry the chillies and ginger rather slowly in the oil or ghee for a few minutes. Turn up the heat slightly and add the cumin seeds. Fry, stirring, until they begin to pop. By this time the ginger and chillies should be slightly crisp and well cooked. Serve the lentils in individual bowls and spoon some tarka on to each bowl.

RATATOUILLE QUICHE
FLAVOURED WITH CUMIN

crust
200 g/7 oz wholewheat flour *or* a combination of wholewheat *and* plain white
100 g/3½ oz vegetable margarine
4 tablespoons cold water

filling
500 g/1 lb aubergines
1 tablespoon cumin seeds, roasted
1 medium onion, finely chopped
2 green peppers weighing together about 250 g/8 oz, finely chopped
3 tablespoons vegetable oil
4 cloves garlic, chopped
250 g/8 oz tomatoes, chopped
250 g/8 oz mild Cheddar *or* Cheshire *or* Gouda cheese, grated
salt
2 level teaspoons hot *or* sweet paprika
2 level tablespoons sesame seeds

Make the pastry in the usual way (see p. 218) and chill it in the refrigerator for 15 minutes.

Grill the aubergines whole, turning them until they are completely soft. Put them under the cold tap and then take off their skins. Roughly chop the flesh, put it in a sieve with a sprinkling of salt and leave on one side. Preheat the oven to 180° C (350° F, gas mark 4)

Grease a 25 cm (10 in) circular flan or tin dish and line it with the pastry. Grind the roasted cumin with a pestle. Fry the onion and peppers in the oil over a medium heat for 10–15 minutes. Add the garlic and tomatoes. Press the aubergines in the sieve with the back of a wooden spoon so that the bitter juices are squeezed out and add them, with the roasted cumin, to the pan. Cover the pan and leave it to cook over a low heat for about 20 minutes.

Combine the grated cheese with the ratatouille mixture. Season with salt and paprika. Put this filling into the pastry case, top with sesame seeds and bake for 25 minutes. Serve hot or cold.

KASHMIRI PULLAO

This method of cooking rice is popular in Northern India and Iran. The rice is cooked with spices and other ingredients in a tightly lidded vessel, which means that none of the flavour is lost. Fine-quality rice such as basmati is often used. Serve the dish with a vegetable and yoghurt or raita.

500 g/1 lb long grain brown rice
4 tablespoons vegetable oil *or* ghee
1 level tablespoon black cumin seeds
2 medium onions, finely chopped
3–4 small chillies, chopped
200 ml/⅓ pint hot water
3 teaspoons salt
125 g/4 oz almond halves
125 g/4 oz cashew halves
125 g/4 oz raisins

Soak the rice in cold water for 30 minutes. Heat 3 tablespoons of the oil or ghee in a large heavy-bottomed saucepan and fry the cumin seeds for 1–2 minutes. Add the onions and chillies (minus their seeds) and fry for a few minutes more. Drain the rice and add it to the pan. Briefly stir fry the mixture before pouring in the hot water. Add 2 teaspoons of the salt and cover the pot with a tight-fitting lid or a piece of foil pressed tightly round the rim.

Simmer on the top of the stove very gently indeed (you may need to use a heat-diffusing pad) for 25–30 minutes. Add a little more water 10 minutes before the end of cooking if the rice is too dry – with this dish, it is probably better to start off with too little water than too much. When the rice is sufficiently cooked, take the pan off the heat and set it aside for 10 minutes with the lid still on.

Meanwhile, toast the almonds briefly under the grill. Heat the remaining oil in a small frying pan and fry the cashews with the remaining teaspoon of salt. Set the nuts aside and fry the raisins for only 1–2 minutes, so that they swell up. Turn the rice mixture out on to a serving dish and briefly mix in the nuts and raisins.

CUMIN BISCUITS

These plain, savoury biscuits have an unusual flavour which goes well with cheese. This recipe makes about 15 biscuits, so double the quantities if you want to make more (one egg will still be enough, however).

350 g/12 oz wholemeal flour
1 heaped teaspoon salt
150 g/5 oz vegetable margarine
2 tablespoons white cumin seeds, lightly roasted
1 egg, beaten
a little vegetable oil

Preheat the oven to 190° C (375° F, gas mark 5). Mix the flour with the salt and then rub the margarine into the flour. Stir in the roasted cumin seeds. Add the egg and vegetable oil to make a pliable dough. Roll out to just under 1 cm (½ in) thick and cut out the biscuits with a pastry cutter. Bake on a greased tray for 10–15 minutes or until just brown underneath. Cool on a wire rack.

Fennel and anise

Sweet fennel is a tall, perennial plant with feathery leaves and strong-tasting, aromatic seeds. It grows easily in England and the leaves are a useful addition to summer salads. The seeds, however, generally need a warmer climate in which to ripen. They are noted for their digestive properties and often used to be cooked with fish 'to consume their phlegmatic humours', as the herbalist Culpeper put it. At the end of an Indian meal they are usually offered, sometimes with a little sugar, as a digestive. In my opinion the flavour of fennel seeds is rather too dominant, though, for frequent inclusion in vegetarian cookery.

Florence fennel is a cultivated variety of the wild herb, grown especially for the swollen 'bulb' at the base of its stem. It is a delicate-tasting vegetable, especially good when served with a white sauce or au gratin.

Anise is related to fennel, though the seeds are a little sweeter-tasting. Both contain the aromatic oil anethole, as does the completely unrelated but similarly flavoured star anise or aniseed, which can be ground up and used to flavour cakes or desserts, especially those containing dried fruit. The flavour goes well with carrots, and there is scope for using it with other root vegetables like parsnips or turnips.

FLORENCE FENNEL
AND MUSHROOM SOUP

Fennel and mushrooms combine well in this delicately flavoured soup. A little aniseed is used to emphasize the taste of the fennel.

90 g/3 oz vegetable margarine
1 large onion, chopped
1 large bulb fennel, chopped
300 g/10 oz mushrooms, sliced
300 ml/½ pint boiling water
1 level teaspoon aniseed, ground
200 ml/⅓ pint milk
white pepper

garnish
fennel leaves *or* parsley, chopped

Heat the margarine in a soup pot and fry the onion and fennel over a medium heat for 10 minutes. Add the mushrooms to the pan and stir fry for 1–2 minutes. Add the boiling water and the ground aniseed. Cover the pan and simmer the contents for 30 minutes. After this time liquidize the soup, then return it to the pan and stir in the milk. Simmer for a further 5–10 minutes, season well with pepper and serve. Garnish with chopped fennel leaves, if available, or chopped parsley.

FLORENCE FENNEL WITH CARDAMOM SAUCE

500 g/1 lb fennel bulbs
seeds from 6 cardamom pods
60 g/2 oz vegetable margarine
3–4 cloves garlic, crushed
1 heaped tablespoon plain flour
300 ml/½ pint milk
salt
pepper
fennel leaves, chopped
2 heaped tablespoons grated Parmesan cheese

Boil the fennel bulbs in salted water until just soft. Grind the cardamom seeds in a mortar. Melt the margarine and fry the crushed garlic and ground cardamom seeds for 2–3 minutes. Stir in the flour, then gradually add the milk, stirring all the time. When the sauce has thickened, take it off the heat and season with salt, pepper and chopped fennel leaves. Preheat the grill to hot. Slice the cooked fennel bulbs and put them in a gratin dish. Pour the sauce over them and sprinkle the grated cheese over the top. Place under the hot grill for 5 minutes and then serve at once.

Fenugreek

Fenugreek is really a legume, but it is generally used as a spice. The small seeds are rectangular rather than round and have a strong, rather 'meaty' taste. In Indian cookery they are generally used finely ground and lightly roasted. Curry powders sometimes include too much fenugreek, giving them a rather musty flavour – fenugreek is best used in small quantities, in combination with three or four other spices. Alone of the 'curry' spices fenugreek has a rather too powerful smell which tends to hang in the air if used to excess.

Fenugreek leaves, which are often used in Indian vegetable dishes and chutneys, have a strong and interesting taste. The seeds can easily be sprouted and eaten like mung beansprouts.

Nutmeg

Nutmeg and mace, which is the dried outer covering of the nutmeg, come from a South-east Asian tree. They have a similar flavour, which is widely employed in both European and Far Eastern cookery. Nutmeg is useful in savoury dishes as well as sweet ones: it is well known as a component of mixed spice and as a flavouring for cakes, it is also delicious with certain cooked green vegetables like spinach, leeks and Brussels sprouts. Milk and cheese dishes, too, are often enhanced by a flavouring of nutmeg. Except in baked dishes, nutmeg is usually added towards the end of the cooking time.

Nutmegs should always be bought whole and grated, just before use, directly into the dish which they are to flavour. Whole nutmegs should be stored in a screw-top jar, where they will keep in good condition almost indefinitely.

CARROT AND NUTMEG SOUP

2 onions, chopped
4–5 cloves garlic, chopped
60 g/2 oz vegetable margarine
700 g/1½ lb carrots, chopped
500 ml/18 fl oz water
1 tablespoon salt
1 level teaspoon nutmeg, finely grated
black *or* white pepper
150 g/5 oz Greek yoghurt *or* 150 ml/¼ pint single cream

garnish
parsley *or* coriander leaves, finely chopped

Fry the onions and garlic in the margarine for about 5 minutes. Add the carrots and water. Stir in the salt and half the nutmeg, and bring the mixture to the boil. Cover, and allow to simmer for 45 minutes. Then sieve or liquidize the soup, return it to the pan and add the rest of the nutmeg. Season to taste with pepper, take the pan off the heat and stir in the yoghurt or cream. Garnish with the parsley or coriander leaves, and serve hot.

SPINACH AND LEEK TART FLAVOURED WITH NUTMEG

crust
250 g/8 oz wholewheat flour
125 g/4 oz vegetable margarine
4 tablespoons cold water

filling
500 g/1 lb spinach leaves, stripped off the stalk
200 ml/⅓ pint milk *plus* 2 tablespoons
250 g/8 oz leeks
30 g/1 oz vegetable margarine *plus* 15 g/½ oz
2 cloves garlic, crushed
60 g/2 oz plain white flour
125 g/4 oz Gouda *or* Gruyère cheese, grated
60 g/2 oz Parmesan cheese, grated
½ teaspoon nutmeg, grated
black pepper
salt
1 egg, beaten
30 g/1 oz sesame seeds

Make the pastry in the usual way (see p. 218) and set it aside in the refrigerator while you make the filling. Preheat the oven to 180° C (350° F, gas mark 4).

Cook the spinach to a puree with the 2 tablespoons of milk. Wash and finely chop the leeks, then blanch them in boiling water for 5 minutes. Melt the 30 g (1 oz) margarine in a pan and fry the garlic for 1–2 minutes. Stir in the flour and gradually add the 200 ml (⅓ pint) milk, stirring all the time to prevent lumps forming. Mix in the grated cheeses, then the pureed spinach and the leeks. Season with nutmeg, pepper and salt. Take the pan off the heat and add the beaten egg. Roll out the pastry and line a greased 25 cm (10 in) flan dish. Pour in the filling, top with sesame seeds and dot with the extra 15 g (½ oz) margarine. Bake for 35 minutes. Serve hot or cold.

Spicy tastes: Nutmeg

LEEK SOUFFLE
FLAVOURED WITH NUTMEG

500 g/1 lb leeks
90 g/3 oz vegetable margarine
60 g/2 oz plain white flour
250 ml/8 fl oz milk
1 level teaspoon salt
white pepper
½ teaspoon nutmeg, grated
75 g/2½ oz Parmesan cheese, grated
4 eggs
15 g/½ oz fresh breadcrumbs, finely grated

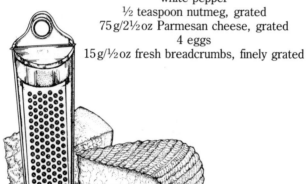

Preheat the oven to 200° C (400° F, gas mark 6). Wash and trim the leeks and cook them in boiling, salted water for 5 minutes. Put them in a liquidizer with a very little water and blend. Make a thick sauce by melting the margarine and stirring in the flour. Add the milk gradually, keeping the heat low and stirring all the time to prevent lumps forming. When the sauce has thickened take the pan off the heat and stir in the pureed leeks, salt, pepper, nutmeg and most of the cheese. Separate the eggs and stir in the yolks.

Thoroughly grease a 1.5 litre (2½ pint) casserole dish and scatter the bottom with half the breadcrumbs. Beat the egg whites in a separate basin until they are stiff. Make sure that the oven has reached the required temperature, then take a large tablespoon of the stiffened egg whites and beat it in with the rest of the ingredients. Fold in the rest of the egg whites as lightly as possible with a metal spoon and pour the mixture into the soufflé dish. Top with the remaining grated cheese and a generous sprinkling of breadcrumbs. Put the soufflé into the oven immediately and bake for 25 minutes (if the top of the soufflé seems to be browning too quickly, cover it with a piece of foil). Serve at once.

DUTCH TOAST

This dish tastes more interesting than the simple ingredients suggest – the nutmeg seems to work some strange alchemy on the other ingredients! Serve it with a green salad, or with leeks or courgettes.

a 500 g/1 lb wholemeal loaf
600 ml/1 pint milk
1 teaspoon salt
pepper
½ teaspoon nutmeg, grated
1 egg, beaten
350 g/12 oz Dutch cheese, thinly sliced *plus* 30 g/1 oz, grated
1 bunch spring onions, chopped
15 g/½ oz vegetable margarine

Preheat the oven to 170° C (325° F, gas mark 3). Cut the loaf into slices about 2 cm (¾ in) thick and then cut them in half. Grate the end crusts as breadcrumbs. Mix the milk with the salt, pepper to taste, nutmeg and egg. Grease a shallow casserole dish. Briefly soak half the bread slices in the milk mixture, then place them in the bottom of the dish. Add a layer of cheese slices and spring onions. Soak the rest of the bread and make a third layer, finishing off with another layer of cheese. Pour any remaining liquid over these layers, and top with the grated cheese and a few dots of vegetable margarine. Bake for 30 minutes.

Saffron

Saffron has been cultivated in the Eastern Mediterranean and the Near East for thousands of years, and in Britain since the Middle Ages. It is made from the dried stamens of *crocus sativus* (not the wild meadow crocus, which is poisonous), and tens of thousands of stamens are needed to make a single ounce. As these all have to be collected by hand, saffron is an expensive commodity and has often been sold adulterated with cheaper substances.

It has always been valued for its distinctive, somewhat bitter flavour and for its brilliant yellow colouring properties. In the East, yellow is associated with happiness and good fortune, so saffron and turmeric have always been much in demand, especially for festive rice dishes.

You only need to use a minute quantity of saffron to achieve flavour and colour, which is fortunate in view of its cost. It should first be steeped in warm water or milk so that it is thoroughly diffused throughout the dish in which it is used.

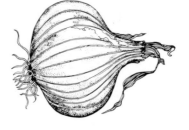

SAFFRON RISOTTO

This is a speciality of Milan which makes a good lunch dish when served with plenty of green salad. I have used brown rice here instead of the usual white.

2 onions, chopped
60 g/2 oz butter *or* vegetable margarine
350 g/12 oz long grain rice
600 ml/1 pint hot water
2 pinches saffron soaked in 150 ml/¼ pint warm water
60 g/2 oz Parmesan cheese, grated

Fry the chopped onions in the fat for about 5 minutes. Add the rice and fry, stirring, for 2–3 minutes. Pour in half the hot water and leave the rice to simmer until the water is nearly absorbed. Add the rest of the hot water and repeat the process. Finally pour in the saffron together with the soaking water and cook until this liquid too has been absorbed. The finished risotto should be moist, but with the rice grains still separate. Lightly mix in the Parmesan cheese and serve.

Spicy tastes: Saffron

PERSIAN RICE WITH SAFFRON, CARROTS AND ALMONDS

Persian 'polo' rice dishes are authentically made with basmati or other fine-quality rice which is soaked, boiled and then steamed. You can also use a good-quality long grain brown rice.

500 g/1 lb basmati *or* long grain brown rice
2 pinches saffron
100 ml/4 fl oz milk
125 g/4 oz vegetable margarine
1 onion, chopped
350 g/12 oz carrots, cut into matchsticks
1 good tablespoon honey
125 g/4 oz split almonds
2 teaspoons salt

Wash the rice, then soak it for 30 minutes. Boil it in plenty of salted water for about 15 minutes, by which time it should be about three-quarters cooked.

While the rice is cooking, steep the saffron in the milk. Melt 60 g (2 oz) of the margarine in a pan and fry the onion and carrots in it for 10 minutes. Stir in the honey. Toast the split almonds under the grill. Drain the rice and mix it well with the saffron milk and salt.

Melt the remaining margarine in the bottom of a large pan and make a layer of half the saffron rice. Arrange the onion, carrot and almonds on top and then cover with the remaining rice. Set the pan over a very low heat (you may need to use a heat-diffusing pad), cover with a lid or large plate and stretch a cloth underneath the lid to absorb any evaporating liquid. Cook for 20 minutes, by which time the rice should be quite soft.

SAFFRON BUNS

This recipe for Saffron buns, a traditional Cornish speciality, makes about 18.

2 teaspoons dried yeast
150 ml/¼ pint warm water
90 g/3 oz brown sugar
300 ml/½ pint milk
125 g/4 oz vegetable margarine
2 generous pinches saffron
700 g/1½ lb 80% wholewheat flour
1 teaspoon salt
125 g/4 oz currants
125 g/4 oz mixed peel

glaze (optional)
2 heaped tablespoons brown sugar
4–5 tablespoons milk

Dissolve the yeast in the warm water with 1 tablespoon of the sugar, and leave to stand for 10 minutes. Boil the milk, and add 60 g (2 oz) of the margarine and the saffron strands. Allow to cool to finger temperature before adding the yeast mixture. Mix together the flour and salt, then stir them into the yeast mixture. Mix in the currants, peel and the rest of the sugar. Knead well, and leave the dough to rise in a warm place for 1 hour.

After this time, knead again, for about 5 minutes, working in the rest of the margarine as you do so. Leave to rise for a further 30 minutes. Knock down the dough and divide in into 18 pieces. Form each into a round bun and leave to rise, covered, on greased oven trays until they have at least doubled in size (this will not take very long). Preheat the oven to 200° C (400° F, gas mark 6).

Bake the buns for 20 minutes. If you want to glaze them, dissolve the brown sugar in the milk and brush it over the buns while they are still hot.

Turmeric

The turmeric plant is related to ginger, and in both plants most of the flavour is contained in the root or rhizome, which is the part used in cookery. Turmeric can be bought as a whole, dried rhizome, but since this is very hard to grind it is better, in the case of this spice, to buy small quantities of ready ground powder.

Turmeric has a warm, spicy flavour and contains a strong yellow dye which colours any dish in which it is used. It is frequently used in Indian and Far Eastern dishes for both its colour and taste – always, as far as I know, in combination with other spices. Indian cooks often tend to overdo the turmeric; I prefer to use between a pinch and a level teaspoon in a dish.

Dried mushroom flavours

CHINESE BLACK AND SHIITAKE MUSHROOMS

EUROPEAN MUSHROOMS

Chinese black and shiitake mushrooms

The full, rather 'meaty' flavour of dried mushrooms is a very useful addition to vegetarian cookery. Since they do not seem to fit into any of the categories of taste and flavour previously described in this book, I have given them a short chapter on their own.

In the Far East, species of fungi such as the Japanese shiitake mushroom and the Chinese black mushroom are specially cultivated for drying. Fungi contain a very high proportion of water, so when this water has evaporated in drying they acquire a highly concentrated flavour: 15g (½oz) is generally enough for a single dish. Shiitake mushrooms – essential for capturing the authentic flavour of many Japanese dishes – can be used even more sparingly.

All dried mushrooms should be soaked in cold water for about 30 minutes before being cooked. Sometimes, for example in bean salads, they can be chopped up and eaten raw and their interesting texture appreciated. They are excellent in casseroles and other slow cooked dishes because they always keep their taste and texture, however long the cooking period.

Dried mushroom flavours: Chinese black and shiitake

SHIITAKE MUSHROOM
AND SPRING TURNIP SOUP

This combination of dried mushrooms and turnips is surprisingly tasty. Turnips are best in the spring and early summer when they are still small.

30 g/1 oz dried shiitake mushrooms
600 ml/1 pint water
4 tablespoons soy sauce, *or* to taste
4 large cloves garlic
2 medium onions
500 g/1 lb turnips
3 tablespoons vegetable margarine
1 small bunch parsley, finely chopped

to serve
English *or* Dutch cheese, grated

Soak the mushrooms in the water with 2 tablespoons of the soy sauce for 30 minutes. Chop the garlic, onions and turnips (finely if you do not want to liquidize the finished soup). Simmer the onions and garlic in the margarine for 10 minutes, then add the turnips, mushrooms and the water in which they were soaked. Bring all the ingredients to the boil, lower the heat and leave to simmer for 45 minutes. After this time, pour the pan contents into a liquidizer if you want a smooth, pureed soup. Return the mixture to the pan and add the remaining soy sauce and the parsley.

Serve hot with an accompanying bowl of grated cheese to sprinkle over the top.

BROWN RICE COOKED WITH
SHIITAKE MUSHROOMS AND SEAWEED

Shiitake mushrooms and dried seaweeds are highly valued in Japan for their health-giving properties. A meal like this is a good one to cook when people have been eating too much rich or sweet food, as at Christmas.

25 g/about ¾ oz dried shiitake mushrooms
10 g/about ¼ oz seaweed, e.g. hiziki *or* dulse
600 ml/1 pint water
1 large onion
3 tablespoons vegetable oil
500 g/1 lb short grain brown rice
90 g/3 oz sesame seeds
125 g/4 oz beansprouts

to serve
soy sauce to taste

Soak the mushrooms and seaweed in the water for 30 minutes. Chop the onion and fry in the oil for 5 minutes. Take the seaweed and mushrooms out of the soaking water (retaining the water), and cut them into small pieces. Add the rice, mushrooms and seaweed to the onion and stir fry them for a few minutes. Pour in the soaking water. Cover the pan with a few layers of cloth, turn the heat right down and leave to cook over a very low heat until all the water has been absorbed (this will take 20–25 minutes).

Roast the sesame seeds under the grill while the rice is cooking. Add them, together with the beansprouts, to the cooked rice mixture when it has cooled a little. Serve with soy sauce.

Dried mushroom flavours: Chinese black and shiitake

FRIED RICE WITH
DRIED MUSHROOMS AND MANGETOUTS

In Chinese cookery, rice is often boiled and then fried with vegetables and seasonings. This dish has a good colour and texture as well as an interesting flavour.

15 g/½ oz dried shiitake *or* Chinese black mushrooms
500 g/1 lb brown rice, long *or* short grain
175 g/6 oz mangetouts
3 large red chillies
5 cloves garlic
2 bulbs lemon grass
3 tablespoons vegetable oil
4 tablespoons soy sauce

Put the mushrooms in a bowl with just enough water to cover them. Boil the rice in the usual way (see p. 214). Top and tail the mangetout pods, slice them diagonally and plunge them into boiling water to cook for about 5 minutes, or until soft. Chop the chillies without their seeds, garlic and lemon grass, and fry them in the oil for 2–3 minutes over a low heat. Add the cooked rice and stir fry for a few minutes more. Add the drained mushrooms and the mangetout pods. Stir the ingredients loosely together and heat the dish through for a few minutes. Season with soy sauce and serve.

European mushrooms

The kinds of European mushrooms most commonly used for drying are the morel and *Boletus edulis* (cèpes and porcini). These mushrooms are usually gathered wild from the woods and forests, since they grow only in association with certain trees.

They are very useful for adding flavour to vegetable stocks and soups, and European dried mushrooms can be used in sauces, especially for pasta. Many cultivated fresh mushrooms are rather lacking in flavour, but they can be improved by the addition of a few dried ones.

BUCKWHEAT COOKED WITH DRIED MUSHROOMS

The Russians, for whom buckwheat was for centuries the staple diet, have a saying that 'You can't spoil kasha [buckwheat] with butter', so you may well wish to add extra butter or vegetable margarine to the finished dish.

15 g/½ oz dried mushrooms
1 litre/1¾ pints water
500 g/1 lb buckwheat, roasted
2 tablespoons vegetable oil
1 celery heart, chopped
90 g/3 oz vegetable margarine
4–5 cloves garlic, chopped
salt
black pepper

garnish
bunch spring onions, chopped

Soak the dried mushrooms in the water for 20 minutes. Remove the mushrooms, retaining the water, and cut them into small pieces. Boil the water in which the mushrooms were soaked. Put the buckwheat in a heavy pan and fry it in the oil for 1–2 minutes. Add the boiling water and the chopped mushrooms and simmer until all the liquid is absorbed, which should take about 10 minutes. Meanwhile, fry the celery separately in the margarine for 5 minutes. Add the chopped garlic and fry for 1–2 minutes more. Combine these ingredients with the buckwheat and mushrooms, season well with salt and pepper, and garnish with chopped spring onions.

POTATO
AND DRIED MUSHROOM GRATIN

2 celeriacs weighing together about 700 g/1½ lb
500 g/1 lb potatoes
10 g/about ¼ oz dried mushrooms
1 medium onion
3–4 cloves garlic
90 g/3 oz vegetable margarine
2 tablespoons plain white flour
600 ml/1 pint milk
1 tablespoon Dijon mustard
1½ teaspoons salt
white pepper
30 g/1 oz parsley, chopped
125 g/4 oz Gouda *or* Gruyère *or* Cheshire cheese, grated

Scrub and par-boil the celeriac and potatoes. Cook the celeriac for about 30 minutes and the potatoes for about 15. Soak the dried mushrooms in just enough water to cover them. Chop the onion and garlic and fry them in the margarine for 10 minutes. Drain the dried mushrooms, chop them and add to the onion. Stir in the flour and gradually add the milk, stirring all the time until the sauce thickens. Add the mustard, salt, pepper, parsley and 90 g (3 oz) of the cheese. Stir well until the cheese has melted, and then take the sauce off the heat. Preheat the oven to 190° C (375° F, gas mark 5).

Peel and slice the celeriac, and slice the potatoes. Grease a casserole dish and arrange in it alternate layers of celeriac and potatoes, pouring some sauce over each layer. Top with the remaining cheese and bake for 35 minutes.

Dried mushroom flavours: European mushrooms

MUSHROOM SAUCE

This is excellent with wholewheat pasta.

15 g/½ oz dried mushrooms
2 medium onions, finely chopped
4 cloves garlic, finely chopped
2 tablespoons vegetable margarine
1 heaped tablespoon plain flour
300 ml/½ pint milk
125 g/4 oz Gouda *or* mild Cheddar cheese, grated
white pepper

to serve
parsley, chopped

Soak the mushrooms in cold water for 30 minutes. Fry the onions and garlic in the margarine for 10 minutes. Stir in the flour and then gradually add the milk, continuing to stir. Chop the mushrooms a little and add them, with the cheese, to the sauce. Simmer over a low heat for a further 10 minutes. Season with pepper and serve with plenty of chopped parsley to sprinkle over the top.

DUXELLES

Duxelles is a mixture of mushrooms and shallots, which is used in French cookery as a base for sauces. Dried mushrooms add extra flavour to the recipe below, from which excellent wine and cream sauces can be made. The mixture can be stored in the refrigerator for several days and the quantities given below are enough to make 3 or 4 different sauces.

A very good, quick sauce can be made by simmering about a third of the Duxelles mixture with 300 ml (½ pint) of water and a wineglass of white wine, seasoned with pepper and herbs.

15 g/½ oz dried mushrooms
150 ml/¼ pint hot water
300 g/10 oz shallots *or* onions, finely chopped
3 tablespoons vegetable margarine
350 g/12 oz fresh mushrooms, finely chopped
1 teaspoon salt

Soak the dried mushrooms in the hot water for 20 minutes. Fry the shallots or onions in the margarine for 5 minutes. Add the fresh mushrooms and the dried mushrooms, plus the water in which they were soaked and the salt. Simmer these ingredients for 15–20 minutes in an open pan until most of the liquid has been boiled off. Cool, and store in the refrigerator.

Alcoholic flavours

VINEGAR
WHITE WINE, RED WINE AND
CIDER

Vine

Vinegar

Vinegar is literally 'sour wine' (*vin aigre*) It is commonly made from red or white grapes, from beer (malt vinegar), cider or, in the Far East, rice wine. The simple chemistry of making vinegar involves leaving an alcoholic substance exposed to the air so that the alcohol combines with oxygen to form acetic acid. The actual process is made more complicated, though, in order to produce a vinegar which is not merely sour but also has more subtle and palatable characteristics. Vinegar readily absorbs additional flavours, and herb or flower vinegars can easily be made at home by steeping the plant material in the vinegar (see recipe for tarragon vinegar on p.131).

In European cookery, vinegar is usually an ingredient of salad dressings and, because of its preservative qualities, a very useful pickling medium. For the latter purpose a wine vinegar, which has a relatively high acetic acid content, should be used. For everyday use I prefer cider vinegar, which has a soft flavour. Malt vinegars should be used only for making pickles and chutneys, and never in salad dressings. All vinegars have antibiotic qualities, but those of cider vinegar are said to be of particular value to health.

VINEGAR PICKLE

This pickle is simple to make. The vegetables are sprinkled with salt and left to stand for a day, after which they are packed into jars and covered with vinegar. Mustard seeds and peppercorns help the preserving process.

90 g/3 oz carrots, chopped
125 g/4 oz cauliflower, cut into florets
90 g/3 oz runner beans, chopped
2 small sticks celery, chopped
2 small green apples, chopped
125 g/4 oz shallots *or* small onions, chopped
3 level tablespoons salt
2 large cloves garlic, chopped
15 g/½ oz fresh root ginger, crushed
about 250 ml/8 fl oz white wine vinegar
1 tablespoon mustard seeds
a few black peppercorns
5 tablespoons brown sugar *or* more for a sweeter pickle

Arrange the carrots, cauliflower, runner beans, celery, apples and shallots or onions in layers in a colander or sieve, sprinkling each layer with salt. Leave for 24 hours, for the salt to draw out the vegetable juices. Then mix the garlic and ginger with the vegetables. Boil up the vinegar with the mustard seeds, peppercorns and sugar. Pack the vegetables into a perfectly clean 750 ml (1¼ pint) Kilner jar and pour over them the vinegar and spices. Make sure that the vinegar entirely covers the vegetables and that it fills the jar right to the top. Press the vegetables well down to exclude all the air bubbles.

Leave in a warm place for 2 weeks. After this time you can transfer the pickle to smaller, airtight jars if you wish, again filling the jars right up to the top to exclude as much air as possible.

This pickle improves with age and should be stored for 1–2 months before eating. After this time, store at cool room temperature, keeping the vegetables covered with vinegar.

Alcoholic flavours: Vinegar

White wine, red wine and cider

Cooking with wine is characteristic of Italian, French and Spanish cookery. Traditional English dishes are sometimes cooked with beer or cider, and in the Far East rice wines are often used to flavour sweet and sour dishes. The use of alcohol in cooking is, in fact, common all over the world except where the prevailing religion specifically forbids its use.

Most people associate wine cookery with the preparation of meat or fish, but in fact many vegetables can also be transformed by being cooked in wine – the smell and taste of wine cookery is much too good to be missed by vegetarians. Vegetables like cauliflower and mushrooms are delicious when stewed with wine and herbs, and a little red wine transforms a vegetable casserole. Wine sauces and salad dressings are also within the scope of vegetarian cookery.

When wine is used in cookery, the alcohol content is usually boiled off but the flavour of the wine imparts a delicious taste to the rest of the ingredients. The better the wine, of course, the better the flavour, but there is no need to be too purist about this. Excellent results can be obtained without spending a fortune.

VEGETABLE AND RED WINE CASSEROLE

500 g/1 lb leeks, sliced
500 g/1 lb parsnips, sliced
250 g/8 oz carrots, sliced
250 g/8 oz mushrooms, sliced
75 g/2½ oz parsley, finely chopped
4 tablespoons vegetable oil
6 cloves garlic, chopped
1 heaped tablespoon plain flour
400 ml/¾ pint warm water
400 ml/¾ pint red wine
1 teaspoon dried thyme
2 teaspoons tomato concentrate
black pepper
1 teaspoon salt

Preheat the oven to 150° C (300° F, gas mark 2). Arrange the leeks, parsnips, carrots, mushrooms and parsley in a large, well-greased casserole. Put the oil in a large pan and add the chopped garlic. Fry for a few minutes before stirring in the flour. Gradually stir in the warmed water and then the red wine. Season with thyme, tomato concentrate and plenty of black pepper, and leave to simmer for 10 minutes. Pour the sauce over the vegetables and season with salt.

Cover the casserole with a lid or with foil and cook in the oven for about 1½ hours. Take off the lid or foil for the last 30 minutes of cooking. (There is never any harm in cooking a casserole very slowly – the longer the cooking time, the more the flavours blend. So if you are preparing this casserole well in advance, do not hesitate to halve the oven temperature and double the cooking time.)

MUSHROOMS COOKED IN WHITE WINE AND TOMATO SAUCE

This dish can be served as an hors d'oeuvre or, with a little more liquid, as a sauce for pasta. First of all make a basic wine stock, and then use this to cook the mushrooms with the addition of garlic and tomato puree.

wine stock
1 small onion, chopped
a few peppercorns
1 bay leaf
1 sprig fresh thyme *or* savory *or* marjoram
a little celery, chopped
1 wineglass white wine *plus* water to make up 500 ml/18 fl oz

3 cloves garlic, chopped
60 g/2 oz vegetable margarine
350 g/12 oz button mushrooms
2 tablespoons tomato puree (from a packet)
1 teaspoon tomato concentrate
salt
black pepper

Put all the ingredients for the stock in a pan and bring to the boil. Simmer rapidly until the liquid is reduced by half. Strain and put on one side.

Fry the garlic (using the same pan) in the margarine. Add the mushrooms, and turn them in the margarine and garlic mixture for 2–3 minutes. Pour the wine stock over the mixture and stir in the tomato puree and concentrate. Simmer gently for 15-20 minutes, by which time the liquid should be reduced to a thick sauce. Season with salt and pepper to taste. Serve hot or cold.

CAULIFLOWER COOKED IN WHITE WINE WITH CROUTONS

6 tablespoons olive *or* vegetable oil
4 shallots *or* 1 small onion, chopped
4 cloves garlic, chopped
1 large cauliflower, cut into florets
about 12 capers
150 ml/¼ pint white wine
150 ml/¼ pint water
1 teaspoon salt
black *or* white pepper
½ small wholemeal loaf for croutons
oil for frying croutons
1 teaspoon plain white flour
3 heaped tablespoons grated Parmesan cheese
bunch parsley, chopped

Pour the oil into a large cast iron frying pan, add the shallots or onion and fry over a low heat for 5 minutes. Add the garlic, cauliflower and capers. Turn the cauliflower in the oil mixture for 5 minutes more, then add the wine and water. Season with salt and plenty of pepper and cover the pan with a tight-fitting lid (a china plate placed over the pan will do). Leave to simmer for about 15 minutes, or until the cauliflower is soft.

Meanwhile, cut the bread into 2.5 cm (1 in) cubes and fry in the oil until golden. Keep the croutons warm in a low oven while finishing the cauliflower dish.

Take the cauliflower out of the pan and add the flour to the sauce. Raise the heat and stir the sauce rapidly for 1–2 minutes to thicken and reduce it. Take the pan off the heat and combine with the sauce the cauliflower, 2 heaped tablespoons of the cheese and the chopped parsley.

Turn the mixture into a warmed dish and sprinkle the rest of the cheese over it. Pile the croutons on to the cauliflower mixture and serve hot.

BUTTER BEANS COOKED IN CIDER

300 g/10 oz dried butter beans
125 g/4 oz vegetable margarine
2 large onions, chopped
4 cloves garlic, chopped
1 celery heart, chopped
500 g/1 lb courgettes, chopped
2 teaspoons salt
2 teaspoons dried oregano *or* 1 bouquet garni
600 ml/1 pint dry cider
1 tablespoon Dijon mustard
2 teaspoons sweet paprika
200 ml/⅓ pint hot water

Put the beans in a saucepan of water and bring them slowly to the boil. Leave them to soak in the hot water for 2 hours. Then change the water, bring the fresh water to the boil and let the beans simmer for 30 minutes. Melt the margarine in a large pan and fry the onions and garlic for 5 minutes. Add the celery and courgettes and season with salt and oregano or bouquet garni. Stir in the dry cider and simmer the contents of the pan for 10 minutes. Preheat the oven to 170° C (325° F, gas mark 3). Put all the ingredients plus the drained beans into a casserole. Stir in the mustard, paprika and hot water. Cover the casserole with a lid and cook in the oven for about 1½ hours or until the beans are soft. Add a little more water during this time if necessary.

CAULIFLOWER AND GRAPE SALAD WITH WHITE WINE DRESSING

90 g/3 oz almond halves, blanched
1 large cauliflower
½ clove garlic
175 g/6 oz small, seedless grapes
1 bunch spring onions, finely chopped
1 bunch parsley, finely chopped

dressing
5 tablespoons olive *or* sunflower oil
2 cloves garlic, crushed
2½ teaspoons white wine
2 teaspoons Dijon mustard
1 level teaspoon honey
salt
white pepper

Soak the almonds in a bowl of boiling water for at least 1 hour (soaked almonds acquire a pleasing texture which goes well in salads). Cut the cauliflower into florets and cook for just 5 minutes in boiling, salted water.

Rub the salad bowl with the ½ clove of garlic. When the cauliflower is cooked, drain it and put it in the bowl. Add the drained almond halves. Wash and halve the grapes, and mix them with the spring onions and parsley into the other ingredients.

To make the dressing, pour the oil into a bowl and mix in the crushed garlic, white wine, mustard and honey. Season with salt and white pepper to taste. Pour the dressing over the salad some time before serving.

DRIED FRUIT SALAD COOKED WITH RED WINE

350 g/12 oz mixed dried fruit (apricots, apples, peaches, prunes, etc.)
300 ml/½ pint water
200 ml/⅓ pint red wine
6 tablespoons concentrated apple juice
juice of 1 large lemon

to serve
Greek yoghurt *or* cream

Put all the ingredients in a large pan and bring the mixture up to the boil. Turn down the heat and let the pan simmer gently for 15 minutes. Leave the mixture to stand all day or overnight.

Serve with Greek yoghurt or cream.

Composite flavours

BOUQUET GARNI AND FINES HERBES
INDIAN SPICE MIXTURES
OTHER SPICE MIXTURES
SWEET AND SOUR

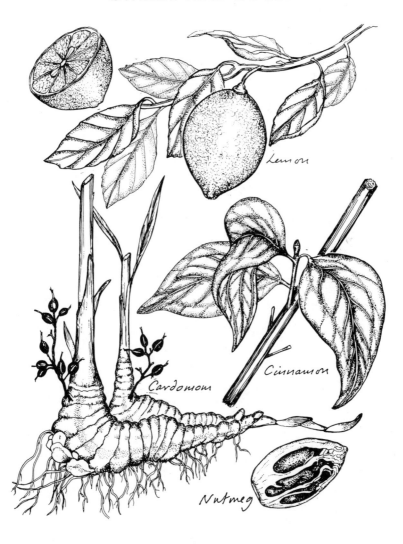

Lemon

Cinnamon

Cardomom

Nutmeg

Bouquet garni and fines herbes

Certain herbs and spices complement each other so well that they have come to be used as a group. French cookery uses these two very popular herb combinations.

A bouquet garni is a bunch of herbs, often tied in a muslin bag, which varies slightly in composition depending on whether it is to be used with vegetables, meat or fish. For vegetarian cookery a bay leaf, a few parsley stalks and a couple of sprigs of thyme will add background flavour to soups and casseroles.

Fines herbes consists of a mixture of fresh parsley, chervil, tarragon and chives, all finely chopped. It is a delicate flavouring used for sauces, egg dishes and mushrooms and can be used in a whole range of vegetable and grain dishes. Fines herbes can be pounded with green leaves such as spinach and watercress to make a mayonnaise base (Sauce Verte). It can also be used in Rémoulade sauce.

It is well worth growing all these herbs in the garden or in pots or boxes and using them throughout the summer.

VEGETABLE STOCK FLAVOURED WITH BOUQUET GARNI

Although vegetable stock may be quickly made from a cube or yeast extract, it is useful to know how to make a tasty one from scratch. It can be used for soups or sauces, or for cooking grains.

1 small onion, chopped
1 bouquet garni
1 carrot, chopped
1 celery stalk, chopped *or* 1 teaspoon celery seeds
a few small pieces dried mushroom
1 tablespoon salt (optional)
a few black peppercorns
800 ml/1⅓ pints water

Put all the ingredients in a pan and bring slowly to the boil. Cover with a lid and simmer very slowly for 1 hour. Strain, and the stock is ready for use.

FINES HERBES SOUFFLE OMELETTE

For each person use:

2 eggs
1 good teaspoon fines herbes – mixture of chervil, parsley,
tarragon *and* chives, all finely chopped
sea salt
white pepper
a little vegetable oil

Preheat the grill. Separate the eggs and beat the whites until they are stiff.
Mix the yolks with the herbs and a little salt and pepper. Fold the egg whites
into the yolk mixture. Heat the oil in a frying pan. Pour in the omelette mixture
and fry, over a medium heat, for 2–3 minutes. Carefully fold the omelette in
half and finish cooking for 1–2 minutes under the grill.

Indian spice mixtures

The word 'curry' derives from a South Indian word meaning to prepare
vegetables, and in Britain the word has come to be used indiscriminately to
denote almost any savoury Indian dish. In India ready mixed and ground curry
powders are rarely used (like sweet mango chutney, they were originally
made for export to England). Instead a selection of spices is prepared to suit
an individual dish. This careful blending of spices for each dish makes Indian
vegetarian cookery at its best the most varied and interesting in the world.

The spices most commonly used are: black pepper, cumin, cardamom,
fresh or dried powdered chillies, ginger, coriander seed, fenugreek, nutmeg,
cloves, turmeric, mustard seeds, kalonji (nigella seed), amchoor, curry
leaves, poppy seeds, cinnamon, asafetida and anardana (dried pomegranate
seeds). Salt is also added, and often a souring agent like tamarind or lemon
juice.

Of these spices, fenugreek and white cumin seeds are generally roasted
before use. Cardamom, cumin, kalonji, fenugreek, coriander, mustard and
poppy seeds are often used whole instead of ground. Coriander and amchoor
can be used in generous quantities because they are mild spices, but turmeric
and fenugreek should be used sparingly (most curry powders tend to overdo
these spices because they are relatively cheap). Nutmeg and cloves, too,
should always be used sparingly because they are so strong. Chillies, which

---

along with ginger and black pepper supply heat to a dish, should be used very much to taste. It is a popular misconception that Indian dishes have to be very hot to be authentic.

Excellent Indian dishes can be made using no more than four or five spices. It is best to get to know a few flavours really well, and then to elaborate. Obviously, the more spices you use, the more variety will be possible. But since Indian cooks have been working on many of their dishes for thousands of years you can't expect to learn this kind of cookery in a few weeks!

SPICY YOGHURT SOUP

A soup made with yoghurt and spices like this one is popular in Gujarat in the west of India.

2 tablespoons vegetable oil *or* ghee
1 large onion, chopped
2–3 green chillies, chopped
15 g/½ oz fresh root ginger, crushed
4 cloves garlic, crushed
2 tablespoons mustard seed, ground
1 teaspoon black cumin seeds
2 teaspoons coriander seeds, ground
450 ml/16 fl oz vegetable stock
300 ml/½ pint yoghurt
1–2 teaspoons brown sugar
2 tablespoons coriander leaves, chopped

Heat the oil or ghee and add the chopped onion and chillies (minus their seeds) and the crushed ginger. After frying these for 2–3 minutes over a very low heat, add the crushed garlic and ground spices. Fry, stirring, for 3–4 minutes. Add the stock and simmer for 15 minutes. Take the pan off the heat and stir in the yoghurt and brown sugar. Add the finely chopped coriander leaves. Warm the soup for a few minutes over a low heat, and serve.

VEGETABLE PULLAO

For a pullao dish, the rice is cooked slowly, with a selection of spices, in a tightly lidded pan. Vegetable pullaos typically include onions, chillies, peas or green beans, but you can experiment with a variety of vegetables. Usually all the vegetables are cooked together with the rice, but I prefer to cook them separately and mix them with the rice afterwards. Serve the dish with a tasty mango chutney.

500 g/1 lb long grain brown rice
1 level tablespoon coriander seeds, ground
1 level teaspoon black cumin seeds, ground
1 teaspoon turmeric
½–1 teaspoon chilli powder (to taste)
a few cardamom pods
1 large or 2 medium onions, finely chopped
3–4 cloves garlic, finely chopped
3 tablespoons vegetable oil or ghee
30 g/1 oz fresh root ginger, chopped and bruised
1 medium red pepper, finely chopped
1 heaped teaspoon salt
200 ml/⅓ pint boiling water
250 g/8 oz fresh peas, shelled or frozen peas
125 g/4 oz mung beansprouts

Soak the rice in cold water for 30 minutes. Mix the ground coriander and cumin with the turmeric and chilli powder. Crack the cardamom pods but leave them whole. Simmer the onions and garlic in the oil or ghee for a few minutes, then add the ground spices and ginger. Stir fry, over a high heat, for a few minutes more.

Drain the rice and stir it in with the rest of the ingredients. Add the chopped red pepper, cardamom pods, salt and boiling water. Cover the pot with a tight-fitting lid, so that no steam can escape (or use a piece of foil, pressed tightly round the rim) and turn down the heat to its lowest setting.

Leave to cook for about 30 minutes, by which time the rice should be soft and all the water absorbed (add a little more boiling water if the rice is not sufficiently cooked, and continue cooking for a little longer). Take the pot off the heat when the rice is ready, and leave it to stand, still covered, for 10 minutes.

Meanwhile, lightly cook the peas in boiling water. Transfer the rice mixture to a serving dish and mix in the peas and beansprouts. You can also remove the cardamom pods at this stage in case the unwary should try to eat them.

PALAK PANEER

This North Indian dish of spicy spinach with cheese demonstrates a typical Indian method of cooking vegetables with strong flavourings, which are offset by the mild-tasting cheese. There are many ways of making a simple cheese from milk: in this case the milk is separated by adding some lemon juice, which imparts a pleasant flavour. It takes only minutes to make this cheese, but start it the evening before you want to eat the dish as two waiting periods are involved. Serve the dish hot with chapatis.

cheese
1.25 litres/2 pints full cream milk
2 tablespoons lemon juice

spinach preparation
1 medium onion, finely chopped
2 cloves garlic, finely chopped
1–2 small red chillies, finely chopped
15 g/½ oz fresh root ginger, chopped *and* bruised
90 g/3 oz vegetable margarine *or* ghee
900 g/2 lb spinach
a little vegetable oil for frying
1–2 tablespoons milk
about ½ teaspoon garam masala

First make the cheese. Bring the milk to the boil, take it off the heat and then add the lemon juice. Leave on one side for the milk solids to separate from the whey. Strain the mixture through a piece of thin, clean muslin and tie the curds up in the muslin to drain overnight. (The liquid whey can be kept for making soup or bread.) Next morning, shape the cheese into a ball, still leaving it inside the cloth. Then let it stand for 1–2 hours pressed between two plates and under a weight (e.g. a cast iron pan). It is then ready for use.

To make the spinach mixture, put the onion, garlic, chilli(es) and ginger in a heavy pan (but not a cast iron one) with the margarine or ghee. Allow to simmer gently for 10 minutes. Add the spinach, washed and trimmed of its thick stalks, and continue to cook slowly for about 15 minutes, stirring occasionally. While the spinach is cooking, cut the cheese into cubes and, in a separate pan, fry it in hot oil so that the outsides of the cubes are just crisp. Add it to the spinach mixture with a few tablespoons of milk. Raise the heat slightly and allow the spinach to simmer until it forms a smooth puree. Add garam masala to taste.

Composite flavours: Indian spice mixtures

GARAM MASALA

Garam masala, literally 'hot mixture', is a combination of warming spices, always added to a dish when it is almost cooked. I imagine this mixture dates from the time before chillies were introduced into India: pepper would have been the main spice used to add heat to a dish, and this 'garam' mixture would have been added as a final seasoning, rather as we add pepper in European cookery.

Most Indian households have their own recipe for garam masala: it usually consists of the stronger, more expensive, spices since not more than 1–2 teaspoons are used at a time. Cardamom, cloves, cinnamon, nutmeg and black cumin as well as black peppercorns are usually included, and perhaps other more unusual ingredients like dried bay leaves and anardana (dried pomegranate seeds) according to personal taste.

Mix up garam masala in very small quantities, as the ground spices will not retain their true flavour for more than a week or two. It is only the work of a few minutes to put the ingredients through a coffee grinder, and it is always useful to have a small supply to add to dishes which lack sparkle.

Here is one possible garam masala mixture, the ingredients of which can be adjusted to suit your own taste:

2 teaspoons black peppercorns
1 teaspoon black cumin seeds
a 7.5 cm/3 in stick cinnamon
12 cloves
seeds from 12 cardamom pods
1 small piece nutmeg (enough to make ½ teaspoon when grated)

Other spice mixtures

The discovery by Europeans of a sea route to the Spice Islands of the Far East, and the subsequent hectic trade in those commodities, has left us with a great variety of recipes which combine spices with our native produce. Mincemeat, fruit cakes and puddings, spiced bread and biscuits are just a few examples. In earlier centuries, spicy meat and vegetable dishes were also familiar in Britain.

A mixed spice combination suitable for cakes may include in varying proportions, ground cinnamon, nutmeg, coriander, ginger, allspice, aniseed and cloves. All these spices, with the exception of ginger which is difficult to dry and grind at home, may be bought whole, ground in small quantities and mixed for use within a few weeks. This will give a better flavour than ready bought 'mixed spice'.

Chinese cookery also uses a mixed spice known as five spices. They are star anise, ground anise pepper, cassia, cloves and fennel seeds. The Japanese seven spice mixture consists of sesame seeds, powdered nori, orange peel, white pepper, sansho pepper, red pepper and white poppy seeds.

APPLE-BASED MINCEMEAT

500 g/1 lb cooking apples
200 g/7 oz blanched almond halves
1 teaspoon cloves, ground
1 teaspoon allspice, ground
1 teaspoon nutmeg, grated
2 teaspoons cinnamon, ground
2 teaspoons ginger, ground
250 g/8 oz raisins
250 g/8 oz currants
125/4 oz mixed peel
250 g/8 oz brown sugar
juice of 2 medium oranges
150 ml/¼ pint brandy
150 ml/¼ pint sweet sherry

Chop the apples into small pieces and pound the almonds in a mortar. Combine the apples, almonds and all the spices with the dried fruit and sugar, and pour over this mixture the orange juice, brandy and sherry. Leave all the ingredients, covered, in a large bowl for 6 days, giving them a good stir each day. After this time pack them into clean jars which you have sterilized in a low oven, seal and leave for about 3 weeks to mature before use.

CHRISTMAS PUDDING

This recipe gives enough ingredients for 3 large or 4 smaller puddings. All the ingredients are simply mixed together and then steamed – the long steaming period can be considerably reduced by using a pressure cooker. Christmas puddings should be made and cooked at least a month before Christmas to enable them to mature.

250 g/8 oz wholemeal flour
250 g/8 oz fresh wholemeal breadcrumbs
250 g/8 oz raisins
250 g/8 oz currants
250 g/8 oz sultanas
125 g/4 oz prunes, stoned *and* finely chopped
250 g/8 oz candied peel
350 g/12 oz muscovado sugar
1 large apple, grated
125 g/4 oz carrots, grated
125 g/4 oz flaked almonds
1 teaspoon nutmeg, grated
2 level teaspoons ginger, ground
2 teaspoons cinnamon, ground
2 teaspoons coriander seeds, ground
1 level teaspoon cloves, ground
250 g/8 oz vegetable margarine
2 tablespoons molasses
juice *and* peel of 1 orange, grated
juice *and* peel of 1 lemon, grated
1 wineglass brandy
300 ml/½ pint barley wine
6 eggs
a little milk

Mix together all the dry ingredients in a very large mixing bowl. Then melt the margarine over a low heat and stir in the molasses. Take the pan off the heat and add the orange and lemon juices, brandy and barley wine. Stir these liquid ingredients into the dry ones. Beat the eggs and stir them in as well. The consistency of the puddings before cooking should be rather moist, otherwise they will become too dry during the long cooking period. Test to see whether the mixture will drop easily off a wooden spoon and, if not, add some milk until the required consistency is obtained.

Spoon the mixture into well-greased basins and cover them with grease-proof paper and cloths or foil, well tied down with string. Each pudding should be steamed in a large pan of boiling water for about 6 hours, unless you are using a pressure cooker, in which case follow the instructions for your particular model. Take care that the puddings do not boil dry or burn. After cooking, cover the puddings with clean greaseproof paper and cloths or foil.

On Christmas Day steam them for a further 1½–2 hours in the same way.

Sweet and sour

The combination of sweet and sour ingredients is particularly typical of Chinese cookery. It probably originated in the Taoist idea of balancing opposites, of achieving the right combination of yin (female) and yang (male) elements. The same concept of harmony lies at the root of Japanese macrobiotic cookery.

Chinese sweet and sour dishes are often flavoured with the following ingredients: vinegar, lemon juice or tamarind, soy sauce, sugar, mirin (a kind of sweet sake or rice wine), garlic, onion and ginger.

CHIRASHI-SUSHI

Sushi is Japanese sweet and sour rice to which various delicately flavoured morsels of vegetables are added. Norimake-sushi is sushi rice pressed around a seasoned vegetable centre and wrapped in sheets of nori (see p.63). Chirashi-sushi is served as a bowl of seasoned rice topped with various delicacies and accompanied by specially prepared condiments like pickled ginger and pickled daikon or radish (which can be obtained from Japanese grocers and some wholefood shops). Chirashi-sushi is easier to prepare than Norimake-sushi, so it is perhaps better to perfect the former dish before attempting the latter. I have used ordinary short grain brown rice, which seems to give good results. If you want to use authentic Japanese rice, consult a Japanese cookery book for details of its preparation.

sushi rice
500 g/1 lb short grain brown rice
500 ml/18 fl oz water
4 tablespoons rice vinegar
3 tablespoons brown sugar
1 teaspoon salt

topping for sushi rice
4 dried shiitake mushrooms
2 tablespoons soy sauce ·
2 tablespoons mirin (sweet rice wine)
100 ml/4 fl oz water
a little cabbage *or* other green vegetable
water *with* soy sauce *or* miso
2–3 sheets nori (seaweed)
2 tablespoons sesame seeds

to serve
pickled ginger
pickled daikon (white radish)
wasabi (horseradish mustard)
extra sesame seeds

Soak the brown rice in cold water for 30 minutes. The cooked rice should be served immediately after cooling to room temperature, so all the accompaniments to sushi rice should be prepared first.

Soak the shiitake mushrooms in cold water for about 30 minutes, then drain them and cut them into small pieces. Simmer them slowly, with the soy sauce, mirin and water, until most of the liquid has been absorbed or has evaporated. Shred the cabbage or greens finely and simmer in a little water flavoured with either soy sauce or miso. Toast the sheets of nori for an instant under the grill, and then crumble them between your finger and thumb. Toast the sesame seeds under the grill, too.

Now heat the measured water to boiling point in a heavy bottomed pan. Drain the rice and add it to the boiling water a little at a time, so that the water remains boiling. When all the rice has been added, turn down the heat to its lowest setting and cover the pan with a few thicknesses of cloth. Allow to simmer until all the water has been absorbed and the rice is just soft. Leave the pan of rice to stand for 10 minutes before emptying it into a bowl.

Mix up the dressing by heating the rice vinegar slightly and then stirring in the sugar and salt. Pour it over the rice and mix it in with a flat wooden spatula. The Japanese usually fan the rice to cool it after mixing in the dressing to make it take on a shiny, glazed appearance.

Cover the sushi rice with all the toppings you have already prepared, and serve with ginger and daikon pickles, wasabi and an extra bowl of toasted sesame seeds. This dish is not so complicated to prepare as it sounds, and the blend of flavours (particularly sweet, sour and salt) is so delicious that it is well worth the effort.

SWEET AND SOUR SAUCE

This very tasty mixture will make tofu appetizing even to those who normally find it unacceptably bland. The sauce is also good for marinating hard tofu. Since tofu absorbs flavours very quickly, you will only need to leave it in the liquid for about 1 hour.

sauce
45 g/1½ oz brown sugar
6 tablespoons warm water
2 tablespoons soy sauce
2 tablespoons rice vinegar *or* cider vinegar
juice of ½ lemon
15 g/½ oz fresh root ginger, finely grated
60 g/2 oz white radish *or* 15 g/½ oz dried daikon (white radish), coarsely grated

250 g/8 oz soft tofu
vegetable oil for frying

Dissolve the sugar in the warm water. Add the other liquid ingredients. Stir the grated ginger and radish into the sauce.

Cut the tofu into 4 cm (1½ in) squares and fry them in hot oil. Serve the sauce slightly warm in individual bowls.

Basic recipes and techniques

BROWN RICE

Cooking brown rice, long or short grain, is a little like baking with wholewheat flour: the grains must be prevented from absorbing too much water and becoming soggy. Here are three methods of cooking brown rice which, in my experience, result in the grains becoming just soft enough, unbroken and well separated after cooking. Different kinds of rice may absorb slightly varying degress of water. I find it best to start off with what is probably just enough, test after 20 minutes of cooking, and add a little more water if necessary.

RICE LIGHTLY FRIED AND THEN BOILED

1½ tablespoons vegetable oil
500 g/1 lb brown rice
600 ml/1 pint boiling water

Put the oil in a heavy-bottomed saucepan and let it heat slowly. Turn the heat up high and add the rice. Stir for 2–3 minutes, until the rice is well coated with oil. Immediately add the boiling water and turn the heat down to its lowest setting. Cover the saucepan with a lid and tie a cloth securely round it (I generally fold a tea towel in four and cover the pan first with this and then with a lid, but take care that it does not catch light if you are cooking with gas). The cloth absorbs all the excess moisture as the rice is cooking, so that after about 25 minutes, the rice is well cooked and just moist enough. Rice cooked in this way may afterwards be mixed with vegetables and seasonings or served with a tasty sauce.

PULLAO RICE

This is a popular method of preparing rice in North India, where long grain rice is generally preferred. Two pullao recipes are given in the book (see p.174 and p.205): basically, the rice is fried with spices and sometimes vegetables, then boiling water is added and the pan covered with a tight-fitting lid. It is left to cook very slowly either on top of the stove or in the oven. A heat-diffusing pad is useful for reducing the heat to a minimum if using the stove top method. I use as little as 200 ml/⅓ pint water to 500 g (1 lb) rice in a pullao dish, but the pan must be sealed with foil or an extremely tight lid so that no steam can escape.

BOILED RICE

Brown rice can be quite awful if boiled in the wrong way, especially with too much water. This method should produce good results.

Soak 500 g (1 lb) rice in cold water for 30 minutes. Rinse and drain it. Have ready a pan containing 500 ml (18 fl oz) of rapidly boiling water. Add the rice only gradually to the boiling water, so that it remains on the boil. When all the rice has been added, turn the heat down to its lowest setting and cover, as in the first method, with a folded cloth and a lid.

Leave the rice to cook until all the water has been absorbed, which should take about 20–25 minutes. This is a good method of cooking rice when it is to be fried afterwards with vegetables and seasonings, or served with a dressing as a salad.

DRIED PULSES

All beans, with the possible exception of the small mung beans, should be soaked for a few hours before cooking. This not only shortens the cooking period but also soaks out the harmful alkaloids, saponins and glycosides which all legumes contain to some degree – though these are most apparent in the larger beans such as red kidney beans and soya beans. After soaking, the beans should be rinsed and boiled in plenty of fresh water until they are soft. Soaking beans in boiling water will help to soften them more quickly; alternatively they can be brought slowly to the boil in a pan of water and then left to soak.

Red kidney beans, soya beans and chick peas can take a notoriously long time to cook even after they have been soaked, so a pressure cooker can be especially useful here. The length of time which various beans take to cook depends on their size and how long they have been stored. The only general rule is that they should be cooked al dente. If making a bean salad, always add the dressing while the beans are still hot – they will then absorb the flavour of the dressing more thoroughly.

Lentils and split peas generally cook more quickly than dried beans, though green and brown lentils can be soaked for up to an hour before cooking. These pulses should be washed very thoroughly before cooking as they are usually very dusty. Lentils should also be picked over for stones. Unlike beans, lentils and split peas are often cooked with just sufficient water for them to become pureed. Individual recipes in this book indicate how much water to use when cooking split peas and lentils.

BEANSPROUTS

Dried pulses are an excellent source of protein, but when they are allowed to sprout they also develop a high vitamin C content. Mung beansprouts are well known, but lentils, aduki beans, chick peas, fenugreek, alfalfa seeds and wheat and barley grains also produce well-flavoured sprouts.

Soak the pulses for several hours in warm water. Transfer them to a bean sprouter (or use a colander covered with polythene). Leave in a warm place and rinse with warm water four or five times a day. The sprouts should appear after 2–5 days. When they are about 1.5 cm (½ in) long they may be eaten or refrigerated for up to a week until required.

SODA BREAD

As well as being leavened by yeast, bread can also be made to rise with a mixture of bicarbonate of soda and fermented milk, i.e. soured milk, buttermilk or a mixture of milk and yoghurt. Soda bread has a closer texture than yeasted bread and a sweeter taste. It is quickly made because it is simply mixed up and baked without needing rising periods.

900 g/2 lb wholewheat flour
2 teaspoons salt
2 level teaspoons bicarbonate of soda
500 ml/18 fl oz soured milk *or* buttermilk *or* a mixture of milk *and* yoghurt

Preheat the oven to 190° C (375° F, gas mark 5). Mix the flour with the salt and bicarbonate of soda. Add the fermented milk and mix well until an even consistency is obtained. Mix the dough by hand but do not knead as when making yeasted bread. Divide the mixture into two round loaves and put them on a greased baking tray. Incise a deep cross on the top of each one. Bake for 35 minutes. Test with a knife blade or by tapping the bottom of the loaves – which should sound hollow – before taking out of the oven and cooling on a wire rack. This bread is good to eat while still warm.

WHOLEWHEAT LOAVES

The main difference between baking white bread and wholewheat bread is that wholewheat flour should be lightly rubbed with vegetable margarine before the liquid is added so that it does not absorb too much water and become heavy. I find that the longer the rise, the lighter the loaf – it is often convenient to make up the dough in the evening and leave it at room temperature, covered with polythene, to rise overnight.

Bread making is the opposite to pastry making in that all the ingredients and utensils should be warm rather than cold. Wheatgerm adds a sweet flavour and, of course, extra vitamin content to any loaf in which it is used, so it is always a good idea to replace a little flour with an equal weight of wheatgerm (e.g. 60 g/2 oz in a flour quantity of 500 g/1 lb).

900 g/2 lb wholewheat flour
2 teaspoons salt
1 heaped tablespoon molasses
600 ml/1 pint warm water
2 level teaspoons dried yeast *or* 2 heaped teaspoons fresh
125 g/4 oz vegetable margarine

Mix the flour with the salt. Stir the molasses into a bowl containing about 150 ml (¼ pint) of the warm water and then add the yeast. Leave it to work, which should not take more than 10 minutes. Meanwhile, rub the margarine thoroughly into the flour. When the yeast is ready, mix it in with the flour and then gradually stir in the rest of the warm water. Knead the dough for about 5 minutes, until it has a uniform elastic consistency. If the dough seems to be too dry (and different flours may absorb differing amounts of liquid) add a little more water. Put the dough in a basin and cover it with polythene. Leave it to rise until doubled in size, or overnight.

Grease two 500 g (1 lb) bread tins. Knock down the dough, knead it for 2–3 minutes only and then divide it between the two tins. Leave in a warm place to rise until the dough has risen up to the tops of the tins (this should not take more than 1 hour at most). Preheat the oven to 200° C (400° F, gas mark 6). Bake for 15 minutes, then turn the heat down to 190° C (375° F, gas mark 5) and bake for another 25 minutes. Test the loaf to see whether it is done by inserting a knife blade into the centre and seeing whether it comes out clean.

Remove the loaves from the tins immediately after taking them out of the oven, and then leave on a wire rack to cool thoroughly. Store in a bread crock or container which is closed but not airtight.

PITTA BREAD

This Middle Eastern bread is made with a normal yeasted dough but is rolled out very thinly just before the second rise and cooked for only about 3 minutes in a very hot oven. Clearly, this method of baking was developed in regions where fuel was in short supply. The only problem with making this kind of bread at home is that you must have quite a large, flat surface on which to allow the pittas to rise. This bread can be served with all kinds of Middle Eastern dishes, particularly dips like hummus, tahini dip and Baba Ghanoush. The quantities given here make about 15 pittas.

1 heaped teaspoon dried yeast
450 ml/16 fl oz warm water
1 level dessertspoon brown sugar
700 g/1 ½ lb wholewheat *or* 80% flour
2 level teaspoons salt
2 tablespoons vegetable oil

Dissolve the yeast with a little of the warmed water and the sugar. Mix the flour with the salt, then add the yeast. Gradually add the rest of the warm water and knead to a smooth dough, working the oil in last. Put the dough in a bowl, cover it with polythene and leave in a warm place to rise until it has doubled in size.

After this time, divide the dough into about 15 pieces and roll each into an oval shape about 0.5 cm (¼ in) thick. Leave the pittas to rise on a surface lightly dusted with flour. Cover them with a large cloth and then with polythene. Leave for 45 minutes to 1 hour. Preheat the oven to 240° C (475° F, gas mark 9). Place as many pittas as will fit on a greased hot oven tray and bake for 3 minutes. Repeat the process until all are cooked.

Immediately after taking the bread out of the oven, wrap it in a damp cloth for a few minutes and then let it cool completely on a wire rack. Unlike other types of bread, pittas should be stored in airtight conditions.

CHAPATIS

Chapatis are the authentic accompaniment to North Indian pulse and vegetable dishes. They are properly made from *ata*, a low-gluten, finely ground wholewheat flour, but if this is difficult to obtain English wholewheat flour, which is also low in gluten, makes a good substitute. Chapatis are usually rolled with a thin rolling pin on a circular stone slab and cooked on a *tava* – an almost flat metal plate. This equipment can be improvised: for example a cast iron pan, very well heated, will do instead of a *tava*. But despite the simplicity of the ingredients, chapatis require some practice before they can be made successfully every time. The quantities given here make about 15 chapatis.

300 g/10 oz *ata or* finely ground wholewheat flour *or*
150 g/5 oz wholewheat *and*
150 g/5 oz plain white flour
1 level teaspoon salt (optional)
about 175 ml/6 fl oz water
a little ghee *or* vegetable oil

Mix the flour with the salt. Gradually add the water, stirring all the time. Knead the mixture very well for about 10 minutes until an entirely even consistency is obtained. Leave the dough to stand, in a bowl covered with polythene, for between 30 minutes and 2 hours (as convenient).

Knead the dough again briefly, and then divide it into about 15 pieces. Heat the tava or cast iron pan very thoroughly. Roll each piece of dough between the palms of your hands with a touch of oil or ghee, flatten it, and then on a well-floured surface roll it into a thin circle about 15 cm (6 in) across.

Place the chapatis on the tava or pan and cook for about 1 minute on each side. As bubbles begin to appear, press them down with a slightly dampened cloth. Chapatis are best served as quickly as possible after being cooked. I think this is the main reason why the custom of Indian women eating after the rest of the family has prevailed!

WHOLEWHEAT PASTRY

Contrary to many people's opinion, wholewheat pastry can be as light and crumbly as pastry made with white flour. When making any kind of pastry it is important to have all the ingredients and utensils very cold. You may not possess a marble slab, on which, ideally, pastry should be rolled out, but always use very cold vegetable margarine and ice cold water, and leave the dough in the refrigerator for a short while before rolling it out. If you use a ceramic dish for baking open tarts, stand it on a metal oven tray: this ensures that the bottom of the pastry crust cooks through and removes the need for pre-cooking. If, exceptionally, you have difficulty in getting pastry dough to cohere, add a few drops of vegetable oil to the mixture. The quantities given below make enough pastry to line a 25 cm (10 in) flan dish.

250 g/8 oz wholewheat flour
1 level teaspoon salt (optional)
125 g/4 oz hard vegetable margarine (e.g. Granose)
4 tablespoons cold water

Mix the flour with the salt (vegetable margarine usually contains some salt so it is not essential to add more). Cut the margarine into small pieces and rub it into the flour using the tips of your fingers. Add the cold water a little at a time, working it well into the dough. Put the dough in the bottom of the refrigerator for 10–15 minutes. Then roll out on a well-floured board.

OATCAKES

As oatmeal contains no gluten, it cannot successfully be made into bread. Fortunately, however, the Scots and Welsh invented oatcakes, which are easy to make, delicious and as nutritious as bread (with a much higher iron content). Traditional oatcakes are made with oatmeal only, though a little wheat flour helps to bind them together more easily. This recipe also uses more oil, in the form of vegetable margarine, than is usual – this makes for a softer texture, which I prefer. The quantities below make 15–20 oatcakes.

350 g/12 oz oatmeal, fine *or* medium ground
125 g/4 oz wholewheat flour
1 teaspoon salt
1 teaspoon baking powder
125 g/4 oz vegetable margarine
200 ml/⅓ pint water

Preheat the oven to 190° C (375° F, gas mark 5). Mix together the oatmeal, flour, salt and baking powder. Rub in the margarine, then add the water. Knead the mixture to form a stiff dough. Roll out, on a well-floured board, to a thickness of about 1.5 cm (½ in). Cut into circles and place on a greased baking tray. Bake for 20 minutes or until just brown underneath. Cool on a wire rack, and then store in an airtight tin.

Oatcakes are often cooked on a griddle instead of being baked in the oven. In this case roll out the dough more thinly and cook on a well-heated griddle for 4–5 minutes each side.

MUESLI

Rolled grains, which can be eaten without further cooking, have become very popular in recent years, especially as breakfast cereals. Oats, wheat, barley, rye, millet and rice are all available in flaked form. When mixed with dried fruit and nuts and served with yoghurt, these rolled grains form the basis of a very nutritious meal. Here is one muesli recipe which I particularly like, though almost infinite variations are possible. When making up muesli, consider the texture as well as the flavour. Mix up a large jar at a time and it will come in useful for emergency meals.

500 g/1 lb soft oatflakes
175 g/6 oz harder flakes, e.g. wheat *or* barley
90 g/3 oz wheatgerm
250 g/8 oz almonds, toasted *and* then ground
90 g/3 oz pumpkin seeds
250 g/8 oz currants
175/6 oz dried apricots, chopped

YOGHURT

Yoghurt is an excellent food because of the benign bacteria it contains, which have been shown to counteract the effect of harmful bacteria in the intestines if yoghurt is eaten regularly. It is easily made at home by mixing a specially prepared culture with warm milk, or, more simply, mixing a little live yoghurt with milk and leaving the mixture to ferment. A yoghurt maker is helpful as it maintains a constant temperature in which the yoghurt can mature, but it is not essential – some people make yoghurt in a large thermos flask.

2 tablespoons skimmed milk (optional)
1 litre/1¾ pints milk
3 tablespoons live yoghurt

Add the skimmed milk to the fresh (this improves the texture of the yoghurt but is not essential) and bring them to the boil. Let the milk cool to finger temperature before stirring in the live yoghurt. Pour the mixture into a yoghurt maker, thermos flask or ceramic bowl standing in a larger bowl filled with hot water. If using the last method, cover the bowls with a thick cloth and leave them to stand in a warm place. Make sure the water in the bowl remains warm. The ideal temperature for making yoghurt is about 40° C (just over 100° F). Leave the yoghurt to work overnight and, when it has reached a good consistency, refrigerate.

Vegan substitutes for dairy produce

The recipes in this book generally recommend the use of vegetable margarine or vegetable oil instead of butter, and include fermented soya products such as tofu and tempe. However some recipes call for dairy products such as milk, yoghurt and cheese, and since an increasing number of people today want to minimize their consumption of saturated animal fats – quite apart from those who do not eat animal products for ethical reasons – the following list is given to indicate existing vegetable substitutes for dairy produce.

SOYA MILK   This may be used instead of dairy milk in desserts or savoury sauces. You may wish to use half soya milk and half dairy milk.

VEGETABLE MARGARINE   Many hard, well-flavoured vegetable margarines, for example the *un*hydrogenated Danish Granose, are now available and in my experience can replace butter in cooking without any loss of flavour. Make sure you are buying a margarine that has not been hydrogenated, as it will have a lower saturated fat content. In fact, using vegetable margarine usually produces a less cloying taste, which is most welcome in baking as well as in sweet and savoury dishes.

VEGETABLE OILS   Like some vegetable margarines, good-quality vegetable oils contain essential unsaturated fatty acids which help to keep down the cholesterol level in the body. Sunflower, peanut and corn oil are all inexpensive, nutritionally useful oils for everyday use. Olive oil adds an authentic flavour to most Mediterranean dishes, and sesame oil is particularly suitable for certain Far Eastern dishes. Special oils such as walnut oil may be used in unusual salad dressings.

TOFU   Tofu, which is made from slightly fermented soya bean milk, is an extremely versatile food with a very high protein content. Its neutral taste lends itself to a great variety of flavourings, sweet and sour.

Soft tofu can be used rather like a soft cheese: for example it can be blended with savoury ingredients, instead of using the usual egg, milk and cheese mixture to form the basis of a quiche. It can also be blended with fresh or dried fruit to make a tart filling or fruit fool.

Hard tofu can be cut into cubes and fried in oil. Served with soups and vegetable dishes, tofu cubes add a high protein content to the meal.

TEMPE   Another fermented soya product, it has been described as tofu cheese. As well as having a very high protein content, tempe also contains vitamin B12, which is extremely rare in vegetable substances. Tempe is delicious when fried in small chips, and can be used in vegetable pasties.

Other soya products which are available from some specialist suppliers include soya yoghurt, soya ice cream and soya cheese.

Useful equipment

PANS

Stainless steel or good-quality enamel pans are preferable to aluminium because minute quantities of the metal, to which some people are allergic, can enter into food cooked in aluminium pans.

CAST IRON PANS   You need these in large, medium and small sizes. The low-priced ware imported from Taiwan is perfectly serviceable.

STEAMERS   Inexpensive white enamel saucepans and steamers combined are imported from Poland. Alternatively, Chinese bamboo steamers are very cheap and can be fitted over an ordinary pan.

WOKS   These traditional Chinese vessels are especially useful for stir fried dishes.

PRESSURE COOKERS   A great help when cooking dried beans and chick peas, which otherwise take a very long time.

BOWLS AND DISHES

EARTHENWARE CASSEROLES   French *marmite* casseroles are said to allow less evaporation and therefore retain more of the flavour of the ingredients. I possess a traditional Spanish casserole made in the potteries of Seville which can be used not only in the oven but also, because of its specially designed base, on a gas or electric ring as well. This kind of dish – flameproof as well as ovenproof – is strongly recommended if you can find one.

QUICHE OR FLAN DISHES   They can be made of ceramic or metal. The former look more attractive when brought to the table, but remember to stand them on a metal oven sheet when baking, so that the pastry is not soggy. A 25 cm (10 in) one serves four people.

MIXING BOWLS   You will need both large and small sizes.

TRADITIONAL BREAD BOWL   A great asset if you are going to make bread regularly, because it is large enough to hold the dough mixture comfortably and its heavy base makes it very stable.

GRATIN DISHES   Dishes to go under the grill need to be more than ovenproof, so it is worth having one or two of different sizes.

BOARDS AND SLABS

WOODEN CHOPPING BOARDS   The larger the better!

MARBLE SLAB   Not essential for rolling out pastry, but something to look out for.

GRINDERS, GRATERS AND BLENDERS

PESTLE AND MORTAR   For grinding small quantities of spices, crushing nuts, etc.

ELECTRIC COFFEE GRINDER   Very useful for grinding spices, nuts etc.

HAND GRATER   For cheese, nutmeg etc. The box-shaped ones will stand firmly on a plate, which helps you to grate the food and not your knuckles.

ELECTRIC BLENDER OR HAND-OPERATED MILL (MOULI)   For pureeing liquid ingredients.

SALT AND PEPPER

TRADITIONAL SALT HOLDER   Ceramic jars with a large circular opening have been desiged in such a way that the salt inside does not become damp.

SALT MILL   Useful for crushing hard salt crystals. Maldon salt crystals are not very hard, so I usually crush them between my thumb and fingers.

PEPPER MILLS   Have two or three in the kitchen, and use them for black and white pepper and coriander seeds.

SPOONS AND SPATULAS

WOODEN SPOONS   For use in non-stick pans and for stirring hot sauces.

SLOTTED SPOON   This is particularly useful for picking out and draining foods that are being cooked in hot water or oil.

SPATULA   For scraping out the last of the cake or bread mix from the bowl.

SLICE   This does exactly what you would expect, neatly and cleanly.

BALLOON WHISK   An old-fashioned implement that cannot be bettered for whisking eggs.

KNIVES

Two sharp knives, with blades about 10 cm (4 in) and 15 cm (6 in) long, are essential. Hachoirs (curved blades with two handles) are also useful for chopping vegetables.

MISCELLANEOUS

ROLLING PINS   You will need a standard size one for pastry and biscuit making. A smaller one is very useful for making chapatis.

COLANDER AND FINE HAIR SIEVE

WALTER FILTER   Improves the taste of most tap water, and filters out most of the fluoride and heavy metals.

YOGHURT MAKER   Not essential, but useful for keeping the fermenting yoghurt at the correct temperature. Alternatively, you can use a large thermos flask.

BEAN SPROUTER   This is better than using jam jars, because it ensures that the sprouting beans are properly drained. Alternatively, improvize with a colander.

MEASURING JUG   An essential, and cheap, piece of equipment which should be calibrated in pints, millilitres and fluid ounces.

SCALES   Even the experienced cook finds a pair of scales indispensible.

Useful equipment

Conversion tables

These tables are only intended as a guide, and are not exact conversions, but they are sufficiently accurate for use in recipes.

WEIGHTS

Metric	Imperial
15 g	½ oz
30 g	1 oz
45 g	1½ oz
60 g	2 oz
75 g	2½ oz
90 g	3 oz
125 g	4 oz (¼ lb)
150 g	5 oz
175 g	6 oz
200 g	7 oz
250 g	8 oz (½ lb)
275 g	9 oz
300 g	10 oz
350 g	12 oz
400 g	14 oz
500 g	16 oz (1 lb)
600 g	1¼ lb
700 g	1½ lb
900 g	2 lb
1 kg	2¼ lb
2 kg	4½ lb

LIQUID MEASURES

Metric	Imperial
100 ml	4 fl oz
150 ml	5 fl oz (¼ pint)
200 ml	7 fl oz (⅓ pint)
300 ml	10 fl oz (½ pint)
350 ml	12 fl oz
400 ml	15 fl oz (¾ pint)
500 ml	18 fl oz
600 ml	20 fl oz (1 pint)
750 ml	1¼ pints
900 ml	1½ pints
1000 ml (1 litre)	1¾ pints
1.25 litres	2 pints
1.5 litres	2½ pints
2.0 litres	3½ pints

OVEN TEMPERATURES

°C	°F	gas mark
110	225	¼
130	250	½
140	275	1
150	300	2
170	325	3
180	350	4
190	375	5
200	400	6
220	425	7
230	450	8
240	475	9

Index